The WASHING MACHINE MAN'S TRAVELS

A washing machine repair man by trade, Andrew Lindsay's true ambition is to raise awareness about environmental issues and the decline of endangered species and indigenous peoples around the world. Unable to find paying work in conservation and disillusioned with the treadmill of modern life, he embarked on paragliding trip to Nepal at the end of 1997 followed by a round-the-world trip. This book is the account of his adventures.

Other titles pending from Andrew Lindsay

Last of the Great White Rhinos
*An ex SAS corporal with an extraordinary passion for
endangered wildlife sets himself up as judge jury and
executioner in a relentless hunt for those at the top of the
poaching trade*

How to Save the Planet
*The definitive layman's guide to what is wrong with humanity
and the way we live, a prediction of where we are heading and
practical – if unpalatable – suggestions on how to get
ourselves back onto a sustainable course*

The
WASHING MACHINE MAN'S TRAVELS

A Round-The-World Adventure Travelogue

Andrew Lindsay

Greenworldbooks

Published by Greenworldbooks in 2005

First published in the United Kingdom in 2005 by
Greenworldbooks,
a subsidiary of worldwidebackpacker.com

Greenworldbooks use recycled materials wherever possible

Printed and bound in the United Kingdom by
Antony Rowe Limited, Chippenham, Wiltshire

ISBN 0-9550083-0-1

Dedicated to Trudy and Penny
   Whenever I felt like giving up
   my promise to dedicate this book to you
   kept me going.

Contents

PROLOGUE

We stood like fledglings on the take off mat waiting for the right thermal to blow through. The windsock fluttered and then maintained a steady angle uphill.

"Go - go - go!"

The canopy came up smoothly and cleanly above my head so I powered through my short run. Well clear of take off, I banked hard right to run parallel with the cliff face and stay in the lift band. I was a bird. I was flying!

Lake Annecy sparkled like a diamond surrounded by jagged mountains and far below, the paragliding shop and landing field were mere dots. Dynamic lift took me high above the takeoff plateau as warm air and wood smoke funnelled up in punchy thermals. It was busy up there and I had to manoeuvre constantly to avoid other pilots.

As I cruised high above the treetops a fellow pilot veered abruptly across my path. Watching him as we came back round to face the plateau, suddenly another pilot was heading straight towards me. We both froze in terror and he flew into the leading edge of my canopy with a loud thwack and sickening rustle of material.

"Oh God – oh God, I'm going to die!" I cried as we spiralled towards the trees, rapidly gathering speed, wind noise increasing. With death an imminent certainty I had time to think clearly.

"This is the worst thing that can possibly happen. We're going to die and I haven't even seen anything of the world yet!"

MASTER PLAN

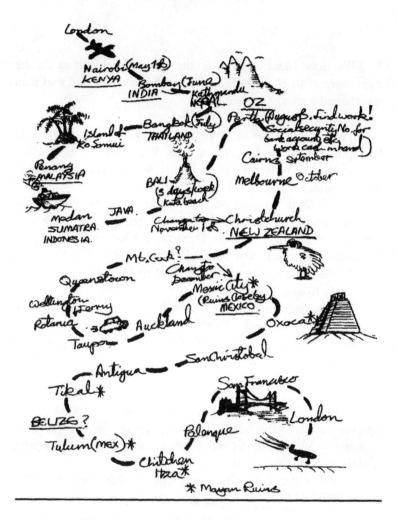

Sketch map at the front of my 1997 diary.
Originally planned for just eight months, the journey
stretched to a year and a half and became a way of life.

AFRICA

ARRIVAL

Stepping off a British Airways 747, the late morning heat hit me in a wave making me giddy and I winced in blinding sunlight. The huge, austere arrivals lounge was busier than Oxford Circus in rush hour and it seemed the entire population of Nairobi had turned out to greet the new arrivals. After the relaxed plane journey the sudden noise and activity were quite overwhelming, so escaping swarms of persistent tour guides with dodgy Hawaiian shirts and serious BO, I joined a group of young travellers sharing a minibus to Upper Hill Campground where the truck tours met.

I pitched tent on the only available space next to an ominous security fence. European students and raucous Aussie truck drivers seemed to make up the camp's population. Everyone wore the latest gear, had the coolest tattoos and seemed to know one another, but in my hiking trousers and thermal T-shirt I felt like a complete idiot. It never occurred to me that most of these people didn't know what they were doing either.

That afternoon in the campsite restaurant I was pleasantly surprised when a young Australian woman came over to join me.

"You look as if you could do with some company," she said.

Ashleigh was going on a six week organised tour and hated the idea of being bounced around day after day in a baking hot, dusty truck. It allowed little freedom of movement and forced you to get along with other tourists while keeping you from meeting the people who actually lived there.

"Normally I do my own thing," she said, "but my dad told me if I didn't do it this way he'd never speak to me again. I've met some of the others I'll be travelling with."

"Nice bunch? Easy to get along with?" I enquired optimistically.

"Quite the opposite I'm afraid. Beer swilling Aussie yobbos."

An 'overlander' truck pulled into the yard to a hail of empty beer cans and a chorus of shouts and laughter.

"Culture!" she exclaimed.

When I showed Ashleigh my intended route with budget and time constraints she was horrified.

"You want to visit all these countries in eight months, with just £3,000?"

Together we thrashed out some ideas juggling dates and figures and my confidence began to return. A three day tour of Masai Mara seemed like a great way to start so I paid the fee and said goodbye to Ashleigh later that evening as her truck pulled away in a cloud of dust.

It was a long hot drive to Masai Mara in the tour minibus through sprawling shanty towns, tea plantations and the open plains of the great Rift Valley flanked by hazy mountain ranges. Small groups of zebra and antelope roamed freely here and there between settlements.

Masai Mara covers around 600 square kilometres and is home to 40 black rhino. We stopped just inside the park boundary and leaving the campsite bickering, I walked to the edge of a crude corral made from sticks. Dusk loomed over the terrain of tall golden grass and bush. There was a musty animal smell on the still warm air and I shuddered at the thought that beyond the fragile barrier we humans were just another item on the menu.

Back around the dinner table a heated debate on aid for Africa raged between a Dutch United Nations economist and a stocky German computer millionaire called Boris.

"I've worked hard for everything I have," said Boris angrily. "Why should I give it away to someone just because they are poor?"

The argument continued with no clear winner until after supper, when the resident group of young Masai came to sing and dance for us. It felt a little contrived because they were paid to do this as part of our tour package, but it was fascinating all the same. Two of the young men spoke very good English and our initial hesitance quickly vanished in an outpouring of questions about the weapons they carried, their way of life, philosophy and beliefs. Tall, desperately slim and very handsome, these quiet-spoken, fearless warriors were supremely adapted to conditions on the African plains. Their hair was plaited and fixed back with red clay, they wore large metal earrings and simple red or tartan shawls draped over one shoulder. Each man carried a long thin spear fixed to a detachable metal point, a wooden club with bulbous carved end and a short wooden drill and block for making fire. The singing consisted of deep rhythmic chants that hypnotised the listener and sent us, as well as the singers, into a trance-like state. Jumping is seen as a demonstration of virility and the men took turns at leaping vertically into the air.

The dancing finished and we were joined by a Canadian woman who was soon to marry one of the young men. Was she really going to give up her Canadian lifestyle to live in a mud hut on a diet of blood and milk? There was a chasm of difference between the two cultures and it would be a huge step. She told us she enjoyed living as a Masai but strongly disagreed with female circumcision. It had been agreed she wouldn't be circumcised herself but she knew of several girls who had bled to death as a result of the practice. I wondered whether it would be possible to keep the traditional way of life while abandoning some of the more cruel or harmful practices.

The young men told us more about their culture. Masai fearlessness is learned from an early age. Only a few years ago village elders would stand over the young victim during male circumcision, watching him closely. If he flinched or cried out in pain he was instantly run through with a spear. Initiation to manhood continued with the young man being taken to a place far from home and left to fend for himself for a month. Finally, he was required to kill a lion with only his spear. Perhaps they should learn to paintball them today because lions are in serious decline.

Western influence has touched the Masai but they have successfully resisted assimilation through their strength of character. They listened to the foreigners quietly and politely while we told them about our religion, education and social system, then when they had heard enough they calmly rose to their feet and walked away. That night while the Masai watched over our tents, I felt a cold shiver as I lay in my sleeping bag listening to the demonic cackle of hyenas and distant moan of lions.

Next morning we set off over rough dusty unmade roads for an all day game drive. The track followed rolling hills of tall golden grass billowing in the breeze, occasionally dipping low to cross streams where brush and trees had found a hold. Crude bridges of logs and boulders were falling apart so passengers disembarked, mucking in to repair the damage while our driver skilfully picked his way across. Wandering off to relieve myself at a particularly awkward crossing the thought suddenly occurred to me, "What an ideal spot for a lion ambush". Zipping up in a cold sweat I quickly made my way back to the vehicle.

We saw the rain coming for hours but there was no avoiding the great grey curtain directly ahead of us. The moment it started our red dust track turned to slime and it became routine to get out and push every few minutes. Rear wheels spun wildly, hurling mud at us until we were covered from head to foot while the rain dripped from our ears and noses and ran down our necks. I cursed, thinking of my Gore-Tex boots buried deep in the back of the van and swore I'd never wear sandals again as they came off for the umpteenth time, red gloop oozing between my toes.

A decrepit two wheel drive Toyota minibus with balding tyres was far from ideal for these conditions. Every time we hit a deep rut the fan belt sprayed water onto the electrics and the engine cut. Our driver kept his cool, wrapping plastic bags around the distributor and gunning the van through the slop like a maniac, until we slammed into a rut so deep that the edge of the berm came half way up the sliding door. The bus lay uselessly on its side wedging the door tightly shut, so we clambered out the windows to push.

Despite a brave struggle we reached a point where slimy clay gave way to loamy, knee-deep mud and the minibus stuck fast. Two miserable hours passed before a young white Kenyan guide came by in a 70's Toyota Land Cruiser. Stepping down, in his khaki shorts and shirt with a huge bush knife strapped to his side, he really looked the part. Our driver handed him a tired looking piece of string for a towrope which the young man threw on the mud with contempt then, taking some business-like chains from the Cruiser, he hitched up and towed us effortlessly the last few kilometres to camp.

The following morning we visited a Masai village. It was very touristy and seemed a bit of a rip-off: the £5 entrance fee was roughly equivalent to a months earnings for a typical herdsman, but it gave us more of an insight to Masai culture. We walked through an opening in the circular kraal fence of acacia branches bent over and woven together, to the nearest house. The walls and roof were constructed from a framework of branches and twigs, covered in cow dung for insulation and waterproofing. If the roof leaked they just slapped more on.

A tall man in his late twenties with braided hair dressed in a brightly chequered shawl, pulled aside the heavy doorway curtain that kept out flies and the morning chill, to show us inside his house. During the heat of the day, he explained, dung walls stayed relatively cool. The largest space, about 10 square metres, was the living room and sleeping area. It was gloomy inside, the only light coming from a single tiny slit window. Several goat skins were laid over a thick mattress of twigs on which children and adults slept together and a number of coarse blankets were folded neatly against a wall for covers. Propped in one corner were prized possessions, a slender elegantly fashioned bow, spear and wooden club. In the partitioned cooking area embers were kept smouldering day and night under a clay stove. Next to this were a number of bowls and spoons beautifully carved from marbled wood. Despite a small vent hole in the roof the room was filled with choking, eye-watering smoke and before long we were forced to leave.

Outside, the owner explained that the cow was the centre of Masai life providing milk and blood, the staple diet. Blood was taken from incisions made regularly in the neck, without long term harm or discomfort to the animal. Cows were wealth and a man's status in the tribe related directly to the number of cattle he owned. Cattle and goats were grazed during the day and herded into the tribal kraal at night to protect them from predators.

The women had gathered wearing colourful shawls, heavy pendant earrings and masses of necklaces made with tiny, brightly coloured beads. They stood in the trampled muddy courtyard encouraging visitors to buy the carvings and beaded trinkets they had made. Ornate daggers and spears were apparently very popular, but try getting one of those on the plane home. Leaving the village we drove north for about five hours to Nakuru town and moved into a decrepit concrete hotel for the night.

A group of four young women joined our party for next morning's game drive in small but intense Lake Nakuru National Park. Now we had a very full minibus. The girls, recently qualified Canadian vets, chattered incessantly, heads and necks battling like giraffes for a better view through the open roof, while cameras clicked and whirred. Above the lake great flocks of pelicans swirled and wheeled in powerful thermals as one fluid organism, wings flashing dark then light. The road meandered through marshes past a lion sitting on a small island with two uninterested lionesses lying beside him. A short distance away waterbuck, their living food, grazed and waded through water and reeds up to their bellies. They seemed to sense that the lions had feasted and were resting.

Thirty rhino were crammed into the small fenced park, one tenth of Kenya's entire remaining population. In a woodland clearing we admired a mature female with an impressive primary horn big as a man's leg, grazing beside her daughter. We stepped out of the van for a break at a quiet open spot by the lakeside but it wasn't long before a herd of aggressive water buffalo made their way over to see off the intruders. Looking down later from a cliff top vantage point the northern lakeshore was pink with a myriad of babbling, squawking flamingos.

Late next morning the rest of the group returned to Nairobi while the Canadian girls and I took a minibus south to Fisherman's Camp on the shores of Lake Naivasha. A couple of hours later we left bands of cheerful waving schoolchildren on the main road and turned down a driveway to the large campground. Workmen slashed laboriously at the lush grass with machetes making it harder for mosquitoes to hide. There was a round wooden restaurant with bamboo tables and chairs set out on a wide veranda, basic but comfortable *bandas* for alternative accommodation and plenty of shade from large acacia trees. With four security guards patrolling the area we felt quite safe and set up our tents close to the lakeside.

The receptionist gave us a quick rundown of local attractions so, catching a *matatoo* to nearby Kongoni village police station, we began walking to tiny Crater Lake Wildlife Sanctuary. We hadn't gone very far when passers by warned us that there were robbers en route so the girls wisely turned back to drop off money belts and cameras at the campsite office. Continuing alone, I hid behind bushes when approached by anyone and passed a dried out goat carcass hanging eerily from a tree.

After an hour's walk I arrived at the sanctuary, a tiny wildlife oasis pristine and wild, teeming with a variety of small mammals, lizards and birds. Camouflaged cicadas - giant flying beetles - made an ear-splitting noise like a band saw cutting sheet steel but mercifully they preferred the low tree cover of the crater perimeter and were soon out of range. Black and white colobus monkeys with long flowing hair, played and squabbled in large shady trees by the trail. Approaching the lakeside through dense swathes of reeds there was a loud monotonous whine and the air was thick with mosquitoes. Giant bird-eating spiders with spiky mottled brown bodies stretched their glistening webs across the track but made little impression on the clouds of manic biting insects. As I clambered up the crater's side and out through surrounding parkland a large male *kudu* turned to stare at me from further up the track and it felt wonderfully invigorating to be walking so close to herds of antelope, gazelle and zebra.

banda - hut.
matatoo - minibus that only sets of when completely overloaded.
kudu - largest African antelope. Males have long twisted horns.

The sky slowly darkened and finally burst into heavy rain, so I caught a lift in the sanctuary's Toyota pick-up with the park wardens who had been cutting firewood from fallen branches. Heading back down the track to Kongoni we came across the Canadian girls, wet through and looking pretty wretched. The veggie truck they had hitched with was stranded up to its axles in a lake of mud, so they piled into the tray and we drove back to camp.

ROBBERY

It must have been around 3am when I heard a faint K s s s . . .
K s s s . . . K s s s . . . followed by a rustling sound. I was
very drowsy and when the noise stopped I figured the cow or
monkey that had been touching my tent had gone away. I dosed
off to sleep again but was woken a few minutes later by a
similar noise interspersed with heavy drops of rain.

T a p – K s s s . . . T a p . . . T a p - K s s s . . .
T a p - K s s s . . .

I shot upright. This was wrong! And just as my eyes started
to focus on my day-sack lying by my feet, it scrunched up and
disappeared through a hole slashed in the tent.

"Baboons. They've got my day-sack!"

"Help!" I yelled at the top of my voice, "Help!" again and
again.

Tearing at the tent door and flysheet, I bowled out and was
running in the direction of my day-sack wearing just my boxer
shorts. My heart sank to the pit of my stomach when I saw two,
three, then four robbers roughly my size with a good head start,
but my whole world was in that bag and I wasn't going to let
them get away with it. Adrenalin surging, I sprinted after the
one still on my side of the deep ditch running parallel to the lake
and soon caught up with him. Leaping across he stumbled at the
other side.

"You're mine, bastard," I thought as I prepared to jump the
ditch and take him.

W H A C K !

In full stride something hit my left hand with terrific force,
thumping it against my side. Under the dim moonlight blood
started to flow freely from a large flap of skin lifted up below
the knuckle. Enraged now, I prepared again to jump. My
assailant, still crouching on the ground, drew back his arm ready

with another rock. He blended into the darkness but I was sure he could see me clearly. The next invisible missile could smash into my face or take out an eye. Two of his mates splashed furiously through the lilies at the waters edge towards the campsite boundary but could have turned and attacked if it came to a fight. The tent slasher had a knife and what if the others had machetes? As I thought about it the stone thrower got up and bolted. It was impossible to follow in bare feet so I raced back to the tent for my sandals, but it was all over bar the shouting.

Three security guards arrived a few minutes later and reluctantly agreed to go through the thorn bush and cactus boundary to the neighbouring plantation. We searched for over an hour, but it was hopeless. Even if the thieves were still lying low we would never find them.

"Christ, they've got everything!"

I desperately wanted to get into the office and call the police but the guards didn't have a key and told me it would be a waste of time anyway. Even if the station had been manned, the police had no vehicles. Dismally I dragged up my sleeping bag and shredded tent. Shocked and bewildered the girls picked up theirs and we moved into the bandas.

There was one more distasteful task to be performed before retiring to our hut. Karen, the most together of the Canadian vets, insisted on thoroughly cleansing and dressing the wound on my hand.

"I was wondering when we'd get to use our fantastic medical kit," she said enthusiastically. "You're not going to faint are you?"

I felt queasy as she drew back the flap of skin, scrubbing bare meat under a running tap at the outdoor washbasin. When she was certain the wound was scrupulously clean she dressed it, wrapping my hand in bright orange horse bandage.

My brain was on overload. There was such a lot to think about. Traveller's cheques would eventually be refunded even though the robbers also had the receipts...but my passport? My budget had been dreadfully low anyway and it would cost too much to replace everything. Visions of going home after only eight days filled my mind, but there was nothing to go back to. No home, no job and no money. Desperately tired, I knew I had to get some sleep - it was going to be a very difficult day - but it was impossible to empty my head.

Just before dawn two shots rang out followed by a loud splashing from the lake. A while later one of the guards knocked on our door and returned my day-sack. I was speechless. Out of gratitude I gave him all my remaining cash - around £10. My wallet, containing the cash and miraculously a $100 traveller's cheque, were in my trousers which I had rolled into a pillow. Peering into the bag there, where I'd crammed them the night before were my passport, camcorder, camera, binoculars, spare clothing, multi-fuel stove and address book. Had the guard shot one of my attackers or had they simply dropped the bag while fleeing? In quiet moments later these thoughts would haunt me but right now there was just exhausted elation. All of a sudden there was a real chance I could continue my journey.

Around mid morning Tom and Ann Carnellis, the campsite owners, gave my slashed tent to their handyman, a little old man with an ancient pedal powered Singer sewing machine in a ramshackle hut and he began the repairs straight away. From their comfortable bungalow I called American Express, the local CID and the British Consulate, while Ann made some tea. They hadn't had a robbery for over ten years and assured me I had just been incredibly unlucky. As we waited for the police I started to feel slightly more relaxed.

"That ditch by the lakeside, what's it for?"

"To keep the hippos out of camp," Ann told me as she poured the tea. "A few years ago we had a nasty attack on some guests, so we dug the ditch."

"What happened?" I asked, more curious than ever.

"A couple and their young son were camped by the lake, pretty close to where you were. One evening they went to eat at our restaurant but stupidly, left the child behind in the tent. When they came back, a hippo was standing between them and the tent. The child woke up screaming so the father tried to distract the hippo, but it ran him down and bit into his backside."

I smirked thinking of the great lumbering beast biting into the poor blokes arse.

"He nearly bled to death before we could get him to hospital. Hippo attack is the second biggest cause of death among tourists in Africa."

She never did say what the first was!

A couple of hours later the CID turned up in a fruit lorry. An athletic looking constable in immaculate blue uniform, shiny boots and beret carrying a cane, a plain-clothed detective and another dressed in a smart green suit. They mulled over the crime scene, went to where the rock was thrown and followed the robbers' escape route, while the suited detective took notes. Then, the four of us squeezed into the cab beside the driver - my knees uncomfortably over the gearshift - and we drove to Kongoni police station.

In a tiny breezeblock hut on the edge of a high walled compound, the constable filled out an official incident report and listed my stolen items. Air ticket, traveller's cheques, Berghaus rucksack, boots and around £450 in cash. It was big news and his colleagues popped in from time to time to ask me questions about life in Britain, the royal family and British politics. Behind an upended beer crate on the floor to my right, lived around a dozen tiny quivering bats. It was incredibly odd to see these secretive creatures in such an accessible place but they must have felt secure, as nobody ever bothered to spring clean or disturb the 'furniture'.

While I wasted the morning at the police station, the girls cycled round nearby Hell's Gate nature reserve. In the afternoon

I took a matatoo to Elsamere, former home of naturalist Joy Adamson. Joy Adamson had been a prolific artist and I wandered inside the old colonial house with its polished hardwood floorboards and staircase, admiring her stunningly lifelike paintings of Kenyan tribes and wildlife lining the ground and first floor walls. Witchdoctors, chiefs and fearsome warriors wearing wild headdresses of ostrich feathers or leopard-skin capes carried an array of spears, clubs and bows. Many of the tribes depicted had already vanished and the big game that once roamed freely with the changing seasons was now confined to a handful of national parks.

Outside I had cream tea on the substantial lawn with other visitors who had just watched the ageing 'Born Free' video. Many years ago on that same lawn, Joy had reared and played with Elsa and the orphaned lions we saw in the film. The Canadian vets arrived full of their day's adventures on clattering bicycles. At Hell's Gate, one of them had her camera stolen by a young park security guard who offered to 'look after' her bag while she went to the edge of a ravine for a better view. When the girls complained an older guard beat him up and returned the camera.

That evening I decided to celebrate the return of my multi fuel stove by cooking noodles with sardines. The girls donated a large sachet of vegetable soup and we set up candles, bowls and cutlery on a table between the bandas, ready for the feast. Carefully following the instructions I allowed a small amount of petrol to trickle onto the burner tray, set the valve to start, pumped the primer several times and then, lighting a match moved it cautiously towards the nozzle. Whoosh!

"Jesus Christ!"

Flames roared upwards threatening to engulf the overhanging thatched reed roof as petrol squirted from the nozzle onto the table. The girls searched frantically for something to smother the fire but the cylinder pressure soon dropped, the inferno died back to a more manageable flame-thrower and as the stars and chirping crickets came out we settled back to enjoy a congealed pudding of piping hot fishy noodles.

In bustling Naivasha town the following morning I parted with the girls, who were leaving for Nairobi before going on to Zanzibar and a friendly hotelier cashed my only remaining traveller's cheque. Now at least I had enough cash to get back to Nairobi, sort my affairs and survive the next few days.

Early in the afternoon I rented a heavy single gear bicycle and puffed and sweated my way around Hell's Gate. A pillar of rock tall as a small block of flats, stood like a sentinel at the trackside entrance with a sign at its base warning visitors they climbed at their peril. The dirt track ran along a dry river bed flanked on either side by jagged granite cliffs over much of its length. A zebra bolted from some nearby bushes braying noisily in alarm as I trundled along on my rickety bike. Suddenly I felt very alone. Would it always leave me feeling so empty: meeting people, making good friends only to part a few days later?

Some Masai youths dressed in bright red and yellow tartan shawls, wandered past taking little notice of me as they laughed and joked to one another. Near the exit a ranger told me that leopards occasionally wandered through the park although sightings were rare.

"They especially like chasing white men on bicycles," he told me with a grin.

Back at the campsite restaurant that evening a massive South African introduced himself. He was taking a short break from chartering his powerful motorboat for marlin fishing off the Tanzanian coast. He'd heard about the robbery and wanted to know the full story.

"I'd have kept going, mun," he said a little insensitively, when I'd finished. "Jumped the ditch and beat the living shit out of 'im!"

I wasn't offended. He clearly meant it and anyway, he *was* twice my size. I'd lost my bottle and that was that.

* * *

The cramped two hour bus ride back to Nairobi began in sunshine. Sitting over the engine compartment I rotated bum cheeks every two minutes to the amusement of fellow passengers, when the thinly padded surface grew unbearably hot. A seat became available as the rain started, dripping through the broken window seal onto my lap.

Torrential rain hammered the sprawling grey city and its streets were awash, so I took a short taxi ride from the central bus station to Nairobi Youth Hostel. Built into the hillside, steps led down to a TV and games room on my left as I entered. Rainwater gushed from a far corner of the ceiling and the parquet flooring curled, ankle deep in water.

The place looked deserted apart from a heavy-set African student in her late twenties who introduced herself as Agnes. Agnes offered to wash my shirt and pants for me - I hadn't realised I smelled so bad - and took me to the local police station social club a few blocks away where we chatted over a beer. Muggings and violent crime were rife, she told me and it certainly wouldn't have been safe to go there alone after dark.

Next morning at the British Consulate, an intimidating top security building surrounded by high walls, razor wire and armed guards, the administrator was very friendly and helpful, sending a fax to my brother for replacement gear: spare water canteens, clothing and a small first-aid kit.

An ibis cried from its roost in a tree as I walked back up Haile Selassie Avenue under a filthy grey sky. It looked like the scene from 'The Killing Fields' when refugees poured out of Saigon. Battered cars, trucks, hopelessly overloaded matatoos and buses were grid-locked and belching thick choking smoke into perpetual rain. Thousands of desperately poor people milled between the stationary vehicles or trudged with sandals and worn out shoes through mud and debris at the roadside. A stream in torrent marked the spot where pavements used to lie. This was Nairobi. No wonder the ibis cried.

Often, despite enduring hardships, people were just plain friendly and genuine, like the fruit seller near the youth hostel who always chatted and joked with foreign visitors, or the woman who inadvertently poked me in the face with her oversize umbrella. Ever so polite and apologetic.

Back at the hostel I had dinner with Cheryl, a cheerful young woman whom I had seen several times mooching around the hostel. She and a group of fellow Canadians had recently attempted to climb Mount Kenya but were beaten back from the snow covered summit by driving sleet. Cheryl had worked in the townships for the past six months with street kids and she told me some of her stories.

"Two of the little boys were cold," she said, "so I gave them warm clothes to wear. When they changed I saw their bellies swollen like footballs, from hunger."

When a businessman was killed in nearby Machakos district the street kids were blamed and a number of them promptly rounded up and flung in jail. Cheryl went to visit - she worked with some of the 'suspects'. Inside it was almost too dark to see but there were up to thirty kids in one cell. Aged thirteen to sixteen, they looked no older than ten, their bodies stunted from solvent abuse and malnutrition. Small hands gripped the cell bars and she heard their pitiful cries for help.

A group of orphaned pre-pubescent girls were caught at a water hole with some adolescent boys. Apparently the older boys would pay a shilling to 'play'. When Cheryl walked into class, the girls were lined up in a kneeling position while their feet were beaten with metal rods.

Cheryl told me she was mugged in Nairobi and later had 400 Kenyan shillings stolen from her bag by a supervisor. It was too much to bear when the woman blamed the kids. That was when she left to climb Mount Kenya.

With a number of traveller's cheques refunded and sporting a cheap but colourful replacement rucksack, I set off in high spirits one morning to visit Lake Victoria. I took a matatoo to the 'country bus station' on the far side of town but as the minibus slowly emptied and we entered a particularly derelict area I was warned repeatedly I would get robbed.

"*Mzungu*, you have a heavy rucksack," said the bus tout, a sinister grin on his face. "We make it lighter for you," and he drew a forefinger across his throat in a cutting motion.

The country bus station was a bombsite. Rubble, mud, deep puddles and a sea of frowning faces that all seemed to focus on the only white man. Muggers don't like attacking in broad daylight. If they're caught in Kenya there is a real danger they will be beaten to death by the public who have had enough of them. But if there was a big enough gang, the traveller could be knocked to the ground, rucksack straps slashed. Complete strangers were now stepping onto the bus, smiling cynically.

"Come on, mzungu, we take you where you want to go."

"I don't bloody think so!" I thought. Maybe they were only joking but it wasn't worth the risk, so I stayed on the matatoo and returned to the youth hostel.

A small, tough looking Japanese biker had moved into the male dorm on my return, his rucksack and pannier bags were padlocked to a bedpost. He'd been on the road for two years and expected to be riding for another year still. To get there he had ridden across Canada and the States, then shipped his bike to South Africa. From Cape Town he made his way up through Namibia and across the Caprivi Strip, riding undaunted into war torn Burundi. After Kenya he wanted to ride across Egypt and on to Europe. Must have had an arse of leather.

mzungu - white man or woman.

28

"Any trouble with the rebels in Burundi?" I asked.
"Oh, Burundi quite safe," he replied jovially.
"Yeah, sure!"

* * *

It was a three hour journey in a cramped Peugeot estate taxi to Kisumu town on the north-eastern shore of Lake Victoria. Nearby, Donga campsite was sheltered by tall deciduous trees whose leaves rustled noisily on the warm breeze. The cool waters of Lake Victoria spread out across the horizon and lapped against a small wooden jetty at the edge of camp. Near the entrance stood a great steam boiler and massive cast iron gear wheel, rusting remnants of an old sugar mill from the distant days of industry and empire.

Morris and Benjamin worked at the camp and were refreshingly gentle in their approach as they touted for business, guided tours and the like. There were no other tourists and feeling vulnerable I asked them repeatedly about camp security. They assured me everything was cool and introduced me to *Umzui* the security guard, a wily old chap with silver-grey hair and a stubbly beard. Umzui wore a stifling combination of green Wellington boots, heavy grey trench coat tied at the waist with cord and a purple beret. His pleasant demeanour to mzungus belied the fact that he would probably kill any local intruder with the metal *rungu* he carried. A hammercop - curious African bird, big as a raven with a pterodactyl head - flew back and forth to its squawking young nesting in the crown of a baobab tree at the edge of camp. A good omen, I decided.

When I had pitched tent the two young men took me on an obligatory boat ride to see some hippos. Morris and Benjamin were in their early twenties. Morris was tall, lean and muscular.

Umzui - old man.
rungu - club with slender body and bulbous end.

His comrade Benjamin, was almost a head shorter and slightly built. They seemed unfairly matched on the oars as we struck out against a stiff breeze in the heavy wooden boat and I worried we might steer around in circles.

Vast Lake Victoria rippled with silver waves like fish scales. We watched giant brown and white kingfishers skimming the shallows and a white headed fish eagle perched high in a dead tree, surveyed its territory. Cormorants stood on fallen logs drying their outstretched wings and barely a stone's throw away, two female hippos with young gaped their massive pink, tusky jaws for the camera just at the right moment. Benjamin told me they wouldn't dare row so close to the highly territorial male.

Dhows on the pale blue horizon had large triangular sails set for Uganda. The scene was tranquil, almost idyllic, but what was that green stuff floating all around? Someone introduced water hyacinth to Lake Victoria a decade ago and it is so prolific that great islands of it now blow across the water. Some years it totally chokes the lake, cutting off the oxygen and killing huge numbers of fish. It was everywhere. As he worked his oar Benjamin told me the authorities were going to buy a specially adapted dredger from Israel to hoover up the problem, but I got the feeling it would be like mowing a lawn with a pair of nail clippers.

Benjamin suggested I went with him to Donga Village for supper that evening and as dusk fell we passed men working on long wooden fishing boats with high curving prows, repairing their nets. We huddled bolt upright on awkward wooden stools, the only diners in the tiny whitewashed restaurant. Distant flashes of lightning threatened stormy weather and the wind blew papers and receipts around inside, but Benjamin assured me the rain wouldn't reach us until later.

Service was painfully slow. I couldn't help thinking it was because I was there: wealthy white man, descendant of the old colonials, but eventually our meal arrived. First ugali, a tasteless chunk of boiled mashed maize that we ate with our fingers. Then scuma-weeky, chopped green cabbage boiled then stir fried with oil, chilli and herbs. The name means stretch out the week, as the leftovers can be added to day after day to make it last. Finally a pair of tilapia, grilled fish the size and shape of a perch, were placed on the table.

We squelched back to the campsite serenaded by crickets and frogs. Oil lamps lit kiosks and clay walled homes with thatched roofs along the way. No electricity here. A terrible crying and wailing came from inside one house as we passed by and I figured someone must have died.

"A funeral," Benjamin told me. "They drink *pemba*, make party. Would you like to see?"

"Er, no thanks," I told him, thinking that would be a bit too much of an intrusion.

Having a strong interest to learn about Kenya's nature and wildlife I was keen to visit Kakamega forest half an hour's drive away, a tiny remnant of the central forest belt that only two centuries ago had stretched from the west to east coast of Africa. After breakfast next morning I said goodbye to Morris and Benjamin and was promptly ripped off on the short taxi ride to the matatoo station.

This matatoo was smaller and even more cramped than the usual battered minibuses. An ancient police arrest vehicle with rock hard suspension that jarred over every stone, it still had a reinforced metal grill across the tiny rear windows and I kept sliding off the impossibly narrow wooden bench seat. During the excruciating journey my young neighbour befriended me explaining it was his duty to see I was safe. At Kakamega village he took me to the local sports club where a stooping grey haired old man introduced himself. Lucas said he would guide

pemba - soupy home brewed beer.

me as far as Kakamega forest but I had to tip him and pay for his fare and fags. He cost me 600 Ksh in the end. I'd had enough and blew my top when the girl in the adobe park office asked for yet more money.

"I've been robbed of almost everything I had in Naivasha. I've been ripped off coming out here. Everyone looks at me and says, 'Mzungu. Ah we can steal from him'. Mzungu doesn't mean white man," I told her, "Mzungu means, I'm a target - steal from me!"

She looked pretty bewildered and when I'd finished my tirade I humbly apologised and paid.

"You must learn to relax," she said knowingly, "or you won't survive in Kenya."

Eunice, my demure guide, accepted my apology and began telling me about Kakamega forest as we set out along a narrow trail into the green gloom, pointing out different types of vegetation and wildlife. We stepped through mighty tangled root systems of parasitic strangling fig trees, growing down like giant cages from the crown of the host tree - now vanished - where the seed was originally dropped by a bird or monkey. Mahogany trees with mighty towering trunks and sturdy buttress roots were home to elusive blue monkeys, red-tails and colobus high in the uppermost branches. Our muddy track meandered through thick undergrowth as we brushed against broad dripping leaves and hanging vines, past landmark trees and shrubs. Eunice knew them all.

Kakamega forest covers roughly 240 square kilometres in south-western Kenya and is packed with a stunning variety of mammals, reptiles and birds. Eunice told me that before the mzungus came certain trees were considered sacred, among them, mahogany. This was all that was now left in one intact, heavily threatened section. She explained that even within the park confines the forest was raided daily for firewood and building materials. It was hard to believe that at this late stage the area wasn't better protected.

Lucas was gone when I emerged from the forest but near the park exit I met Frederick, a bicycle-taxi rider in his mid teens. Bicycle taxis are very basic machines, black with heavy steel frames and only one gear. I sat astride a firm, narrow leather pad on the rear rack which became torture after only a few minutes. Frederick huffed and puffed along the sandy track pedalling me back to the main road, where I waited with a bunch of people on their way home from a hard day's work on the tea plantation.

ORPHANS

It was just as well I set off early for the Sheldricks' place. I had read so much about them and was keen to visit but trying to find a matatoo to get me there only resulted in total confusion. Everyone I asked said they had never heard of Daphne Sheldrick, her rhino orphanage, or even of rhino.

"Rhino. It's a bloody big animal with horns coming out of its head!"

"I know wut e rhino ees!" said the matatoo tout indignantly. The other passengers smiled at my lack of cool. Meanwhile, we were so tightly squeezed inside - people leaned across in front of my face with their bums against the sliding door - that I didn't even notice when the guy sitting next to me slipped his hand into the front pocket of my day-sack resting on my lap and stole my glasses. I can see pretty well close up without them, but I did need them for viewing wildlife.

Finally I spotted a sign to the 'elephant and rhino orphanage', got off and turned down a long bush lined track. The place had once been a farm with machinery and outbuildings strewn here and there. A tall slim woman in her late forties, dressed in jogging trousers and T-shirt, emerged from the veranda at the rear of the well-appointed bungalow. Daphne's daughter Jill seemed happy to talk about her work to the small group of visitors that had gathered.

Not many people could boast of having a national park for a back garden. Around forty black rhino were squeezed into neighbouring Nairobi National Park's forty-six square kilometres, a very high density for such territorial animals and the Sheldricks' latest charges came from there. It felt quite strange knowing that only twenty kilometres away was a bustling, sprawling city almost the size of London.

The orphan rhinos, a male and female both around three years old, arrived accompanied by two rangers, at the muddy yard overlooking bush-land dotted with small trees that trailed off into the distance. Standing as high as a man's waist and weighing almost half a ton, they loved to be tickled and scratched by their devoted guardians. One by one we were invited forward to touch them. Big round muscular bodies, coarse but sensitive skin. Even in these youngsters one could feel a great sensibility and mystery. Normally we could never get this close and it was a great privilege.

The female, Jill told us, was separated from her mother when cattle were brought into the park by local herdsmen. She was heard squealing pitifully for hours. Her mother was spotted careering through the park several kilometres away in a state of exhaustion, a spear protruding from her side.

The mother of the male had limped up to the Sheldrick's house one day and collapsed, too ill to move. After veterinary attention she recovered a little but her front right leg had been badly injured by a snare and there were spear wounds on her body. She hobbled about on three legs for several months until one day one of the rangers noticed she was pregnant. She gave birth to a healthy male calf but was in great distress afterwards and had to be put down.

Jill explained that her mother built the orphanage and her stepfather, David Sheldrick, had founded Kenya Wildlife Service in the early forties, gazetting the large area that became Tsavo East in 1948.

"Up until then it had just been hunting, hunting, hunting, everywhere," she told us. "My stepfather was a man of great vision. He knew even then that if something wasn't done fast we would lose everything. He lobbied the government and officials but got absolutely nowhere. Then he had an idea and wrote articles to all the major newspapers.

'THIS WILDLIFE MENACE' and 'WILDLIFE THREATENS CROPS!'

He wrote:

"Wildlife threatens farms and the very economy of Kenya. Bounties must be placed for the extermination of elephant, rhino and zebra. Why should Kenyan farmers have to put up with such losses? These animals must be shot, poisoned..." He even suggested that herds of elephant should be bombed using aircraft! The response was outrage. People were so horrified that the government finally listened. Things were very tight back then and he was forced to manage all of Tsavo East's eleven thousand square kilometres with only six rangers. It was a major task but in those days it could be done.

Despite his efforts in the last 25 years the world's population of rhinos has plummeted from 72,000 to less than 11,000 because of poaching and human expansion."

We looked at the two calves, playing and nuzzling one another. They laid down on their sides in a sloppy wallow to let the guards scratch their underbellies and the softer skin where the inner thigh joins the body. They were in ecstasy, completely unaware of the desperate plight facing their species.

"We've reared over fifty orphaned elephants," Jill continued, "but we don't have any at the moment and the last two didn't fare very well. One was too small and just didn't make it. The other had a terrible time. After her mother was shot by poachers she fell into a river. We found her up to the top of her head in water. By the time we pulled her out she'd been there for ages. Can you imagine the trauma? A baby seeing her mother killed, tusks hacked out of her head in front of her and then standing, trapped in cold water for several hours!

Elephant babies are totally dependent on their mothers. She rallied round for a few days but we couldn't fight the infection from the cold and ingesting all that water. Antibiotics suppress the bacteria that aid digestion. Not the best thing for a growing baby."

The other visitors dwindled and left so I chatted with Jill as she prepared a special milk and protein mix for the young rhinos. A sparrow hawk swooped in low and fast through the dense tangle of rhododendron branches at the back of the house with a shrew in its talons.

"She always comes here and she always catches something," said Jill's husband ruefully.

We watched as she tore the unfortunate rodent apart.

"She's a lethal killer," said Jill, "but she never finishes what she catches so she's a wasteful beggar too."

Something stung me on the leg and I jumped back instinctively. Safari ants were on the march in broad columns, seemingly everywhere.

"What will you do if they go in the house?" I asked, alarmed.

"Get out the way," said Jill with a wry smile.

There was an astonishing variety of birds in the lush trackside vegetation on the way back to the main road. Red green and blue finches, a hummingbird with surreal gleaming neck feathers, grey shrikes about the size of a magpie bickering in a nearby tree and sunbirds with punky head-crests and long flowing tails. Kites with distinctive 'v' shaped tails circled adjacent fields and high above them vultures scoured the countryside for carrion. From every country you take a lasting picture or memory and in Kenya, for me it was the cra-a-ak, cra-a-ak sound of doves. They had me fooled at first when I thought the deep croaking that seemed to follow me everywhere, even in the small green spaces of the city, had to come from a larger bird like a marabou stork. Now, whenever I think of Kenya I remember that sound.

Back on the youth hostel roof that afternoon I watched mountainous clouds building in the distance as the kites thermalled in the late afternoon heat over Nairobi's grey tower blocks. I chatted with a silver haired man in his fifties optimistically setting out clothes on a line to dry. Dennis was quiet spoken, shrewd and dedicated. A biologist by profession, he'd come to Kenya to volunteer his services in conservation work. Kenya Wildlife Service had no money to supply a vehicle and he must have a vehicle, they told him, otherwise he'd just be lion food. He would also need to find and pay for a guide.

Lion numbers were plummeting in Tsavo National Park as the growing Massai population took ever more game animals for food. In addition, Dennis had a theory that too many safari vehicles were wandering off the official tracks. Tourists bribed their guides to get in close and often blew the predators' cover or scared away game. Driven by hunger the lions searched for easier prey in surrounding ranches and *shambas* among the cattle and goats and were slaughtered.

"So how can I get involved?" I asked him. "Do you need anyone to help with your research?"

"Not possible really. Kenyans are very wary of foreigners taking jobs here, even in voluntary work. They've already told me if I need a support worker it must be a native Kenyan."

His answer was disappointing but no great surprise.

"I've been fascinated about wildlife conservation since childhood," I told him. "I'll be passing through Tsavo in a few days on my way to Mombasa. If there's any way I could be of help…it would mean a lot to me."

Denis stroked his beard thoughtfully for a moment.

"Do you know anything about vehicles?"

"Yes," I nodded enthusiastically, "I used to be a mechanic."

He took a pen and piece of paper from his shirt pocket and scribbled something.

"When you get to Mombasa look me up," he said, handing me the slip of paper.

* * *

shamba - small plantation.

It was early evening. I sat on the patio eating fresh pineapple and mango from the nearby market stall with some of the other hostel guests. During a break in the rain warm humidity brought troublesome mosquitoes with the nightly serenade of crickets, so I washed down my malaria tablets with iodine dosed water. Iodine not only neutralises lethal bugs, it has the added advantage that fellow travellers detest the taste and never ask a second time for your canteen.

Mathias, in his mid-forties, had been living in the youth hostel for several months. His wife and kids lived in Britain while he studied in his native country. He was on the prowl looking for conversation and joined us while we ate.

"When I walk into Nairobi I see so many young men just standing around with nothing to do, wondering how they're going to make another shilling to feed themselves."

"Yes," sighed Mathias, sorrowfully. "It's a terrible thing, such high unemployment."

"But why have such big families when you know most of your kids will never find work?"

"You see," he said after some thought, "we have always had big families, dating back to when child mortality was very high. There are no pensions so children are expected to provide for the parents in their old age. A large family is still a sign of prosperity and wealth."

"Prosperity?" I gasped. "Kenya's population is growing exponentially but it can't support everyone now! What on earth will it be like in twenty, fifty years?"

"For any real hope of improvement we need a change of government," said Mathias, "because Moi and company are much too corrupt. If things ran efficiently they would never be able to embezzle as much as they do."

Ten years ago, he told us, for even suspicion of anti-Moi thinking, people were taken off into the forest and murdered. Many disappeared that way. That night at the youth hostel we debated loudly, but I hoped Moi himself crouched behind the patio wall and heard us. Then I really put my foot in it. Talking about the first white settlers I blurted out,

"The worst thing those morons ever did was bring religion and education to Kenya!"

I knew it was wrong even as I said it. Mathias's smile vanished, his face stiffened and his tone was suddenly very serious.

"Actually I am an elder of the church..."

Profuse apologies were urgently needed.

"I mean they were morons because they didn't try to understand native beliefs and culture."

No, that didn't sound like an apology.

"I'm sorry, I didn't mean to knock religion. I was out of order."

Mathias saw that I didn't mean any harm and when he'd lightened up again he told us a little about his family and background.

"My Uncle was the last medicine man in our village and he had a lot of wives. It seemed that every woman who went to his house for treatment ended up being his wife."

Several years ago Mathias had been a criminal prosecutor in Nairobi.

"I honestly believed that people who committed crimes wanted to go to prison because life was so much easier inside, so I dedicated my life to sending them there as efficiently as possible."

Rising late next morning I started to pack for Mombasa. With my remaining kit stowed, I assembled important documents on the bed... but where were my replacement traveller's cheques? I scoured the bunk bed and dorm but there was no trace. Bastard! They must have been stolen while I took a shower.

Back again at the American Express office in Nairobi town centre they gave me a thorough grilling. Two half-hour sessions on the phone to a very cheeky and unsympathetic oriental sounding female, half way across the globe. Finally I'd had enough.

"Listen, we can do this all day but what I need to know from you is, God forbid, if I lose any more cheques, will your company still replace them?"

"Why," asked the Amex clerk, "are you thinking of having some more stolen?"

I hit the roof, giving her a right earful and then let rip at her manager too.

"I'm stuck out here with my arse in the breeze and the very last thing I need is your insulting, unhelpful clerk accusing me of cheque fraud!"

At the police station on the other side of town chaos and anarchy reigned as dodgy looking characters queued and milled about. Who was guarding whom? Who actually worked there? I asked a smart looking man in a suit where to go for my theft report. He shook his head and gave that annoying clicking sound Kenyans make with the tongue against the palate when they are disinterested. Someone nudged my arm pointing out that the guy in the suit was waiting to be charged. Ushered into a side room I chatted to the lad in front of me.

"So, what did they steal from you?"

"All my money... but I caught him," and he pointed to the tall, gangly bloke with crooked teeth leaning against the opposite wall.

"Well done!" I exclaimed, remembering how I'd let my robbers get away and shook his hand warmly. While we waited in the small interview room for a detective, offenders and victims sat uneasily together. Looking sinister in dark flared collar shirt, drainpipe pants and white socks, the wide-boy robber started to harass his victim.

"Why you bring me trouble?" he implored, as though he really was innocent. "You come to me and ask my help. I am free man. Why you bring me trouble?"

On and on he went repeating the same old nonsense until finally, outraged at the situation his victim snapped.

"Why don't you shut the fuck up?" he shouted, glaring wildly.

The robber glared back and pointed a bony finger, "I not shut the fuck up. I am free man!"

"Not for long my friend, not for long."

Moments later the two were escorted away for questioning.

A young detective calling himself Mutia, arrived to write me a fresh report for the missing £600 traveller's cheques. He looked up between writing.

"England?"

"Yes," I told him.

"London," said Mutia, more as a statement, because London was the only place of note in England.

"Yes. Outskirts of London."

Mutia paused for a moment,

"Tell Tony Blair he must help us in Kenya. Former British colony. He must help Kenya!"

"That was more than forty years ago," I reminded him. "Kenya must look after herself now and anyway, what's the point of Tony Blair sending money to Kenya when the money's stolen before it even leaves the plane? They're not stupid in the West. They know what goes on here."

"Yes, yes," agreed Mutia, mercifully not offended. "It is a big problem here. We must sort it out. We need help."

He signed and passed me the document. I wished there was a way to help. Perhaps the West could take its boot off the neck of poorer countries by writing off their debt to us, but that would imply that we actually gave a damn.

I grabbed the report and was gone.

TSAVO LIONS

A woman died in third class on the way to Mombasa. No fanfare, no mourning relatives, no officials or post-mortem. Early fifties, snuffed out. In the darkness they dragged her past me along the aisle on a blanket. Leaving the body at a station in the middle of nowhere, they stepped back on the train. Someone else's problem now. Life was absurdly cheap in Kenya.

Thoughts soon turned back to my own misery. Unbelievably tired, I was in a sort of waking coma, there really was no way to sleep in third class and the hard upright seats were wickedly uncomfortable. Eyes didn't clear of gritty sleep when I blinked, backside and back ached terribly.

The Cosy guesthouse in Mombasa was a joke at less than the price of a bag of chips for a single room. An utterly ramshackle shag hole. Shredded mesh curtains, grey from decades of grime, billowed on the hot breeze that blew through my broken window. The piss stained mattress rose and fell in lumps and troughs under a torn bed sheet. Home.

A dusty main street led to the town centre of two storey colonial Portuguese merchant dwellings with balconies and shuttered windows. At nearby fort Jesus, built in the 1600s to protect the nation's interest in timber, ivory and slaves, heavy black painted cannon looked out to sea from portals in the two metre thick walls. I recognised a couple of Australian lads from Fisherman's Camp but they were in a hurry, desperately searching for the cheapest possible way to get to Zanzibar. Later that afternoon I went for a refreshing swim in a rocky cove just outside Kilindini harbour and spotted them stretching out on a long motor dhow, heading for the clove island. On my way back to Cosy I stopped by the office of Kenya Wildlife Service. Dennis wasn't there so I left a note with one of the rangers.

Sitting in the Excellent restaurant that evening I was served by a chirpy waitress who looked and sounded like the lady cop with the squeaky voice in 'Citizens On Patrol'. Her colleague, a grumpy ill natured waiter, positively scowled at the customers and at me, the only mzungu, in particular.

So engrossed in my thoughts and unwittingly frowning at the glass of Tusker beer in front of me, at first I didn't recognise the mzungu who had just entered the restaurant. It was Dennis and he'd brought with him a plump Kenyan wearing a broad smile and a smart tailor made suit.

"Got your message," said Dennis. "This is Mr Mabele, deputy parks administrator for Tsavo. He may be able to help with the matter we discussed in Nairobi."

Mr Mabele's grin widened even further and a bead of sweat rolled down his forehead as he shook my hand vigorously. The two men sat down, ordered food and beer, then Dennis excused himself and walked to the bar where he seemed to be on friendly terms with the barman. Mr Mabele took this as his cue.

"I unde-stand you would like to visit our park as a re-such assistant. This ees not usually pemitted." He paused to let me guess where he was leading, "…but you know, anything is possible here in Kenya."

We haggled for a while, eventually agreeing on the sum of two hundred and fifty dollars for ten days inside the park, plus fifty for the gate keeper. Dennis glanced over and seeing we had concluded our business, rejoined us.

"If that's all taken care of…"
Mr Mabele and I nodded in unison.

"Good."

Dennis explained that his Land Rover kept jumping out of second gear and told me if I could fit a replacement gearbox we could be on our way as soon as it was up and running.

With the pressure off we were able to talk more freely. I chatted with Mr Mabele - Desmond - about his family, home and job. Despite having been fleeced I decided he wasn't such a bad character after all and it was humbling to learn that his monthly salary as a top parks official amounted to little more than I earned back home in a day.

Early next morning I met up with Dennis at the KWS office and after dealing with some paperwork he drove us to the vehicle compound, a disused farm on the edge of town. Inside a ramshackle corrugated iron barn was a shabby assortment of trucks, vans and farm equipment. Space had been cleared around a partially cannibalised long-wheelbase Land Rover, designated as gearbox donor.

Dennis produced a comprehensive tool kit from the back of our vehicle.

"I'm walking back into town, got some more supplies to sort out. Our guide should be along in a little while to help you. His name's Nyerogi," and with that, he was gone.

Having removed all bolts and connections from both gearboxes I lay on the ground, staring up through the donor vehicle's open floor panel, wondering how to lift the heavy lump on my own. In the poor light I was suddenly aware of a pair of eyes in a little black face, staring back down at me. Alarmed, I made to sit up and cracked my head sharply on the bell-housing.

"Bollocks!"

"Sorry boss," cried the stranger, rushing round to see if I was OK. Nyerogi introduced himself when I stopped swearing and we shook hands. He was thin and of athletic build, apart from a small paunch above cut-off jeans. He was in his late thirties, I guessed and stood only around five feet six inches tall. We exchanged pleasantries and I suggested how we might move the heavy gearboxes between the two of us.

"OK boss."

"Nyerogi," I said, "you shouldn't call me that. My name is Andy."

If his skin hadn't been so dark, I would have sworn Nyerogi blushed. His politeness and respect for a complete stranger were quite touching.

The operation went smoothly and we tightened the last bolts as Dennis returned. Then it was time for a test drive into town to collect the new supplies. The three of us spent a good hour loading food, water and equipment into the Land Rover. Care was needed to ensure that fragile items wouldn't be crushed and more frequently needed equipment could be easily reached. As last light faded we parked the Land Rover in the secure KWS compound and walked to the Excellent for supper.

It was an hour's drive along bumpy baked mud roads to the ranger station on the edge of Tsavo. I hid in the back under sleeping bags and a stinking canvas tarpaulin while Dennis handed over visitor's permits and gave my fifty bucks to the security guards. It was agreed I should keep out of sight despite my arrangement with Mr Mabele just in case any officials showed up unexpectedly, but when we were well inside the park I sat up front with the others.

The scenery was wonderfully different, this was the animals' domain. No farms or agriculture, no towns, villages or people. Trees and bush-land gave way to rolling hills covered in waist-high elephant grass. In every direction there was some form of big game to be seen. Antelope, a large herd of buffalo by a tree lined river and easiest to spot of all, giraffe in the distance. Dennis stopped the Land Rover and checked our position on the map against his global positioning system before explaining its basic operation to Nyerogi and myself. Nyerogi was not only a likeable character, he was very knowledgeable too and suggested we visit an area of marshland surrounded by hills a few kilometres away, a favourite ambush site for lions.

The marsh area had good access from a dirt road in the south and it seemed an ideal place for us to observe the effects of tourist activity on lion behaviour. We took up position on the tallest hill, leaving the vehicle just out of sight of the marsh. Dennis set up a tripod for powerful binoculars and another for a camera with an enormous telephoto lens. Nyerogi and I put up the tarp as a sun shelter and beneath it laid out a table for maps and writing equipment, chairs and cooking gear.

"Nyerogi, can you fetch the laptop and the maps?" I asked, fumbling with a stubborn guy rope. "They're up front under the passenger seat."

"OK bwana makubwa." he replied with a wry grin and went to find the items.

I looked quizzically at Dennis.

"Big white boss," he translated.

Enough said.

The grass had been grazed back to knee height on the hilltop and it was easy to spot any unwelcome visitors, but we kept a sharp eye out all the same. It was a hot muggy day and the sun struggled to break through the haze. We could see the whole valley from our vantage point and with the binoculars no movement could escape our attention. Sharp eyed Nyerogi barely needed them and soon spotted a pair of mature lions about two kilometres away on some raised ground.

Before long an open top Land Rover brimming with tourists appeared from the western end of the marsh. They were nowhere near the official game trail and from the map it was hard to tell which road they had actually taken to get there. The Land Rover bulldozed its way through elephant grass and scrub, stopping in front of the soft ground. We couldn't see the number plate but the company logo was clearly visible so Dennis took photographs for evidence. The driver waited twenty minutes or so, then seeing nothing, skirted round the area and headed out to the east.

Around 10am the two large males, now accompanied by four lionesses, moved purposefully towards the marsh from the eastern valley. The males dropped out some 400 metres from the marsh while the females continued, becoming almost invisible among tall reeds. Their target seemed to be a herd of buffalo with small calves and a group of four zebra on our side of the marsh, but it seemed odd to approach from the wrong side. They were giving themselves a lot of very difficult ground to cover.

Dennis made another entry in his logbook as a pair of tourist minibuses came in on the official south road. As soon as they entered the floodplain both deviated off-road, pushing new tracks through the grass. They stopped to allow their passengers time to film and take photographs.

Another half hour had passed when Nyerogi, who had wandered to the edge of our hill, came bounding towards us.

"Boss, boss!" he hissed, forgetting in his excitement what I'd told him in the vehicle compound.

"Look boss!" He pointed to an area at the foot of our hill, imploring us to see. Dennis found it with the powerful binoculars and made an agreeable sound. Not to be left out, I scanned the area with my pocket binoculars taking line of sight from Nyerogi's outstretched arm. A twitch of tail, the flick of an ear, then sleek, urgent movement through the long grass. Two more lionesses were closing on the buffalo, right beneath our noses. They were clearly from the same pride, moving in to spook the buffalo across the marsh to their waiting companions. The hairs stood up on the back of my neck and I could hardly believe the scene of life or death unfolding before our eyes. It was impossible not to get caught up in the spectacle of it and the three of us looked on like Romans lusting for gladiators' blood.

One of the bus drivers spotted the two conspicuous males and both vehicles drove towards them just as a third bus appeared trundling down the south road. We watched in disbelief as the first two pulled up barely a stone's throw from the two males. Meanwhile, our two females had closed another fifty paces on the buffalo but were running out of cover as elephant grass gave way to patchy reeds and open water. Infuriatingly, the third bus made its way over to join the others - where there's a crowd there's usually something to see. Its driver stopped half way between the marsh and the other vehicles but from this position he was too close to the ambush group.

The babbling sound of excited tourists carried, distorted by the hot breeze, to where we stood. To the ambush party it must have been intolerable. A zebra brayed its alarm call and buffalo and zebra began slowly moving to the western edge of the marsh. Whatever happened, they weren't going to run towards three white vans and their noisy occupants. The male lions, sensing it was all over, stood and slowly wandered down to where the females still lay hidden. Now zebra and buffalo moved in earnest to reach dry land. The lionesses didn't move, it wasn't worth the energy. The ambush had taken all morning to set up and this was the best area for miles around. Where else could they go? Dennis looked up from his binoculars.

"It's worse than I thought," he said blankly.

We spent the rest of the day observing and making notes. It was late afternoon before the large pride finally moved out, hungry, their efforts wasted. At one point we'd counted six vehicles. None of them kept to the official road and their fresh tracks flattened the grass in all directions. I felt a little guilty as we cooked up rice and tinned stew. For us it was easy. With light fading we packed away our food and cooking gear and retreated to the Land Rover's roof platform to discuss the day's events.

"We'll stay here for two more days to make sure it wasn't just a fluke," said Dennis, "and then I'd like to visit that water hole to the east you mentioned, Nyerogi."

Competing prides of lions roared and bellowed throughout the night interspersed with the hideous cackle of hyenas.

"Since Richard Leakey left KWS ten yees ago theh has been much less control in the parks," Nyerogi told us. "This place is pretty useless for hunting now but the lions steel fight ova it every night. It ees theh instinct. Theh tradition!"

Inside I snatched fitful sleep, bedroll and sleeping bag laid out on top of our supplies, while Dennis and Nyerogi fared little better on the roof.

Day two followed much the same pattern and we counted thirty-five tourist vehicles before dusk, only two of which kept to the official road. The first arrived at dawn so the resident pride was never able to set up a daylight ambush.

On day three no lions came at all, so accurate data would clearly require a longer period of observation. Instead, we counted a staggering forty-two vans and trucks. It was a curious kind of nature watch, observing our fellow humans as if they were merely another species of game.

Late in the afternoon a group of four African rangers chanced by our hilltop in a shabby Nissan Patrol and stopped for a visit. Dennis showed them his papers and they didn't seem too concerned that my details weren't listed. One of the guys recognised Nyerogi and they chatted for a while in Kikuyu.

It looked as though the rangers had one uniform between them, substituting the rest with assorted civilian garb. One wore the olive green combat trousers, another the jacket, a third the beret while the fourth sported army boots and webbing. They all carried very businesslike bolt action Enfield rifles though. Thomas, the youngest of the group, allowed me to inspect his gun and I lined up on fake targets in the marsh while Dennis and Nyerogi demonstrated the binoculars and impressive camera.

"Good job the tour companies don't have many four wheel drives," commented Dennis as I pretended to nail a grazing wildebeest, "otherwise they'd all be up here as well."

I told Thomas we had seen tour buses going off road and spoiling lion ambushes. He replied that there weren't enough rangers to cover Tsavo properly and his group were actually dealing with the more urgent problem of poachers hunting for bush meat. Thomas had never been to school and learned to speak English through the job. He was twenty years old and had been with the ranger service for four of those. The rangers left us late in the afternoon.

We chatted again that night on the roof. It was Dennis' turn to sleep in relative quiet inside, so I wanted to be as tired as possible before turning in. I asked Nyerogi about his background and people.

"I am Kikuyu," he announced with considerable pride. "Theh are eighty-five different tribes in Kenya and more than feeftee diff-erent dialects but Kikuyu is the lagest."

Nyerogi's family had lived in the tiny village of Shombe about eighty kilometres north of Nairobi, for several generations. Although they were Kikuyu his great grandfather had been a Bushman, which explained Nyerogi's modest stature. He had a wife and four children and enjoyed home life, but all the males in Nyerogi's family had inherited a nomadic wanderlust. It was his love of the Bushman's way of life that kept him away from home, often for months at a time. Being a registered tracker with KWS carried prestigious status and he showed me the official cap badge and identity card he kept in a hide pouch tied to his waist. As a young man, he told me, he had worked with the last of Richard Leakey's controversial Anti Poaching Units.

"In those days I saw a lot of action. It was like a war with poachas from Uganda, Sudan and Tanzania.

I rememba one patrol back in 1984. I was with six rangers on the trail of a gang who had butchered many elephants near Lake Turkana. The poachas weh heavily armed and led us into a trap. Three of the rangers weh keelled straight away, I was shot in the stomach," and with that, Nyerogi pulled up his t-shirt. Grabbing the kerosene lantern that stood between Dennis and myself, he held it to his abdomen to reveal the dearly won small, purple scar. Dennis sat back lazily against a bedroll and lit his pipe. He'd heard the story before, but I was enthralled.

"What happened? How did you get away?"

"One of the poachas came over to steal the dead ranger's weapons, so I waited 'till he was close and then I keelled him with my spear!"

He picked up the spear laying beside him and held it aloft, triumphantly.

"Bloody hell!" I gasped.

"The shooting went on fo a while. Eventually the pochas got scared and ran away."

Nyerogi had many such tales of close encounters with poachers. Even more hair-raising were his stories of hunting rogue elephants and man-eating lions but some of them, I would say, bordered on the fantastic. Dennis had worked closely with Nyerogi for two months now and was well aware of his exceptional storytelling ability. He took much of what Nyerogi said with a pinch of salt. No one, however, doubted Nyerogi's skill as a tracker. It was eerie the way he could read the faintest trail signs, shallow paw or hoof depressions. It made little difference if the ground was soft or hard. Folded grass stems, a freshly broken twig. Pungent scent marker sprayed by a leopard on a tree trunk or secreted on a bulrush from the eye of a water buck. He told us what the animals were thinking and by doing so, predicted when the leopard would return to finish its kill in the fork of a baobab tree, or when it was time for the baboons to visit a water hole to drink. He was a genius.

Out of earshot Dennis told me, "Nyerogi could track the ghost of a butterfly across a lake!"

I listened intently to everything he said and tried to learn as much as I could about bush-craft.

"Tomorrow," I told him, puffed up with a pretend air of importance, "I'll show you how I make fire without matches."

Nyerogi nodded his approval.

In the morning we drove to the waterhole Nyerogi had recommended and to our horror, it was much worse than the marsh area. An absurd Picadilly Circus where humans stayed safely inside their vehicles while the animals fought over the limited territory in between. A water hole is naturally a muddy place but there in the summer heat, constant churning from vehicle tyres had turned the area into a dust bowl. The dust blew around whipped up into hot, blinding whirlwinds adding to the torment of zebra and wildebeest.

By mid-afternoon we stopped counting when we reached sixty vehicles and drove a kilometre or so straight into the bush for shelter and quiet. Dennis noted our observations in his journal and Nyerogi went with me as a sharp eyed lookout while I cut and collected the materials I needed:

A branch thick as my thumb and as long as my arm with a piece of para-cord tied loosely between the ends to form a bow. A shorter rounded length of softwood for a drill, fashioned with a gentle radius at one end and a point at the other. A short block for a hand-held bearing and a base of hardwood. A bit of shaping and fine tuning and you have what you need to make fire. A bow-drill.

Peeling the loose bark from a dead vine as Ray Meers had shown me on one of his *woodlore* courses the previous year, I rubbed the fibres between my hands until they became fine and wispy. Folding them over and over on themselves to make a tight springy bundle, this would be my tinder. We walked back to the Land Rover where Dennis had finished making notes and gathered a pile of dry twigs for kindling. Dennis had thoughtfully set out a ring of stones as a fire break and filled the billycan ready for a brew.

The pressure was on as I knelt down and looped my drill into the bow cord, supporting it between bearing and base. Working the bow back and forth as fast as I could, a small plume of smoke soon rose from the drill base but I hadn't anticipated how much harder any exertion was in the fierce

woodlore - In addition to his TV work Ray Meers runs courses teaching the art of surviving and thriving in the outdoors.

African heat. I stopped working the bow and checked under the drill base for smouldering embers. The tiny pile glowed for a moment and died. I tried again but now I was tired and my arm ached. I tried again and again but the glow from the little pile of embers always died before I could drop it onto my tinder.

In total frustration I stood and walked around the Land Rover a couple of times, cursing and shaking the cramp out of my arms. Then I knelt down and tried once more with renewed vigour. Smoke billowed from the drill base but this time I kept working the bow despite aching arms and shoulders, until my inner sense told me it was time to stop. Picking up the base with its tiny glowing beacon, I carefully tipped the embers onto the tinder. Blowing a jet of breath across it, there was a puff of smoke. I drew a deep breath and blew again…a small cloud of smoke…and again…and…fire! The tinder burst into flames. Holding it by the edge, I placed the ball of burning tinder under the kindling and stood back, exhausted but triumphant.

Nyerogi looked on impressed and then held up a green plastic Bic lighter.

"In Kenya, we use thees," and he flicked a small flame into life from the thumbwheel. Dennis and Nyerogi burst out laughing. A moment later I tossed the bow into a thicket and joined in.

Two more days at the water hole produced an alarming picture as larger game and predators alternated control over the hotly contested site. When the elephants became so hungry they could no longer defend the territory they reluctantly moved on and lions moved in. Starved down to the rib cage, different prides fought viciously over the worthless muddy wallow while flocks of tourist buses came and went, ensuring that no kills were ever made.

Within a two kilometre radius, Nyerogi led us to the remains of three lions in varying states of decomposition. It was hard not to get emotional when, out patrolling the surrounding area we came across a ragged emaciated young female by an outcrop of rocks. Driving closer we saw the reason for her pitiful moans of distress. Three tiny cubs lay lifeless on the grass beside her. Sad empty bags of fur, abandoned by the rest of the pride in times of extreme shortage. Yet there we were, surrounded by game. Nyerogi looked on impassively. His spirit and all his knowledge told him, 'This is how it is, you can't change it', but I knew inside he boiled with rage, like Dennis and me.

Our final port of call was a pair of cattle ranches three hours drive away along the northern perimeter of Tsavo. To the ranchers, straying lions had become a menace and despite paying increasing amounts on round-the-clock patrols, they were losing more cattle then ever. When they realised Dennis was there to help and not just tell them not to kill lions, they began opening up sharing information about sightings, attacks on livestock and confirmed lion kills. One rancher took us to an outhouse behind his barn and flung open the door. Peering through the gloom inside we counted twelve lion skins.

"It was a bad year," he told us.

It was late and he invited us to stay for dinner. We ate grilled ostrich steaks on a large wooden veranda, sipping whisky and soda, and talked well into the night.

It was finally time to make our way out of the park. Dennis admitted he would have been happy to have me stay longer but we were low on supplies and there was the constant worry of a run in with park security. I had one last meal together with Dennis and Nyerogi back in the Excellent restaurant, then I bade them good luck and farewell.

Note: Since the departure of Erup Moi, Kenya Wildlife Service has developed into a highly motivated and effective force for national parks management and conservation.

KENYA COAST

Catching the early morning bus for Malindi further up the coast, I stepped off half way at Kanamai Youth Hostel. The place had dorm space and basic but comfortable double rooms for more than sixty guests arranged in ground level blocks around a grassy courtyard but I was the only visitor. The emptiness created an eerie atmosphere as if an outbreak of some deadly disease had driven everyone away.

The Kenyans in the church at neighbouring Kanamai Conference Centre were having afternoon choir practice as I sat on the covered patio, gazing out at the endless Indian ocean and perfect blue sky. Strong choral vocals against a fast, complex drum beat. It was almost midday and the tide was all the way out. Breakers pounding the coral reef over a kilometre away made a constant booming roar. A woman's voice called the next tune and in perfect unison, they changed the melody. In this wonderful setting the sound they made was truly uplifting. They slowed down the pace and shushed like a steam train pulling into a station. Voices called out, then a murmur rose to a noisy babbling hubbub. One of the campsite workers paused from sweeping up leaves and told me,

"They are praying."

Sure enough, they were. It was just their way of doing it.

I skipped lunch, walking instead with two lanky local lads, Salim and Mohammed, out to the reef. Anyway, the staff didn't want to cook for just one mzungu. There was a definite route to follow; the causeway of dead coral was submerged from ankle to knee-deep masked in places by seaweed and if the lads hadn't guided me I would never have made it. For the unwary all manner of spiny urchins, moray eels - Salim called them moran - and other stinging, biting nasties, lurked in cracks or under stones waiting to end your holiday or at least send you to hospital.

We walked for over an hour. The young men assured me that the bleached white coral had been dead for many years and we weren't really doing any harm. Nor were the scattering of fishermen over by the live coral beds where we were heading. Crunch, crunch, crunch.

At the living reef we were suddenly surrounded by splashes of brilliant pink, green, purple and red just below the water's surface. Giant puff balls, fragile lace patterns, multi-layered fan shapes and spiky antler coral. Here and there, exquisitely coloured fish hid or hunted between the layers and branches. Sadly, even here many of the coral tips had turned white and died. The reef was under attack from global warming, pollution up and down the coast and from fishermen who dragged their anchors across it and over-fished it.

Later that afternoon I walked slowly south down the beach. Jagged brown pockmarked limestone, like a magnified Aero chocolate bar, rose as high as a two storey house above the sea, severely undercut by pounding surf. Waves swept in, trapping air in the hollows with a whoomph-crash, shooting spray high into the air. Above me a lone tree looked as though it had grown there since the beginning of time. Mighty roots burrowed deep into the rock face and its enormous trunk curled upwards to a massive canopy of broad waxy leaves. I stopped to watch a strange bird about the size and shape of a cuckoo with a black Zorro eye mask, speckled chest and long barred tail. It seemed perfectly at ease as I approached to within a few paces and gaped its beak as if to call, taking a chest full of air, but made no sound.

The following day I nursed my sunburnt back sitting under the canvas patio shelter. The tide was in and fiddler crabs played tag with the surf while a sand wasp tirelessly flicked out sand from a tunnel it was excavating for its young. As the tide began to retreat I walked north along the coastline bordered with coconut palms. People hassled me along the way trying to sell trinkets or wood-carvings, while others just asked for money. After about an hour I reached a wall of rock protruding down to the sea with just a narrow weathered gap to walk through. A bunch of kids played naked in the waves and a man in his mid-twenties, dressed in shorts and a flowery Hawaiian shirt wandered across washed up palm branches and seaweed to intercept me.

"Why you no go through gap?" he demanded in a bullying tone that took me by surprise.

"Because I don't want to," I told him, remembering the warnings I'd heard about muggers on the beach. He had a dreadful stammer and we went awkwardly through the usual banter.

"Yu – yu – you from England?"

"Yes."

"London?"

"Yes."

"I th – th – think m – m – maybe you help me."

"How can I help you?" I asked, slightly ruffled, wondering what was coming next.

"I think m – m – maybe you give me shoes," he stuttered, nodding down at the sandals I carried by my side.

That struck a nerve. Kenya had robbed me and left me with nothing but sandals for my feet and now this bloke wanted to take those as well.

"Why should I give you my shoes?" I asked, a sense of outrage giving me renewed courage.

"Because I - I think maybe you have spare shoes. M - m - maybe you give me."

He seemed to think the world and in particular foreigners, owed him a living.

"Why should I give you my shoes?" I asked again, regaining control of the situation.

"OK," he finally conceded, "m - m - maybe I not understand."

"Easy mistake!" I told him, beating a hasty retreat.

On the way back I picked up some driftwood for a rungu, rapping it sharply on a rock to check its strength. It would be dark soon but the next hustler who wanted my sandals, binoculars, or the shirt off my back, had better have a gun!

Walking back to the main road next morning I got into a rhythm despite the rucksack straps aching on my sunburnt shoulders. Rachel, a student who worked part time in the shop at Kanamai camp, kindly offered me a lift and her mother drove while I shared the back seat with her aunt. I agreed to go with them to church, realising too late that it was all the way back down in Mombasa.

"So what do you think of my country?" asked Rachel as we bowled along.

"Well, you have a corrupt government, exploding human population growth and desperate poverty. I can't understand why the people just accept things the way they are."

Rachel was shocked. "Andy, there are things you must understand about Kenya. Five years ago the price of bread was five shillings. Last year it was ten. This year we pay twenty shillings for a loaf of bread, but when the price is too high, Kenyans will just eat something else."

Rachel paused for a moment to let me absorb what she was saying.

"We need a revolution, but before that happens here we will have to reach rock bottom and poor, unemployed and hungry as we are, we haven't reached that level yet. We don't even know where that level is! You talk about caring for the environment, for our children and our grand children. The average Kenyan doesn't think further than how to feed themselves tomorrow."

I felt a kind of helplessness predicting the serious problems the country was heading towards, but all thoughts and concerns for the future evaporated as we drove past lines of shanty market stalls on the outskirts of Mombassa.

Inside the plain, modern church spirits soared with joyful music, wake-you-up - shout-as-loud-as-you-can preaching and glowing warmth and fellowship. Men and women who had so little, still managed to put on a fine suit or brightly coloured dress and hat to look their best. The main choir sang sweet harmonies and the special guest choir dressed in long golden robes, had a potential hit on their hands. I imagined that morning in every big town across Kenya, similar choirs singing like angels.

The sermon was heavy going at times. A highly animated preacher spoke each sentence in English, translated immediately into Ki-Swahili by his faithful sidekick. He shouted a lot and all too often built up to a great crescendo, only to stumble for the right word at the punch line. The topic of the sermon was: it's not where or how you worship but who or what you worship that matters and the point was shouted home again and again.

The service ended and I said goodbye to Rachel, making my way to the nearby bus stop. The empty Malindi bus sat on tick-over for fully half an hour, then someone - not the driver - jumped into the cab and revved its nuts off for a further twenty minutes in the searing afternoon heat.

People slowly trickled onboard attracted by the frightful noise and billowing smoke. It seemed odd because it wasn't like selling vegetables or clothing, where a low price or colourful display might tempt you to buy. You either wanted to go to Malindi or you didn't. The engine didn't like it either and by the time we finally pulled away the main bearings had started to knock ominously. From almost empty the bus was now overcrowded, rows of seats impossibly close together, so I forced my knees down into the least excruciating position.

Half an hour into the journey the monotony was broken quite unexpectedly. As we pulled out to overtake a huge tipper lorry in front, he suddenly swerved directly across our path turning down a side road.

"Oh shit!"

Our driver hit neither horn nor brakes - probably neither worked - we turned tight inside the curving truck, but not tight enough to make the side road. The truck driver spotted us slamming on his brakes and we sailed past him straight into the forest. Smashing through dense undergrowth and creepers we came to an abrupt halt, breaking the bough of a large tree.

Before the dust and steam had settled everyone filed off and started jabbering all at once. I jumped out of the driver's door to inspect the damage and take photographs. A stout chassis member in front of the engine had folded neatly in half. The sump was stuck up on the unfortunate tree stump but it wasn't leaking and looked retrievable, so I asked a middle aged man sitting on a suitcase who seemed reasonably in control of himself,

"Why don't they use the truck to pull the bus off the tree?"

We watched as our driver and fellow passengers attempted to wrench open the cab doors to get to the terrified truck driver.

"In Kenya we don't do it like that," he said, dryly.

Grabbing my rucksack from the dead bus I threw it onto the other Malindi bus, which had miraculously appeared. Ten minutes later, with the others still squabbling, we were off and with slightly more leg room. Nice one.

From the moment I set foot in the small seaside town of Malindi I was followed by a young man, more Arabic-looking than African, in his early twenties. He barked questions at me as we walked into town.

"You look for hotel?"

"No thanks."

"Where you want to go?"

"I don't need any help thanks."

"You want cheap hotel?"

"Please, leave me alone."

"You want hashish?...You want girl?...You want boy?"

"Piss off!" I yelled, furious at the insinuation, but he persisted hovering a few paces behind, always in the corner of my eye. There were no other tourists in Malindi. They had all been scared off by a fear of escalating violence and by people like him. Faces glowered at me from inside corrugated iron shacks filled with wooden carvings nobody wanted as the beach road turned in towards the centre of town, away from the cheaper guest houses. Turning to walk back again my shadow was there, but I'd had enough.

"Why are you following me?"

"I not follow you. I go this way."

"What d'you mean you're going this way. You've been following me ever since I got off the bus. I've got nothing to give you. You have nothing I need. I'm the only tourist left, you've scared all the others away and now you're pissing me off too!"

He stopped following. I had made an enemy and I felt awful about that. It seemed like the whole of Kenya was falling apart and everyone blamed westerners.

Da Gama's guesthouse stood facing the Indian Ocean and a serene horizon. Francis, the young manager, was friendly and always willing to talk with his only guest. That evening he helped me catch up on world news. Then, out of the blue, revelation!

"...President Moi personally sacked David Weston, last Thursday," he said.

"You're kidding?"

David Weston was the new head of Kenya Wildlife Service. It was like a pantomime unfolding, where the plot was so utterly predictable you couldn't believe it would happen that way...until it actually did! Moi had stuck some crony in Weston's place and changed the law so that he and his friends could steal land from the precious national parks for 'development'.

The following morning I visited nearby Gedi ruins, site of an ancient fortress and long lost culture. The crumbling perimeter wall and buildings were made from smoothly carved stone blocks, now reclaimed by cool, shady, Arabuko Sokoke forest. The settlement was mysteriously abandoned less than five hundred years ago at a time when the surrounding area was still part of a giant central African forest belt.

A green and brown patterned lizard, about a foot long, darted across my path and wedged itself in a crack in the wall. Trying to examine it more closely I had almost tugged it free when suddenly its tail came off bloodlessly in my hand. I leapt back in horror as the disembodied tail writhed and squirmed dementedly. Lizards can re-grow their tails and will shed them in an emergency to evade predators. All the same, I couldn't help feeling it must have been pretty painful.

Peering down a deep well in the central complex, a round barn owl face stared back up from a chink in the brick lining. I rested on an upturned tree trunk whose roots enveloped a heavy stone block like a giant fist and a troop of macaque monkeys gathered in the branches overhead. Some of the females had babies clinging to them and kept a watchful eye while the males moved about to get a better view of the intruder. They still remembered a time when tourists visited regularly bringing titbits and treats.

I left the ruins and was shown around a series of large net enclosures in neighbouring Kiepio butterfly farm by Sally, a Voluntary Services Overseas worker from England.

"Local people are paid to collect butterflies from the forest and bring them back here to lay eggs," she told me, "and the pupae are sold to collectors around the world. The project benefits the local community and gives them a real incentive to preserve the forest."

As we inspected magnificently patterned butterflies in various stages of development, Sally explained that this was one of the best chances the remaining forest had for survival.

Malindi architecture had a visible Arabic influence with plain whitewashed plaster walls, flat roofs and small secretive windows and the town was split evenly between African and Arabic descendants. There was a sharp contrast that afternoon as I left the uncertainty of the Christian sector to walk among Moslem men in white drapes and women covered from head to foot with eyes peeping through black letterbox veils. It was clear from the men's faces that they were either indifferent or disapproved of westerners but despite this, I felt completely safe and knew no one would mess with me there.

By the edge of the reeking fish market, I watched while timber was manually loaded onto a great wooden dhow. The ship had a huge single mast that seemed to grow out of its cargo and a spacious bridge above the crew's quarters. Sinewy porters carried great planks up an enormous, perilously springy gangway, their backs glistening with sweat. The planks probably weighed as much as the men who carried them and they used their shirts rolled up like doughnuts on their shoulders, to protect them from their spine-crushing burden. I suddenly felt humbled that my life was so much easier.

That evening as I sat talking with Francis outside the guesthouse, drinking cold beer and swatting mosquitoes, a battered old Mercedes drew up and out hopped a huge Arabic guy. Hassam was a friend of Francis and he sat down to join us. After they'd caught up on one another's news Hassam turned to me asking the usual stuff; where are you from? What do you do for a living? Then he asked me about my religious beliefs and whether I was married.

"Of course, Moslem faith is the one true faith!" he said with an air of absolute authority.

"There are many people who would give you an argument about that," I told him. "I'm not convinced one hundred percent myself, but I guess I believe more than not."

"Why do you not believe?" demanded Hassam. "It is because inside, you know your Christianity is not the true faith! You can not sit in the middle on this matter my friend. Read the Koran. Read the Koran. When you have faith, everything comes to you. Success..." and he stroked the heavy gold chain and Rolex that adorned his thick wrists. "I have my business and it goes well. God has smiled on me. A good wife...someone to wait at home for me and bring up my children. Your English women have no respect for their husbands. They argue with them, don't do their housework and bring shame on them. If my wife is like that I give her this!" and he slapped his fist in gesture.

I thought about it and just for a moment of sheer self-indulgence - aside from the violence of course - it almost seemed like a good idea. An arranged marriage. Gone was the uncertainty of searching for the 'right woman'. A devoted wife who would always do everything I asked and never complain...and that's when the bubble burst. I couldn't imagine a situation where one's partner was utterly subservient, not free to have their own opinion. Such a relationship would be unspeakably dull. If Moslem married life was so great, how come Hassam spent his evening sipping coffee here with us?

Unfortunately I missed the early morning monthly guided tour of Arabuko Sokoke forest so I waited in the visitors' centre until Tansy, the tour leader in her early thirties, finally arrived back with a small entourage of guests and local guides. Tansy had set up the Kiepio butterfly farm project a couple of years earlier and she told me more about the forest. Home to more than 600 types of tree and 200 species of bird, it held the second highest biodiversity of all the forests in Africa. The forest management team were preparing to charge visitors an entrance fee and run more frequent guided tours to help fund the cost of conservation work, but Tansy was not happy about the idea.

"It's nice to have somewhere in Kenya where people don't have to pay to get in. It would cost more to build the infrastructure than we could take at the gate and we're only visited by a small number of people."

It was too late to start the main nature trail so Tansy suggested a shorter walk for me. A little way down the track the forest canopy closed in and a large falcon, with dark barred chest markings turned and flew off silently through the treetops as I approached. Shortly afterwards my heart jumped when a large black snake shot out from under fallen leaves just a few paces ahead and hurried across the trail. A dozen or so golden-rumped elephant shrews - rabbit sized long-legged rodents with long pointed snouts - scampered for cover among weedy saplings and ferns and in the clearings, black drongos, with trailing tail feathers three times their body length rose and swooped for insects with rollercoaster flight. Standing motionless I watched an adas duiker - tiny forest deer - as it foraged by the trackside up ahead, before disappearing into a thick tangle of shrubs. Passing a lake thickly overgrown with reeds and white flowering lilies, a large white egret hunted for fish while vervet monkeys chased one another and chattered noisily in the branches above me.

Early next morning I said goodbye to Francis, walked to the bus station and promptly at 7am our driver stepped into the cab and we set off, back to Nairobi. After the torturous rail journey the bus surely had to be a better option for my return, but the road west of Mombasa was in a shocking state. The broken tarmac surface, little wider than our bus and completely washed away in places, zigzagged into the distance, its broken edges dropping down on either side to dusty mud tracks. Every so often there were potholes deep enough to swallow a bus wheel and shear axles or wheel studs so buses and lorries meandered wildly from one muddy track, up over broken tarmac to the other in search of the least punishing course. Often we found ourselves on the wrong track facing a row of oncoming trucks, one in each lane - a sort of oversize chicken run. Someone would have to give way! Progress was often reduced to a crawling pace while passengers bounced violently around and dust swirled inside, coating everything and everyone in a fine red layer.

Bush and dense undergrowth lined the roadside for much of the journey. A leafy mantle of bindweed covered everything, blending the different levels together and its white flowers were so dense in places they looked like a layer of snow.

When we hit road works the detour took us on a wide sweeping arc of freshly bulldozed red ochre and the vegetation on either side was completely covered in bright red powder. Suddenly we were engulfed in an enormous swirling dust cloud, churned up by a passing lorry. Unable to see anything at all outside our driver brought the bus to a shuddering halt, throwing his hands in the air with disgust. It was going to be a long drive to Nairobi.

Having finally organised my replacement air ticket to Bombay and with the bulk of my travellers cheques refunded, I felt able to relax. At the youth hostel the young American in the neighbouring bunk asked if I'd like to see a new film with him in town.

"It's about a famous American legal battle that took place at the end of the nineteenth century," Stephan told me.

At breakfast on the patio, we watched as an unusual looking group marched up to the front desk. A thick set young man in smart grey suit and flat-top hair cut, led five girls wearing head scarves and dowdy ankle length dresses. All carried a single black book, but no luggage. Not your typical backpackers.

"More of your countrymen I think, Stephan."

Stephan shot me a disdainful glance and went over to check them out.

"I don't believe it," he said, when he returned. "They're missionaries from Oregon, come to show the Kenyans how to live. The guy is nineteen years old and the youngest of the girls is only seventeen. How can they tell these people anything? What can they possibly know about life?"

In town Stephan and I filed into a packed cinema, the only whites in the audience and quickly made our way up steep steps to the last available seats. Emotionally charged and based on a true story, we watched 'Amistad'.

It came to the point where the captain of the illegal slave ship, discovering he had seriously underestimated the amount of food and water needed for the journey to America, ordered his crew to balance the equation and a number of slaves were tied helpless to a weighted rope. My stomach heaved and I felt physically sick as men women and children were dragged screaming off the deck into the ocean. A murmur of angry voices rose from the audience. Malevolent faces with fiery white eyes craned round to glare at the mzungus and I wished my seat would swallow me up.

"I think they're going to lynch us," whispered Stephan as he scrunched down low in his seat, white knuckles gripping the armrest, but we survived our misadventure, slinking out before the end of the film.

On our way back to the hostel we were passed by swarms of people eagerly heading towards the distant muffled sound of trumpets and drums. They seemed drawn as if by an irresistible force and before long, burning with curiosity, we joined the lines of jostling bodies streaming from the city, arriving at a grassy bank overlooking a large oval athletics track. The music grew loud, there was even a section of screeching bagpipes, but the crowd was tightly packed and even from our vantage point is was difficult to see what was going on. Through gaps in the bodies we watched hundreds of soldiers in green khaki, steel helmets and jack boots, then blue uniforms, sinister dark glasses and berets and finally, fancy red tunics with lavish helpings of gold braid, march past to the pompous rhythmic melody. I asked my neighbour what was going on and he explained that President Moi, after announcing he had decided to stand for another four years of office, had declared a national day of celebration.

The soldiers stamped past, white gloved hands swinging back and forth not quite in unison, followed by a cavalcade of black Mercedes and Daimler limousines. There was no cheering or applause from the huge crowd, just a noisy hubbub that might occur whenever you get 20,000 people standing close together. The president was incognito, like a rumour behind darkened windows. I guessed he liked the idea of being able to look out at his subjects and didn't want to make himself an easy target. The last car crept away with the fading music, the crowd began to disperse and the president (if he'd really been there at all) left the stadium.

The first leg of my journey was over and as I waited in the departure lounge for my flight to Bombay that evening I was joined by a young traveller from Dublin called Eugene. We sat together on the half-empty plane and I told Eugene the story of my robbery at Lake Naivasha.

"I can beat dat one," said Eugene with a grin. "At Dakar my rucksack was nicked before I even got out'a de airport!"

INDIA and NEPAL

MUMBAI
(Bombay)

It was stiflingly hot and humid as Eugene and I ventured outside the deserted airport building and we wondered what on earth it would be like when the sun came up over Bombay. Squeezing into a cab our driver knew only two speeds; too fast and stop, so the tiny black bowler hat shaped vehicle squealed and swerved along broad empty streets towards the city centre with its terrified passengers. Suddenly, a young woman appeared from nowhere stepping blindly across our path. The cab screeched to a halt in a cloud of tyre smoke, barely grazing her hip and if she hadn't arched her body out the way at the last instant, she'd have been a gonner! Our driver and the woman glowered at each other for an embarrassing moment before we accelerated away again.

We sped past endless rows of dilapidated concrete apartment blocks, sporting broken shutters and crumbling balconies draped with washing. By the time we reached the ornate colonial city centre the sun was already up and the roads snarled with smoking, grid-locked traffic.

India was experiencing a heat-wave which took it up to an unbearable forty-five degrees. Eugene suffered terribly with his pale, heavily freckled skin, blue eyes and curly red hair and we sweated buckets as we carried our heavy rucksacks through swarms of jostling pedestrians, past kiosks selling juice from freshly crushed sugar cane, limes and oranges. Settling in a cheap guesthouse near the city centre we threw down the packs and collapsed, exhausted on our beds.

A short walk from the guesthouse people lived in shanty houses made from old doors, tarpaulins, rugs and any other materials to hand. At one end our street was littered with human excrement and it was difficult to find a clear path through the mess.

In the afternoon I went to explore the museum, always a good place to start in a new city. Near the entrance a smartly dressed man about my age walked up and before I could stop him, thrust a tiny baby into my arms. He ran back to his family and quickly snapped a photo of me holding the infant before taking a number of family shots with me, looking rather bewildered, in the middle. This strange ritual was repeated half a dozen times over the next few days. Back outside a couple of hours later the afternoon heat was oppressive. By the Gateway of India, a massive stone archway that stands looking out to sea in front of grandiose colonial hotels, I was cornered by an eight year old girl, sent begging by her parents. The charming, bright little hustler told me she had never been to school and taught herself English by chatting up tourists. It was always a dilemma whether or not to give to beggars, but in her case it was hard to refuse.

Next day Eugene and I moved into the Salvation Army youth hostel a few blocks from the sea front where the poorest of the low budget travellers hung out. The dorms were simple corridors with bunk beds end to end on either side and looked like the prison block in Midnight Express. Scraps of clothing were strewn randomly or hung on lines to dry. Colourful printed sarongs were stretched in front of lower bunks where people lay in bed or made love in the midday heat and a thick haze of hashish smoke hung in the corridors. In ours, a large noisy fan suspended from the ceiling spun eccentrically, swirling the air into a miniature tornado, but it made no difference. It was stifling! I laid out my ground sheet and sleeping bag liner to fend off ravenous bed bugs and mosquitoes.

One of the beauties of the place was that you couldn't tell who was what simply by looking at them. Boy, girl or something in between. Poor or rich pretending to be poor. Intellectual or non intellectual. An anorexic skinhead with bare chest and arms covered in tattoos, babbled loudly with his mates in a phoney American accent. Absurdly hyperactive for his shocking physical state and the energy sapping heat, he boasted about fights he'd been in and 'cracking heads'.

After a cool wash under a dribbling broken shower head I returned to the dorm to find bone-head and his mates were gone.

"Amazin' guy," said Eugene enthusiastically. "He says he's from Columbia and he's been all round Asia, payin' for his trip wid illegal kickboxing contests."

"He'd be hard pressed to crack the skin off a rice pudding," I thought to myself. He looked as if he was on drugs and I decided not to let my valuables out of my sight during my stay.

With five classes of travel on Indian trains, the thought of having to endure fifth or cattle truck class for the sixteen hour journey to Delhi, made me shudder. In third class and below there were no fans and no guarantee of a seat. The traveller may as well take a gun and shoot himself in the head instead.

Foreigners had to purchase tickets in advance from a special tourist ticket office. Applicants join a queue to receive a numbered card, then wait patiently for their number to be called. On hearing your number, approach the first desk to receive an official ticket chitty and join the next interminable queue. Having reached the second desk, present your chitty with passport for stamping. Mercifully, the next queue is a seated affair - a kind of reward for having persevered thus far - and the applicant plays a game of musical chairs edging slowly forwards. At the third and final desk, hand over cash and ticket chitty to be stamped with a final seal of approval and you are awarded, 'The Ticket'. It's a long drawn out procedure but failure to comply would surely result in unbearable misery.

Later that afternoon I chatted with a Frenchman in his late twenties as our small wooden boat chugged through sparkling choppy waves towards Elephant Island. Martial looked like some turn of the century archaeologist in smartly pressed beige trousers, sleeveless angling jacket and panama hat. He was staying in relatively luxurious accommodation during a short break from his job as a professional photographer. I wondered what he'd make of the Salvation Army Youth Hostel.

The island's main attraction was a medieval Hindu temple dating from 680 AD, which had been carved straight into solid granite leaving mighty stone pillars to support the hillside above. To one side of the entrance was a fabulously detailed frieze of the Hindu god Vishnu, as tall as a double-decker bus with an Elephant's head, a woman's body and six flailing arms. She sat cross-legged contemplating her subjects who stood around her. A large pack of mongrel dogs now shared residency with a troop of macaque monkeys while outside, two grubby little girls swore and taunted us when we refused to take their photograph with the scenic temple backdrop and pay them for the privilege.

On the boat ride back I talked to a girl from Switzerland and asked if she'd like to join us for dinner.

"That would be nice," she said, enthusiastically. "I have to ask my friend, but it should be OK."

"You're travelling with your boyfriend?"

"Yes."

"Oh…" I said, with a look on my face that so obviously meant, 'Well what's the point if you're going to bring your boyfriend?'

The girl's face dropped and Martial looked away in embarrassment but luckily, with the helpful excuse of the language barrier I managed to squirm out of my tight spot and we were still on speaking terms.

We arrived back at the jetty and she announced, "Here is my friend," introducing the good looking Indian guy she'd been talking to earlier on the boat. When she explained the dinner plan to him he exploded with rage, screaming at her in the middle of the crowd.

"You talk to these guys when my back is turned and already you want to fuck with them!"

With that he threw their room keys up the concourse and gave her another tirade of abuse.

"Hey look," I told them, "if it's going to be a problem don't worry, we'll do our own thing."

"I'm sorry," said the girl, quite distressed. "It is a problem."

Martial and I moved away but stayed a while within earshot, just to make sure she was OK.

That evening Martial and I joined Eugene and another youth hostel resident for supper. Our food arrived sizzling on cast iron dishes and we huddled round our dimly lit table on bright orange bench seats. Rows of overhead fans stirred the hot humid air and the sound of wailing Hindi singers on nitrous oxide soothed our ears.

Real Indian food doesn't have the colourful, creamy sauces we have come to expect in the west. It's mostly dry yellow curry paste with lots of lentils, chick peas, runner beans and chillies and variety comes not so much from taste as from different grades of hot. There are usually chapattis to mop up with and copious amounts of plain boiled rice. Diners at neighbouring tables ate with the fingers of the right hand (the left was used for other functions), occasionally looking up from their food to stare at the ignorant foreigners as we wolfed down our food with spoons.

Eugene took a mouthful of the hairy mango chilli things from one of the condiment bowls.

"Hot?" I enquired politely.

He was silent for a moment, then reached for his cold beer with an urgency taking long deep gulps.

"Yeah…But its a creeping heat!"

Walking back to the hostel rats appeared from cracks between paving slabs, holes in walls and sunken gutters and began taking over the streets. Hundreds of bed frames with meshed twine bases were set out on the pavement because it was just too hot indoors and the rats scurried over them and their occupants.

INDIA BY TRAIN AND BUS

Eugene had decided to stay a while in Bombay but my plan was to head north to Delhi, so we said goodbye and I made my way to the railway station. Women in brightly coloured saris sat on the floor or milled about mithering heaps of small children, while their husbands struggled with impossibly large amounts of luggage. As the train crept slowly towards the platform buffers, a bedlam of shouting, jostling humanity converged at either end of the coaches, attempting to force their way on board before the occupants had a chance to leave. After franticly searching up and down the enormous train I finally tracked down my coach. The wrong number had been posted next to the door. It was due to leave at any moment but there was no way the panic stricken mob would clear in time, so I forced my way onboard crushing past women and children. This was no time for gentlemanly behaviour.

Reaching the first couchette the aisle was a scene of utter chaos; luggage strewn from floor to ceiling, bodies everywhere. Two European looking women were jammed up with enormous rucksacks, trying to reach our couchette from the far end.

"Gimme the bags or you'll be stuck there all day!" I called to them.

New Zealander Penny, Australian Trudy and I rough handled the rucksacks onto a top bunk and quickly grabbed our places. People with unconfirmed seats constantly tried to squeeze alongside us; women carrying babies, cheeky men who swore blind that we were in *their* seats.

"I claim this seat for England, Queen and country. Piss off the lot of you!"

This was second class. The padded benches and back rests would pull out later to form bottom and middle bunk beds, vital for a long journey. Three large ceiling mounted fans stirred the air sufficiently to evaporate sweat from skin and prevent the occupants from expiring.

On the bench facing us were a couple in their late thirties and their obese daughter of eight or nine. Disinterested mother wrapped in a brightly coloured sari with a ripple of spare tyre on her bare tummy, picked her nose. Father put a scab covered foot on our seat, between the girls.

The train rattled over an old iron suspension bridge with broken wooden boards beneath the tracks. The river below was covered in plastic bottles, chunks of polystyrene and garbage. In between were a few exposed areas of stagnant green slime and oil. It looked as if the nearby town used the waterway as an open sewer and it was hard to imagine how it could sustain any form of life higher than bacteria.

Penny spoke above the trains rhythmic clatter, drawing my attention from the window.

"That seems like an unhealthy relationship."

I looked up from my rambling thoughts at the scene on the opposite bench. Father caressed and fondled his plump daughter in an overly affectionate manner. Mother stared out the window, disinterested. To begin with I wasn't so sure about Penny's insinuation, but later that morning mother stepped up to the top bunk and father stepped up the fondling. Trudy and Penny were disgusted and made their feelings quite plain.

The train occasionally slowed and crept into stations along the journey, coaches shunting and lurching with backlash the last few metres. Food sellers hopped on board and walked up and down the aisle, loudly advertising their wares. Freshly made chapattis were OK and fruit was safe enough when peeled. Samosas were probably OK but it was best to avoid anything containing meat. The cha man was a favourite, filling tiny plastic cups from a heavy pewter urn with sweet, warm, refreshing tea.

By late afternoon I had burned myself out talking and the girls clearly needed a rest, so I wandered to the end of our carriage and stood in the open doorway while India's countryside rolled out before me. I hadn't been paying much attention to my surroundings or my feelings but all of a sudden the hairs stood up on the back of my neck as I realised, I'm here! Despite its problems, this was an amazing country. Vast and complex, a land of utter extremes. High mountains to arid plains. Incredibly rich to desperately poor. I had never seen tones and sunset like this before and as the train rattled on relentless, I was thrilled to see tiny flashes of peoples lives. Farmers returning to the village from the fields carrying manual tools. No machinery here. Children shouting and playing in muddy pools. Emaciated white cattle with jagged protruding hips and bulbous shoulder humps grazed alongside elegant egrets with slender stabbing bills.

Magnetised to the spot for more than two hours, I was finally brought back to the present when a young Sikh tapped me on the shoulder and introduced himself. Rajesh spoke good English and told me he was on his way to Kashmir. He said it was a beautiful region and suggested I should go there too, but I reminded him that a group of tourists, kidnapped by Kashmiri separatists several months earlier, were still missing. It really wasn't a good time for foreigners to visit. Rajesh invited me several coaches down to meet a Hindu friend of his and it was great to see that a friendship between two young men with such different faiths could endure here in India.

When I finally returned to our couchette, a lady-boy was sitting in my place beside the girls. I squeezed in between them to try and edge him out, but he was cheeky and motioned for his friends to join him.

"No, no," I said firmly. "this bench is only meant for three, look!" and I pointed to the brass number discs above each seat, and to my ticket. Just then the guard, a small balding man in his early fifties, walked by and immediately started shouting at them to leave the coach. They refused to budge, poking fun instead which infuriated him even more. He stormed off down the train, returning a few minutes later with two soldiers carrying bolt action rifles and long battens. The ladies rose to their feet protesting loudly and received a few sharp whacks across the shoulders and buttocks, before being prodded and bullied out of the coach.

Darkness closed in around the dimly lit train and I realised I had almost forgotten about our incestuous neighbour opposite. Penny was struggling to clear rucksacks and bags on the top bunk to make a nest for herself.

"I've got so much gear up here, I could do with another bunk," she said, exasperated.

"That one should be free soon," Trudy commented, referring to the child's middle bunk. "Daddy's bound to want to sleep with his daughter!"

...And he did, inviting the little girl down to join him. She complained she was hot and in the poor light we watched gobsmacked as he leaned forward, flipping her skirt up over her chest and smoothing her tummy. Then, feeling up higher, he groped her tiny breasts. Now I was disgusted too. I wanted to punch him in the teeth, but that wouldn't change him and it wouldn't change anything in India. He deserved to be in prison, but I was the one who'd get arrested. Mother grunted, half asleep. She couldn't give a toss. She hated her old man and was probably glad she had a daughter to divert his attentions.

Trudy told me the problem of incest and general child abuse was widespread in India. Bombay had large numbers of child prostitutes in the red-light district and the authorities estimated that around sixty percent of them were infected with Aids.

Late the following morning our train rumbled into the sweltering shanty hubbub of Delhi. Trudy and Penny had been there before and made a beeline through milling crowds to their favourite guesthouse. We walked down impossibly narrow streets strewn with pungent rotting litter and a chaotic tangle of telephone wires and power cables sagged between dusty concrete blocks no taller than five storeys. At ground level the streets were lined with drab grey offices, open fronted greengrocers, fast food restaurants and odd assorted stores. There was the scooter store, piled high with oily bits of two-stroke engine, broken frames and wheels. Then there was the pan store, crammed with copper and galvanised pots and pans of every conceivable shape and size. Another appeared to sell nothing but front wings for the tiny black Morris Oxford taxis. Just as a three wheel truck piled high with building waste rammed its way past, squashing pedestrians into doorways, we escaped, entering the glass fronted Vivek Hotel.

In a small, plain, fifth floor room I took a *mandi* wash because none of the showers worked and then called in on the girls to see if they were ready for dinner. You could hear the howl of their air conditioning fan all the way down the hall. Working the handle the door flew open and a small cloud formed where frigid air-conditioned air met the humid 35 degrees of the hallway. At the head of the bed was a very large wall mounted fan like the ones used in wind tunnel experiments, going full tilt and it blew the girl's wavy blonde locks over their faces. The room looked as if a grenade had gone off inside and I thought they must have taken both overstuffed rucksacks and simply tipped the entire contents all over the bed and floor.

"Wow, you ladies sure like to make yourselves at home!" A flying pillow caught me on the chin.

"We'll be ready in five minutes," said Trudy.

A thick grey haze hung over Delhi's sprawling suburbs as we stood on the hotel roof later that evening watching a weary orange sun cough and splutter its last, but our attention was

mandi - wash with a jug and bucket of water.

distracted by a plume of black smoke billowing from a few blocks away. The plume became stronger and wider until it formed its own cloud, blotting out the last remaining light. We watched hypnotised for more than an hour but there was nothing we could do and no sign it was getting closer, so we went to bed.

Before breakfast next morning I went looking for the source of the fire. An entire section of a neighbouring street had been cordoned off and workmen struggled feverishly to remove a giant mound of rubble and ash. The fire had claimed a four storey building. Most of its front wall had collapsed onto the street exposing the charred carcass of rooms, joists and tangled cables, but a passer-by explained that mercifully, no one had been hurt.

The girls had decided to spend the day shopping so I booked myself on a coach trip - Indian style - to the Taj Mahal and Agra Fort, symbols from a mystical time of kingdoms and great battles.

The coach set off early on the three and a half hour ride to Agra. Its large fixed windows amplified heat like the panes of a greenhouse, there was no air conditioning and fans mounted at intervals below the luggage racks didn't work.

After an hour or so we came to a standstill at road works and the temperature soared inside. It was as if molten lava was filling the coach from the floor upwards, I felt nauseous and sweat ran in rivulets from my nose and cheeks. Tempers flared and passengers shouted at the driver. He sat impassively for several unbearable minutes until suddenly he snapped round to face us, exploding in a screaming tirade.

"What's going on?" I asked my neighbour urgently and he did his best to explain in broken English as the coach once again juddered forward.

"He say, someone threw baby out of bus. Road too narrow for him to go round."

I asked him to repeat what he'd said because I couldn't believe I'd heard him correctly but when he did, I still couldn't believe it. By the time I made up my mind to make our driver stop and investigate we were several kilometres further down the road and it didn't seem like such a good idea any more. "Is it alive or dead?" I wondered. "Has anyone else gone to check? Surely the world must stop while this is sorted out?" I felt like I was watching events from inside a glass bubble and life carried on around me as though nothing at all unusual had happened. Every passing second took us further down the road. I did nothing and now it was too late.

Several hours later still shell-shocked with disbelief, I discovered that our itinerary included not two, but seven historic sites. To a foreigner the tour might have seemed inexpensive, but for locals it cost an arm and a leg and I suppose the operators had to pack in plenty of value to attract them. We hurried through magnificent forts, temples and shrines where young Indian men wearing long black trousers sniggered at my pale stork's legs. Bustle, bustle, bustle, barely half an hour at each site, then racing on to the next.

In the evening we passed through a sleepy village on narrow, tightly winding streets, barely wide enough for our huge coach. The cab threatened to demolish jutting corners and tear down overhead wires while overhanging branches banged against the windows and rattled along the roof. Chickens, goats and children got in the way so our driver honked the horn again and again in frustration. I covered my face in shame as we shattered the sacred tranquillity, passing through like a noisy, smoky, whirlwind.

On the last section of the trip our new tour guide staggered onto the bus, completely pissed. He swayed dangerously, eyes zooming in and out of focus as he shouted his commentary, all in Urdu, gesturing towards important sites left and right which nobody could see…because it was pitch black outside!

We stopped at yet another very impressive floodlit fort - very nice - and stood outside a Hindu temple in the great courtyard while our guide rattled away again in Urdu. I listened for a while hoping he'd say at least something for the Englishman's benefit, but no, so I picked up my precious sandals and padded into the temple alone. On my way out again having satisfied my curiosity, the rest of the group were just entering and the guide stopped in front of me.

"Why you not leave sandals outside as I have been telling you? What the hell do you think you are doing? This is holy place, you cannot be walking here with these filthy things!"

In another town some time later, we followed matey to a local Hindu shrine resembling a miniature theatre, lit by hundreds of candles. Sitting cross-legged on the floor, we formed a semicircle around a tiny stage hidden by curtains. Our friendly guide chatted briefly with the curator who delivered an impassioned speech, in Urdu, to the group. Then, with a single sweep, he hauled back the curtains to reveal two large plastic dolls clad in ornate traditional costume, among a clutter of artefacts: polished brass urns, incense burners, more candles and layers of brightly coloured cloth. As the collection tray came round I quietly got up and made my escape. Travelling on to our next stop, Krishna's birthplace, I was refused entry by armed police because of my unsightly bare legs, so I took the opportunity to snatch some food.

At 3am the bus driver finally dropped me somewhere in Delhi.

"But you promised you'd take me back to Pahar Ganj!" I grizzled, visions of wandering the streets for hours, getting mugged or even worse.

"Yes, yes!" said the driver, anxious to get off to bed. He motioned down the street on the left somewhere and his mate nodded vigorously in agreement. There wasn't much choice. Even if they'd wanted to, the bus would never make it down those narrow streets slung with a bird's nest of wires and cables, so reluctantly I stepped off and the bus sped away in a cloud of smoke.

There wasn't a soul around and wandering down deserted streets that all looked exactly the same I soon realized the nightmare potential of my situation. Suddenly, three large dogs appeared from nowhere, barking furiously. I tried to get out of their territory but they kept coming closer and closer, snapping viciously, trying to get in a bite and pinning me against a wall. Surely their owner or a neighbour would come to help at any moment…but no one came.

Shaking with fear I swung at them with my feet and fists, the dogs moved back enough for me to reach a nearby rock. I hurled it at the biggest, most aggressive animal catching him squarely on the shoulder and he yelped, running off a few paces. The others backed off a little and I picked up more ammunition then, slipping past the barking dogs I made my way quickly down the street and eventually passed a restaurant I recognised. The bus driver had been right after all.

With more than a tinge of sadness next morning, I hugged Penny and Trudy goodbye outside New Delhi station and boarded the train to Gorakhpur, north of Varanasi. From there I caught a bus to Sonauli, last Indian town before the border and walked the short dusty road into Nepal. Another bus stood ready to take the mixed group of travellers on a bumpy, sleepless overnight trip to Kathmandu. One of the numerous bus touts disappeared with our tickets so the handful of westerners jumped on early to find ourselves good seats. A while later as other passengers filed onboard a tout came over to me.

"You move please."

I had specially chosen the seat directly behind the driver's cab because all the others were much too close together and I knew what that was like. It was also highly likely I'd be moved from whatever seat they put me in next. Messing about was standard procedure.

"No, I'm sorry. I need this seat for legroom."

"This seat reserved," insisted the tout. "You move please."

"No. I like this seat," and I turned to face the window, determined to have no further part in the conversation. Behind me the small group of foreigners joined the rebellion, also refusing to move. Maybe they really did have allocated seats for us, but what system there was fell apart and there was shouting and screaming as two Indians pushed their smaller Nepalese neighbours around and pinched their seats. The bus moved off, arguments still raging, but eventually it settled down to a faint murmur of discontent. We made a couple of brief rest stops but I stayed rooted to my spot.

Suddenly there was uproar and I woke as the bus pulled to a halt. Two young men were dragged off into the darkness by the other passengers and beaten senseless. We had stopped near a police check post and the lads were pushed in that direction, punches and kicks raining down on them all the way. I jumped off too. Whatever they had done this was a bit bloody unfair.

"Hey. Pack it in!" I yelled, as one of the guys reeled from a vicious punch to the back of his head.

For a frightful moment I became the centre of attention, but it had some effect and the bulk of the crowd left off while the lads were dragged into the station.

Someone explained, "They stole camera."

Sure enough the lads, possibly disgruntled at losing their seats, had climbed on top of the bus during a rest stop and stolen a camera and purse from one of the foreigner's rucksacks.

"OK," I told him, feeling a little responsible, "but don't bloody kill them for it!"

The Nepalese have a very strict moral code and theft by an individual is considered a slur against the entire race. After a long and heated discussion the police dragged the two young men from the station. Apparently they were not prepared to take responsibility if either should die in custody and they had no money to pay for medical treatment. The other passengers decided not to let the two back on the bus, instead having a whip-round to pay towards medical costs or further transport. All of a sudden our driver clapped his hands loudly, shouting, *"Jam-jam!"* and everyone filed obediently back onboard.

jam-jam! - hurry hurry!

KATHMANDU

Our bus trundled into sleepy Kathmandu at dawn and I took a noisy motorised rickshaw to Kingsland Guesthouse in the city centre. Kathmandu instantly transports the visitor back in time with its crumbling clay and adobe dwellings and primitive way of life. The city was just waking and skinny cattle, goats and chickens wandering broken potholed streets were joined by decrepit smoky vehicles and swarms of people with round, olive skin faces.

Kathmandu is a treasure trove of ancient wooden Buddhist temples with multi-tiered roofs, corners curled upwards to the sky, Hindu shrines beautifully carved in wood, or simple stone phalli where offerings of blossom, rice and incense are placed to ensure fertility. The low rise city is dotted with monasteries inhabited by purple or orange clad monks and their western students, colourful markets selling trinkets and clothing, and lazy tourist cafes. The people are friendly, tough and genuine. Many of the beautiful carved wood and clay buildings are falling apart due to lack of money and neglect. Open rubbish tips by the side of the street reek appallingly, everything crumbling or unfinished, but most visitors like the place the way it is, warts and all, because our modern hippy culture fits so well with its tremendous character and powerful spirituality.

One morning I met an American visitor who told me there was a fascinating monastery within walking distance on the northern edge of town, so we set off together after breakfast. Suburban sprawl petered out into a single row of simple adobe houses and workshops. There was the butchers. A man stood in an open doorway struggling with armfuls of buffalo offal, some of which flopped onto the filthy floor while flies buzzed around desperate to complete their lifecycle. Further along young and old women sat on stools teasing wool into thread with wooden spinning wheels while inside, other members of the family dyed it and weaved it into cloth. The street turned uphill and on a sharp bend we looked into an open-fronted workshop the size of a small garage. Two men worked alongside half a dozen small boys ranging from about eight to thirteen years old, as they hammered sheets of copper into plates and bowls.

Form the brow of the hill we saw the monastery, like a fortress in the distance. As we entered, loud chanting in the form of deep, repetitive mantras echoed from various Spartan stone buildings. We sat at a table in the courtyard and talked with a middle-aged Tibetan monk, wearing a red cloak and sandals. He spoke very good English and told us he'd spent eight years in notorious Drapche prison, where he was regularly beaten and tortured for the crime of handing out pro-democracy leaflets. After release he escaped the oppressive Chinese occupation by walking across the snow-covered Himalayas to Nepal, but several of his companions died along the way. He explained that the Chinese had banned religion, completely destroyed most of the ancient Tibetan monasteries and tortured or killed anyone who spoke out against them. He couldn't understand why the rest of the world was so indifferent to the suffering of his people, barely eighty kilometres to the north.

Someone told me it was possible to hire a taxi all day in Kathmandu for less than £10. It seemed like a great way to see the city so I got up early next morning and stumbled downstairs into the guesthouse courtyard, almost walking straight into the rear end of a massive bull elephant. The animal let out a deep resonant rumble of annoyance when it saw me in the corner of its big white eyes and I jumped back to the relative safety of a stone gatepost. High up on its back sat a leathery skinned *mahout* in mouldy tweed jacket and *topi*, barking two-syllable orders which resulted in slow, careful movements forwards or

mahout - elephant trainer and guardian.
topi - traditional hat shaped like an inverted flower pot.

back. The old man stood confidently and hacked at the drooping branches of an enormous courtyard tree, like a giant oak but with broad waxy leaves. Another terse command and the great animal raised its trunk. The mahout walked over its forehead in a rather undignified manner and, grabbing a handful of each ear, clambered down using the trunk as a staircase before gathering up the fresh cuttings. The heavy duty gardening team were doing some large scale pruning and any foliage that wasn't bundled up and piled onto the elephant's back was happily consumed before they moved on to the next job.

I found a taxi just around the corner, a badly battered, ancient Datsun Cherry driven by a middle-aged man in a black leather jacket that was two sizes too small. We trundled off over cobbled potholed streets, some so narrow that oncoming cyclists were forced to dismount and pedestrians flattened themselves against walls to let us scrape past.

Before long we stopped on the main street outside an arched gateway to the Buddhist temple of Patna. In the middle of a large courtyard surrounded by three storey houses and shops stood the great whitewashed temple, as big as the dome of Saint Paul's, resting on a massive square base. A magnificent gilded tower with pointed spire, stood on top of the dome glistening in strong sunlight and on each face were painted the all-seeing eyes of Buddha that look into the souls of mankind. My driver said I could call him Chum - his real name was quite unpronounceable to foreigners - and he cheerfully began telling me about the temple in broken English.

Built into the sides of the base were a large number of ornately carved wooden cylinders or prayer wheels on vertical spindles, 1,000 exactly according to Chum, each one containing a prayer written on parchment. Chum explained that we must walk clockwise around the base and spin as many of the wheels as possible in order to activate each prayer and release its goodness into the world. On one side a broad column of steps led up to a whitewashed clay annexe, inside which was the daddy of all prayer wheels. The massive red, bell-shaped wheel with huge gold embossed characters was taller than a man and spun slowly on smooth bearings, clicking sedately like a giant bicycle ratchet.

Back outside we watched as an old man carrying a bucket climbed a rickety wooden ladder leant against the huge dome and proceeded to splash yellowy orange liquid over the nice white surface. Apparently the slurry was an offering containing lentils, curry powder and flower petals.

Leaving Patna we made our way to Pashupatinath, an area of Hindu temples on the other side of town. Parking up we crossed a broad stone bridge high above a stagnant river and scaled a long flight of steep steps. On our left was a series of seven stone temples, consisting of four pillars supporting a heavy domed roof. Inside each was a granite plinth gently curved like a plate, adorned with candles and small dishes of rice or yellow and orange incense and in the centre of that was a large granite phallus. Hindu women placed offerings in the hope of bearing many children but I couldn't help feeling that with exploding population growth, high unemployment and desperate poverty, that was the last thing the country needed.

Standing beside one of the temples was an old chap, sweaty face painted with red ochre, matted dreadlocks down to his waist, wearing only a baggy loin cloth like an oversized nappy.

"Sadhu," said Chum in a reverent tone. "Holy man."
The man muttered something and frowned at me, thrusting out a filthy hand in an aggressive begging motion. He didn't act very holy.

"This man carry great weight from penis," Chum continued, nodding at a large bronze bell at the man's feet. "You want to see?"

"Er, no thanks Chum," I said, edging away as the man pulled out his knob and started limbering up, stretching the foreskin like some deranged party balloon. Secretly I was curious to see if his willy would snap off under the weight, but I wasn't going to pay good money for it.

Catching our breath at the top of the steps our attention was drawn to some beautiful and very lifelike murals including a distinguished looking sadhu with a bushy grey beard and moustache, features dusted white with chalk powder. He wore a funny turban-like hat, material gathered up and flopped over to face the front and sat in the lotus position, palms turned upwards. Just then a familiar face walked by staring back at me and I suddenly realised it was the man in the picture.

From here we had a perfect view of the massive complex that extended well into the city on both sides of the river, multi-tiered yellow, red and blue walled temples vying for the tallest and holiest position. Below us on the opposite bank of the hazy river, people were preparing mounds of sticks in front of a line of long, low sheds.

"They burn bodies," said Chum. "Throw ashes in river."

We continued our taxi tour in the mid-afternoon heat, but as the road became jammed with swarms of pedestrians we were forced to a standstill. Chum hopped out to see what was going on and a moment later motioned for me to join him, abandoning the car in the middle of the crowded street. Up ahead a noisy crowd had gathered in a square and over the tops of jostling heads I could see a fight contest was taking place on a raised boxing ring. Two skinny lads in red shorts, vests and padded head guards were busy knocking ten bales out of one another, occasionally wrenched apart by a plump, finger wagging referee. Spectators roared at every big flurry of punches and the overcrowded square looked ready to burst at the seams. Young would-be boxers sat astride a balcony, tightly packed one behind another because there wasn't room to sit side by side. They clung to every inch of the pillars and open widows in an ornate wooden temple on my left, while rooftop crowds on my right overflowed onto telegraph poles and a handy tree. The gong went at the end of the bout before any major damage was done and when the referee held the victor's arm aloft a great cheer went up. We stayed for two more matches before pushing our way back to the car and carefully reversing out of the tight spot.

The 'monkey temple' was our last port of call. It was early evening and as it wasn't too far from the guesthouse, I thanked Chum for all his help and let him get on his way. A long, steep stairway led up the side of a rocky pinnacle to the temple complex where a large golden central spire, similar to the one at Patna, stood gleaming in the orange sun. A large troop of macaque monkeys, from which the site gets its name, played and squabbled in surrounding shrines, ignoring aloof temple cats and the steady flow of inquisitive tourists. There was a marvellous panoramic view of the entire city and as the sun slowly settled causing the temple spire to glow like fire, the chaotic music of car horns wafted up on the warm night air.

Next day while visiting Tamel district on the other side of town, a rain shower started and I watched from the shuttered window of a beautiful wooden café built on three levels, as tourists scurried into the temples of Durbar Square for shelter.

Later that afternoon, after halving the asking price but still paying double the going rate, I clambered into a motorised rickshaw to head back to the city centre. The machine was an ancient, canvas-enclosed trike. Based around a scooter engine and front end, it had a clunky handlebar gear change and bits of framework welded on here and there to give it shape.

My driver, shirt and T-shirt rolled right up above his paunch for cooling purposes, pulled away sharply and swung straight across the path of heavy oncoming traffic. Small motorbikes, cyclists and taxis swerved or jumped on their brakes, squeaking by and somehow avoiding collision. We vied for position with other road users amid the machine gun clatter of unsilenced two stroke engines, shrieking hooters and filthy choking smoke.

Brahmy kites with forked tails circled and swooped over an empty park on my right. On my left, ancient impressive *stupas* and temples with gilded roofs peeped out between crumbling brick and concrete shops selling everything imaginable. A bloke finished taking a dump over a drain, stood and pulled up his pants. Mange-riddled bitches with scarred faces and teats down to the ground scrounged through the open rubbish tips, almost ready now to drop the next litter of unwanted pups.

Spine-jarring bumps, alarming noise, smell of rotting vegetation and filth. A huge bull with massive horns and heavy neck wattle stood motionless in the midst of traffic and chaos on a broken ankle, hoof broken back, too painful to move. Swarms of people bent on suicide, crossed in front of the relentless torrent of vehicles. A bus drew perilously close belching thick black smoke and repeatedly sounding its air horn.

'If you don't get out the way you'll come off much worse, I don't give a shit!'

We stood our ground, relentless, missing a guy with his entire family on a tiny scooter by less than a gnat's cock. In the city centre the traffic was completely jammed so I got out, still shaking and walked. I felt like kissing the ground in relief. I couldn't understand why I loved the place so much.

Sitting in a rooftop café that evening overlooking the tourist centre of Kathmandu I studied a map of Nepal, wondering which trek to do. Pale skinned westerners wandered the streets below, head and shoulders taller than their rugged Nepalese neighbours. The guy at the next table asked to look at my map, then he joined me and we discussed possible routes.

Mike, a PE teacher from the Peak District was around five feet ten inches tall, unassuming, tough and extremely fit. After only a short discussion we decided to team up for our trek and went for a beer in the Tom and Jerry Bar to celebrate.

stupa - dome-shaped Buddhist shrine.

Mike and I spent the following morning sorting out money, new walking boots for me and trekking permits. In the permits office we met a group of young women: Dunja from Croatia, Isobel from Spain and Nicolett from Italy. They hired themselves a guide and agreed to let us join them. Whether our meeting was chance or fate I was pleasantly surprised at how easy it seemed to become part of a trekking party. I couldn't imagine walking the mountains on my own.

ON TOP OF THE WORLD

Early the following morning our little group boarded a bus for Dunche on the southern edge of the Himalayas and the start of the Langtang trail. It was an unbelievably bumpy ride up hair-raising unmade mountain roads and after a bone-shattering nine hours we arrived at Dunche village, wobbled into Langtang View Guesthouse and crashed for an hour to recover.

As its name suggested, the guesthouse had a magnificent view of snow covered Langtang Himal and the congruence of three great valleys. Peering through the stone arch entrance our hillside dropped sharply down to a deep gorge before rising again into vast towering mountains, giving one a tremendous feeling of space. They looked close enough to touch but were actually several kilometres away. A group of four men sat cross-legged by the trackside with an air of relaxed self assuredness about them as they smoked clay pipes under wide brimmed hats. They were Sherpas, supreme climbers of the Himalayas and among the toughest of Nepalese people.

After breakfast the following morning we packed and set off for Syambru village, a full day's walk away. The first leg of the trail took us steeply down a treeless mountainside covered in dry grass and thorn bush, before crossing a deep ravine on a narrow footbridge of steel cables and alarmingly loose wooden boards that bounced and swayed with every step. Far below Langtang river thundered over a waterfall jammed with fallen trees like scattered toothpicks.

Dillip, our guide, was in his early twenties, taller and heavier built than most Nepalese. Originally from India he was loud, craved attention, constantly interrupted conversations and said he preferred life in the city. For all that he was a character, cheerful, upbeat and always giving encouragement.

As we began the long ascent it was soon clear I was the slowest walker with Nicolett a close second. The trail, often hellishly steep and cut into the side of the river gorge with crude stone steps, presented no obstacle to the mountain people and I had to move aside as a young woman carrying three great planks of wood from a strap around her forehead, jogged past. At first I kept asking myself why we punished our poor bodies this way. My shirt and shorts were saturated with sweat. Muscles burned like fire before turning to jelly and I stopped frequently to gasp for air while Isobel, Dunja and Mike raced on ahead like gazelles, adding insult to injury.

Being slower had its advantages however. It gave me time to absorb the incredible atmosphere of my surroundings and I enjoyed Nicolett's company as we walked together. I began to see the mountains as much more than merely another physical challenge to be overcome. This was my life, this was what life was about and it felt more real than anything I had done before. The walk was becoming a spiritual experience and I knew that Nicolett felt the same way.

If you have even a modest level of fitness your body slowly adapts to the sudden massive demands and you start to recover more quickly at every pause. I got into a walking rhythm, it became as compelling as breathing and everything in my head, all my worldly worries, fears and concerns started to evaporate. Looking down the steep gorge to the thundering river and across at vast, timeless mountains towering up the other side gave me a constant feeling of awe and I began to realise how utterly insignificant I was. It had been so long since I allowed myself such clear thinking, free of constraints from people and the rat race back home. I felt as if my life was a great building that had stood neglected, crumbling for decades. Today it had been completely demolished and was now being rebuilt, stone by stone.

After the robbery, with Canadian vets Melanie, Karen, Alexa & Morag

Benjamin tries a little fishing while Morris paddles, Lake Victoria

'Don't put your foot on
these', warns Salim

Cannon at Fort Jesus,
Mombassa

Bush bus, Malindi

Feeding time at the Sheldrick's Rhino Orphanage; three of the five rhino species are on the verge of extinction

Some matatoos are in a really bad way – this one incredibly still worked!

Pahar Gange, New Delhi

Sacred cows, Agra Fort
(Red Fort)

Agra Fort

Taj Mahal seen from Agra Fort

Durbar Square, Kathmandu

Himalya from Langtang,
Nepal

View from
Langtang, Nepal

Nicolette
making
friends

Taking a break from the
gruelling business of
breaking in a pony

Nepalese women gambling with shells

Glacier at the top of
Langtang trail

Heading back down
the trail

The 'frog and
goat' man

The trail hugged the side of Langtang river gorge winding up and down, again and again. It snaked through steaming forest close to the raging river, crossing back and forth a dozen times on swaying single track suspension bridges with flimsy wooden slats. Occasionally we encountered groups of porters dressed in sandals, baggy pants cut off above the ankle, waistcoats and topis, carrying impossibly large loads on their backs from forehead straps. A stack of plastic water butts three metres tall tottered by on sinewy little legs and a while later we were passed by a guy carrying a whole flock of chickens in wire fronted wooden boxes. Now and again we flattened ourselves against the mountainside to let donkey or pony trains squeeze by; up to twenty beasts at a time wearing bells and colourful head plumes, weighed down with bulging sacks of rice or corn. More than once we had to turn back from a narrow bridge as the animals - which had no reverse gear - started across no matter who was already on.

By late afternoon we reached the pretty village of Syambru, a single line of low-lying houses with coarse dry stone walls, tiny windows and grey slate roofs, clinging to a steeply descending spine-back ridge. We moved into a beautiful pinewood guest house near the top of the village, with a breathtaking view of the terraced slope that dropped away to the river gorge far below and the gigantic wall of facing mountains. An outside staircase led up to the balcony and cosy double bedrooms. Taking off the rucksacks gave one a sensation of falling forwards, footsteps felt springy, lighter than air. Thoroughly exhausted we all took a much needed cold mandi. wash, ordered food and then rested our weary bodies.

Toilets up in the mountains usually consisted of a hole in the ground in a crude wooden shack. Ours fed out into a rice paddy to make use of natural fertilizer but most of the old folks didn't even bother with it, preferring to crap straight in the field. Through the dark hole the white plastic sheet below appeared to be moving so, holding my breath against caustic farmyard smells, I took a closer look. It wasn't plastic sheet at all; the whole slurry-covered bank was seething with squirming maggots.

Having worked out that your pants have to be right down around your ankles otherwise you fall over backwards or worse still, crap in them, I hit on the next snag.

"Where's the sodding toilet paper?" I yelled to Dillip, who I could see milling about outside through large gaps in the shack wall.

"No paper here," he called back. "Use hand and water jug like everyone else!"

Next morning we ate breakfast on the flat roof of Gamesh Himal Lodge, surrounded by spectacular views of terraced mountain slopes and the deep river valley, while our host urged us to buy a locally produced guidebook packed with interesting information about the region. He told us they sold it in order to pay the teacher's wages at the school they had recently built.

It seemed an extremely harsh way of life up in the mountains. The people live on a basic diet of dhal bhat - thick lentil broth and rice eaten twice a day around mid morning and late afternoon, sometimes with turkili - potato or bean curry, or dhido - boiled mashed millet. Everything from building materials to food has to be brought up by porters, donkeys or ponies and a trek to the more remote villages can take several days.

We were getting used to dhal bhat. It's full of carbohydrates and really gets you up the hills, you never get sick from it and it's the only item on the menu where you get endless free top-ups. Some of the more exotic dishes; omelette or pizza, kept us waiting for hours and ended up tasting much the same anyway, especially when, as seemed to happen a lot, the chef was a ten year old girl left to cook for half a dozen people over a simple clay stove with only a single hot plate.

The numerous steep climbs from Syambru to Changtang village were gut-wrenchingly punishing and as we edged ever higher the air became colder. Changtang village lay spread across a broad glacial plain that provided much better arable land than typical mountainside rice paddies. The villagers had a little more money as a result, so most of their buildings had smooth-sided stone and mortar walls and sturdy tiled roofs. Building work continued here and there as we arrived, rafters and battens going up over grey stone shells. Inside one a group of young men sat cross-legged amid piles of rocks, laboriously chipping flat faces with hammers and chisels.

Having spent two long, exhausting days together Isobel had had enough of Dilip's over-the-top humour and constant innuendos. As we entered the village she reached boiling point but Dillip didn't seem to know when to let up. He showed us to a cramped, gloomy guest house with tiny widows made from polythene sheet and a ceiling so low even Dunja, who was the smallest, had to stoop. The ladies were paying a lot for the privilege of Dillip's company and now, to save a few rupees, he'd brought them to the dingiest guest house in town. He tried to make a joke of their annoyance and suddenly, Mike and I had to hold Isobel back as she flew at him, fists flying. She didn't calm down until we found another more comfortable place and settled in for the night.

On day three now more in the routine, I played my favourite CDs in my head and let my thoughts simply drift the way they took me. Light-headed from altitude and exertion, I could feel my spirit mingle with the spirits of the trees in the forest, the lichen covered rocks and the thundering river. I became aware of many past travellers who had walked this and other ancient trails. Their life force still lingered and it was an excellent place to find them, if your mind was open.

Several hours later, high above the tree line, we approached the last ridge before our destination and all heads turned as we gazed open-mouthed at an enormous glacier, slung like a white hammock between distant peaks. All of a sudden misty cloud swirled up the valley engulfing us, there was a sharp chill and it started to drizzle.

It was a huge relief as the first stone houses came into view. The village of Kyanjin Gompa lay on a relatively flat saddle at the highest point of the valley, flanked on either side by towering walls of waterfall-streaked rock. There was no arable farming at this altitude and close to the start of monsoon there was only a handful of trekkers, but in summer the steady flow of visitors provided a regular income for the five or so lodges.

Dumping our bags in plain but comfortable Yala Guest House we walked to the edge of town, crossing a steep snow-melt river bed strewn with beach ball size boulders where we joined Dillip, as he sat on a grassy slope gazing down the other side of the valley. For once, even he was silent as we stared out over the unfolding valley and the next range of snow-capped mountains.

After a brief rest Dunja, Isobel and Mike forged ahead determined to explore a little further, but Nicolett and I were completely finished and hung back. She sat on my lap and I held her close as we rested in the shelter of a giant moraine boulder.

Back at the guesthouse I kept nodding off to sleep by the wood stove where my clothes dried, so I went to bed. Nicolett brought my boots to my room later and I asked her to stay. Of all the bad timing. I was so riddled with cold it was hard to breathe but I wanted her and needed her, now! I lay back and she sat astride my waist lifting her sweatshirt and t-shirt over her head, but my head started to pound, nose filled with snot, streaming and red raw from constant blowing. We kissed, but I couldn't breathe and I felt like shit. 'Bugger!' I tried to explain. We lay quietly in a cosy 'spoons' position for a while, Nicolett with her back to me but I guess she must have felt rejected and before long she pulled on her clothes indignantly and left.

The Langtang Trail

At Yala Guest House, 4,000 metres above sea level, Mike and I were grounded next day by stinking colds while the young women attempted Tchirco-Ri peak, a further 300 metre climb. The break suited me fine and I sat out in the sunshine with Mike, absorbing our glorious surroundings and the achievement of just getting there.

Vultures patrolled high above us while yak calves frolicked and tore around the village. A group of teenagers, collecting boulders from a nearby hillside for building paused to watch the men below breaking in new ponies. The ritual was quite brutal as they took turns riding the animals during the midday heat, working them to a state of complete exhaustion and beating them into action when they paused for breath.

The quarriers made their way up the slope for the umpteenth time that day, singing at the top of their lungs a simple melody that rang around the mountain tops. Their traditional brightly coloured costumes contrasted sharply with the surrounding dry grass and grey stone. Mere dots high above us, yaks somehow clung to the near vertical mountainside and far above them, the rocky peak topped with prayer flags towered over us all.

The horsemen turned their attention to a feisty white pony that bucked and kicked viciously whenever it got the chance. It threw several would-be riders quite spectacularly before weakening. Then, tying a rope to its bridle and with one riding, one pulling, they ran it up and down the hill for the rest of the afternoon.

Reluctantly next morning, we said goodbye to Kyanjin Gompa and began making our way back down the valley. After an hour or so I rounded a bend to find Nicolett crouched by the trackside. Her face was ashen and she looked in a bad way. I tried to comfort her placing a hand on her shoulder but she brushed me away, removing a t-shirt layer despite the morning chill.

"Believe me, you don't want to see this," she said. "Please go."

Walking on I glanced back to see her retching yet again. A little while later I crossed a splashing crystal brook in a deep gully and balanced my way gingerly along a crude, single log bridge. All at once I was hit by a wave of nausea, sweating and shivering. A young man and his wife carried a heavy double bed from head straps, almost running up the steep track towards me. It was all I could do to hang on until they were out of sight then I threw up over the edge, retching uncontrollably. Several minutes later when the crippling stomach cramps subsided I continued on my way, considerably weaker for my first experience of altitude sickness.

We were pretty strung out along the trail, I hadn't seen another soul for hours and was completely absorbed by my thoughts and surroundings. Clambering up a steep rubble section, focusing just a few paces ahead, I almost bumped into a young man walking down towards me. In his early twenties, he wore a heavy black woollen cloak over a coarse flax waistcoat and carried a large *kukri* in a sheath, tucked into a broad waistband. A grey woolly cap sat on top of thick, wild locks of jet black hair and he smiled, baring neat rows of yellow teeth. I wanted to say something, but what do you say to a man leading a billy goat on a piece of twine, while carrying half a dozen large frogs impaled through the head by a sharpened bamboo stake. He showed me his catch of unfortunate edible frogs, some still squirming.

"*Namaste.*"

It was mid-afternoon and I stopped for a rest at a tiny forest settlement on the edge of the raging river. Only a few feet away the mighty river thundered between huge glistening boulders

kukri - broad bladed traditional Nepalese knife with distinctive, oblique 'V' bend.
namaste - hello.

creating clouds of spray. The old guy who brought me lemon tea seemed glad of the company and happy that a tourist made the effort to talk to him. He told me he'd served with the 2nd *Gurkha* Regiment for seven years and had fought the Japanese in 'Burr-mah' and 'Malay'. I wondered what he thought when Japanese tourists walked by today.

That evening as I stared out from the enclosed wooden veranda at Peace Lodge, Syambru village, dense mist rolled away as if by magic, revealing the village and then Langtang *kola* cloaked with neat lines of rice terraces. The place had an amazing affect on my mind making me feel completely relaxed and at peace. Dunja joined me and we watched a farmer on a steep slope far below as he skilfully turned a huge pair of oxen back and forth, drawing a primitive wooden plough across an impossibly narrow terrace.

Next morning I was ready to go before the others and being the slowest, decided to get a head start. Everyone said, 'It's easy, just follow the trail,' but I have a very poor sense of direction and when the trail split I took the wrong route, heading straight up the mountainside. My trail wound almost vertical in places through the eerie gloom of ancient temperate forest where trees formed crooked shapes, their trunks and branches thickly hung with dripping wet moss and lichen.

The climb took nearly all day and almost killed me. On reaching the top it turned cold and a heavy mist drew in. Completely lost I searched round and round the plateau for the right path but luckily, just as I was starting to panic, a villager happened by and pointed me in the right direction. Walking on towards Cholang Pati settlement, Dillip and the girls appeared like ghosts out of the thick grey soup. They'd taken the longer

Gurkha - highly respected regiment of the British army originally made up of men from the Gorku region.
kola - river gorge.

path but got there half an hour before me, while Mike raced on alone.

Completely shattered, we finally reached the tiny village of Lauribiniyak, clinging to the mountainside where a hand painted sign proudly proclaimed 3,600 metres. We had walked for almost eleven hours that day and as the light was fading, suddenly a window opened through swirling mist. Distant peaks at eye level and slightly below streaked with laser beams of light, burst out of liquid cloud that flowed around them. The fabulous sunset almost broke my heart and I didn't know whether to laugh or cry. We gazed in awe from the top of the world until the mist engulfed us once more and the sky turned inky black.

We settled into Evening View guesthouse for the night, extremely basic accommodation that looked like a converted dry stone sheep pen. Warmed by a clay stove, the small living space led on to a row of tiny bed-chambers with curtains for doors and piles of smelly yak wool blankets to slide under. Dillip had passed this way several times before and gave the shy owner a hard time with constant jibing; the place was too cold, the choice of food too basic and everything tasted the same anyway, but he was glad to have us all the same. Huddled around the dinner table with our backs to the stove, we draped a heavy woollen tablecloth over our legs to keep in the warmth and ate large quantities of fried potatoes, a luxury in these parts, washed down with hot tea. It was a relief to see Isobel finally coming to terms with Dillip's boisterous, extrovert manner and the two chatted and joked like old friends.

After climbing steadily for several hours we arrived at Namaste lodge on the shore of Gosainkund holy lake the following afternoon. I had sensed an uneasy distance from Nicolett all morning and as we wandered off to explore our surroundings I was left to wonder what had gone wrong.

The icy green lake was deathly still, roughly twice the length of a football pitch across its widest point and according to Dillip, more than a thousand metres deep. A thin layer of mist clung to the opposite shore and not so much as a bird or the ripple of fish disturbed the eerie silence. Along its shallow edges Buddhist pilgrims had placed stones one upon another, to form hundreds of small shrines that stood out from the water. The lake and tiny settlement on the northern shore were well protected from the elements by a crescent of mountains and some of the stone towers may have stood for many years.

The girls were getting ready for the long push to Dunche and the dreadful bus ride back to Kathmandu. I was determined to walk over Laurabiniyak pass following the same path Mike had already taken to Sundarijal, about another five days walk, but the pass was at 4,500 metres and I already found myself short of breath from the least exertion. If the weather turned nasty I could be in serious trouble.

HIGHS AND LOWS

It was a sad parting with the others. Nicolett still refused to even talk to me and it wasn't the kind of send-off I needed. It was a hard slog in cold driving rain to Laurabiniyak Pass but I reached the saddle surprisingly quickly. The pass was bleak and desolate with no shelter of any kind and the narrow trail meandered over jagged granite outcrops only defined where boulders had been placed as crude steps. Wearing every piece of clothing I had I was cold and wet through, but at least I'd begun the downhill leg.

I felt certain I must be the only person crazy enough to be out there in such appalling weather, when I spotted a young man in plimsolls, black baggy pants and woollen coat, fairly jogging up the mountain towards me. We stopped to exchange pleasantries.

"Where you go?"

"To Gopte," I told him, innocently.

"Gopte empty. Nobody there. You go to next village."

But I'd studied the map. The next village was almost ten hours walk from where we stood.

"No, no. It has too be Gopte," I insisted. "Next village too far! How do you know it's empty?"

The stranger's name was Angdowa and he explained that his lodge, Himali Mendo, was the only one in Gopte. He was on his way to his wife and child in Syambru because it was the start of monsoon and there would be no more tourists.

"Well I have to go on," I told him.

There was no way I was climbing back over the pass and to try for the next village after Gopte, unprepared and in failing light, would be madness. Angdowa thought for a moment and then, still smiling told me,

"OK, I go back to Gopte, make fire, cook dhal bhat," and before I could protest this wasn't necessary, he was gone.

It rained almost the whole day, with only short breaks in thick mist to give an idea of the terrain. Reaching an unmarked fork in the trail I remembered Angdowa assuring me,

"Don't worry, trail easy to follow."
Yeah sure, until it splits and you have no idea which way to go! I studied the map and racked my brain. A wrong decision could have disastrous consequences. Eventually I choose the downhill path hoping it would lead me to the right valley, but as time wore on and after several exhausting uphill sections I began to have serious doubts. I hadn't passed another soul since meeting Angdowa several hours ago and for all I knew no one had been this way for days.

Rounding a bend I heard the thundering sound of a waterfall only to find the gulley was covered over by a crust of snow and ice as wide as a house. Hoof and footprints stopped abruptly at the snow's edge and the trail simply vanished. Had anyone actually crossed here? To fall through would mean certain death. Absolutely terrified, I tested its strength and pressing my body against the frozen snow, very carefully crabbed my way across.

After two more snow-covered waterfall crossings, my nerves were completely in tatters. In some places, where the trail had collapsed into the forest below or where it was just too steep, I had to scrabble on hands and knees, hauling myself up by roots, creepers, or outcrops of rock. I passed wild horses. Just like the bumblebee that shouldn't - according to the laws of physics - be able to fly, horses shouldn't be able to climb near vertical, but they got up there somehow.

Late in the afternoon I came across a work party laying heavy stone steps, clearing fallen trees and re-routing the trail above or below areas of landslide. Slaving away like a chain gang in the cold drizzle they showed no sign of discontentment. Seeing the leech gaiters they wore tucked into their plimsolls I quickly checked myself and found several of the nasty squirming parasites on my boots and socks.

Physically and mentally exhausted and having long given up any hope of finding my destination, the tiny hamlet of Gopte appeared as if by magic through a dense wall of mist, Angdowa standing in his doorway expecting me. I pulled the leeches from my boots and ankles and he hung my wet clothes above a clay stove to dry.

While we waited for the dhal bhat to cook Angdowa struck up a tune on his dramnyn, a crudely carved stringed instrument like a small violin that gave a plinky plonky sound when strummed. The situation seemed so bizarre, perched on a mountainside we couldn't even see for mist and drizzle somewhere in the Himalayas, and I struggled to cope with my sudden change of emotions, from total fear and panic to warmth and companionship. If he hadn't been there I think I'd have gone completely mad.

We talked as we ate. It wasn't easy because Angdowa's English was very poor and I spoke no Nepalese. Angdowa played another tune and sang, then he handed me the dramnyn, "Your turn." I strummed away with a vengeance running through my rendition of Deep Purple, 'Smoke on the Water', Elvis Costello, 'Oliver's Army', and finishing with The Who, 'Pinball Wizard'. Angdowa smiled at my awful singing and we huddled closer to the stove. He turned my boots again to help them dry, the rest of the dhal bhat went down and outside darkness slowly replaced white blindness.

Next morning I said farewell to Angdowa and began the long walk to Kutumsang village in the neighbouring valley. The mist had cleared temporarily and the sun burned through towering clouds to reveal glorious views of tree-covered ridges. As I walked, movement became fluid, I no longer needed to concentrate on pushing myself and eased into my stride.

By late afternoon, however, I was tired again, the thin air making me weak and light-headed. Endless steep climbs and shin-jarring descents had taken their toll and the mist and drizzle had been back for some time. I was going a bit crazy walking hour after hour, never passing another soul, nothing but whiteness in front of my face, constantly mindful that I might fall over some great precipice. As I rested for a while by a temple in the middle of a long incline, small statues of various Hindu gods set back in archways of stone seemed cold and unsympathetic. What on earth was I doing there?

I felt as if I was dying of loneliness, but miserable as I was, I relished the experience. This was the most independent I had ever felt in my life, no one knew or cared where I was and it was something I was doing entirely for myself. The physical pain was mine, I deserved it for making such a mess of my life but my reward was seeing first hand - even if only in glimpses - the greatest scenery in the world.

By the time I reached the village of Kutumsang stretched out along a knife-edge ridge I was completely worn out body and soul. A young woman squatted in the track washing her face and neck over a large copper bowl. She stood when she saw me, tossing back her long black hair and showed me to her house. After a cool mandi wash I lightened up in the company of Nurpu Sherpa, owner of Kutumsang lodge. An ornately carved wooden staircase led to a long balcony overlooking the village and valley below, and as we sat talking from this magnificent vantage point, Nurpu's wife and two sisters with round smiling faces and jet black hair that fell below the waist brought us food and sweet tea. Just before nightfall Nurpu went off to indulge in his favourite pastime and a short while later, he and a friend thundered up the narrow track on horseback. For some time they raced from one end of the village to the other, the walls echoing to the clatter of hooves. No one dared get in their way.

Next day around mid-afternoon, light drizzle gave way to a torrential downpour and the walk to Chisopani turned into an uncomfortable uphill slog. I watched in horror as streams grew into cascading rivers, carving deep gullies and washing the track down the mountainside. On a steep slope below me a family tried desperately to shore up defences against the waterfall tearing through their rice paddy. The young woman nearest shouted something to me as she splashed through mud and hammering rain. Maybe she wanted me to help but there was nothing anyone could do. Finally arriving at the village I quickly found somewhere to stay. The lodge owner spoke a little English and told me that gazelle Mike had passed through a couple of nights ago.

Chisopani village lay in a weather trap on top of a horseshoe ridge and astonishingly, only a kilometre or so down the supply road the mist cleared and the sun was hot enough to burn my skin. I sat on a rocky outcrop overlooking the Himalayan range and a great valley that stretched towards Kathmandu. The valley floor was soaked from monsoon rain and rivers that had burst their banks, and shone brilliantly in the sunlight. Dragonflies with exquisitely gleaming purple and green bodies hovered and darted around me, checking out the stranger in their territory, while I watched mountainous sky-scapes powered by massive thermals rapidly building and changing shape.

Back at the village the rain had stopped, replaced by cool mist. I had a couple of Chang beers in the BBC guesthouse while two men prepared the evenings grisly entertainment for a small gathering of onlookers. In the neighbouring paddock a man held the hind legs of a goat while his mate chopped its head off with a single blow from his kukri. In that same instant the shroud of mournful grey mist fell away to reveal the steeply descending mountainside dotted with brilliant red, yellow and violet wild flowers glowing in a magnificent, fiery sunset.

Early the following morning I walked down through lush rhododendron forest bathed in brilliant sunshine. The track was severely eroded from centuries of use, cut by rainwater gullies as tall as a man, and meandered off out of sight. Clouds above neighbouring peaks formed towering mountains that changed shape with incredible speed, as if alive. Sitting for a while on a berm of baked clay I watched laser beams of sunlight dance over the Himalayan foothills. I have heard that when someone is close to death they see a beautiful green valley that invites them to walk down. Only those who don't enter survive to tell the story, but I imagine it must look something like this.

All of a sudden the clouds closed right in shutting out the sun, it became chilly and I started walking again to keep warm. I wandered through a tiny hamlet perched on a steep slope, completely deserted apart from some chickens and a white baby goat wearing a crimson ribbon around its neck. Looking closer I was horrified to see the fleece around its throat was actually soaked with blood. Surely they hadn't just left the poor creature to bleed to death? Strangely it didn't seem to be in any distress and there was little I could do, so I left.

Further down the trail I stood aside to let a buffalo calf and its mother pass by. Blood streamed from their throats and below the cow's left eye. 'Yuck!' Maybe it was some sick local vampire cult. I passed a pair of bullocks in a rice paddy, same thing and finally it dawned on me; leeches! I quickly checked my clothes for any of the little horrors and found a fat one as big as my thumb, clinging to the back of my knee. Taking the cigarette lighter Nyerogi had given me I carefully singed its bum and when it dropped to the ground, stamped on it with my heel. 'Splatter!' The track and rocks nearby were sprayed with my dark red blood as the overstuffed body exploded.

A few hours later the fringes of Sundarijal were in sight on the floodplain below and I took the last few steps of my descent. Ducks paddled in a filthy stream that ran alongside heavy steel pipes taking water to the city below. Having worked so hard to get up there it seemed such a shame to be coming back down again, trading life in the mountain top dream world for the hassle and noise of the city. This had been one of the most emotional and physically draining experiences of my life but I felt so much richer for the experience; now it was time to move on.

From my steamed up window on a clattering local bus the sprawl of Sundarijal blended into the chaos of Kathmandu. I found a hotel, showered and hung out in a restaurant next to Kathmandu Guesthouse, watching a bizarre mix of humanity go by.

* * *

It was time for me to leave Nepal so I made my way to Kathmandu airport ready for the ten-o-clock flight to Bangkok. In the departure lounge I watched a rat scurry along electrical trunking above a huge painting of a moonlit Himalayan village. A couple of monks strolled in, both in their early 40's, shaved bald and wrapped in orange drapes. They smiled, apparently calm and inwardly content and without realising it my heart rate slowed, apprehension subsided and I began looking forward to the next stage of my journey.

The Thai Airlines Jumbo lumbered into position, wings juddering visibly as we trundled over lumps and bumps on the concrete taxiway. Then it was full throttle, engines screaming and 400 souls were scrunched back into their seats by an immense acceleration force. Seconds later nose wheels lifted and we left the ground on a crazily steep ascent angle before banking hard over right, as if to show everyone face on what the lights of Kathmandu looked like by night. For some reason I felt strangely calm. I guess I was thinking how lucky I'd been already and even if we lost it right then at that most vulnerable moment I could honestly say, life owed me nothing.

We reached our cruising altitude of around 9,000 metres somewhere over the Bay of Bengal, the plane levelled off and the engines settled down to a reassuringly monotonous hum. Thai air hostesses, ever so polite and gentle in wasp-waisted dresses of blue and gold that were too tight around the ankle to be practical, set about wrestling filing cabinets on wheels full of petite meals, up the aisles. One swished past and I caught a whiff of her perfume as she looked back at me and smiled.

Meal time was over, the small bottle of wine I took with my food had gone straight to my head and the sweet smiling hostess was busy cleaning up vomit from a fat kid who'd eaten too much pudding. I stood ahead of the cabin crew seats mid way along our time and space capsule as we floated on towards our destiny, staring out of the window in the emergency door. The sky was surprisingly light above even though there were no stars to be seen and far below where wars raged and babies were born, it was the deepest shade of mauve.

THAILAND and MALAYSIA

BANGKOK

At 3am Bangkok airport was cool and impersonal with walls of glass and slippery marble floors, polished constantly by an army of uniformed attendants. The banks wouldn't open until later, so having no Thai money, I tried to get some rest on an uncomfortable row of plastic seats, away from the menace of flailing brooms.

When the sun came up I set off for central Bangkok by bus. If you can master the Thai public transport system you can get around incredibly cheaply, but when I woke up on the bus some time later I was completely lost and no one spoke a word of English. Why should they? Stepping into a taxi the sudden change from oppressive humidity to frigid air-conditioning made me shiver. The driver seemed unsure where I wanted to go but agreed to help for 100 bhat. Didn't he know that all backpackers must eventually end up on Kau-San road? Gunning the engine he spun the steering wheel, sporting a single unsightly yellow fingernail on his left little finger, the same length again as the finger itself. Perhaps it was considered a thing of beauty here, or maybe just ideal for nose picking.

Almost immediately we found ourselves in grid-locked traffic on an endless freeway. I glanced anxiously at the meter as it ticked past 80, willing it to slow down. Reading my thoughts the driver barged the big luxuriant old Honda over to the hard shoulder and sped down a slip road taking us under the freeway and deeper into choking grey smog. As we pushed and weaved our way between the lines of nose-to-tail traffic I felt sure something was missing, but couldn't quite figure what it was. Then, in an acutely embarrassing move, my driver jammed the Honda at 45 degrees across the path of a new Mercedes, blocking two lanes of traffic and finally it dawned on me, there was no road rage. Not so much as a frown or raised fist. No matter how snarled the traffic got, the car horns stayed silent and tempers never flared. My driver smiled and explained that in Thailand, even if you were deeply wronged, showing anger was considered extremely undignified.

Suddenly ahead of us at the junction, standing on a tiny podium amid the melee of smoking vehicles, was 'The Fly'. The traffic cop wore giant goggles and a black rubber mask with twin side filters that completely covered his face. Arms waved frantically directing alternate lanes of cars to creep forward.

I could have sworn we'd already passed a large office block with distinctive blue marble pillars from the other direction, but almost an hour after setting off and now at least in the right general area, I parted with 200 bhat and walked the rest of the way.

After moving into a two bunk room at Bangkok Youth Hostel, I walked back towards Kau-San Road and was 'picked up' by an unusually friendly local man calling himself Pawn. Pawn tagged along dropping bits of information here and there, as we wandered through a square of magnificently decorated temples with roofs turned up into points at the corners. He told me these were designed to shoot descending demons back into the sky. Inside one particularly ornate temple sat an enormous gilded statue of Buddha as tall as a house.

Pawn told me he was an English teacher, which was odd because his English was bloody awful, and before that he'd been a kick boxer for several years. Then he pointed out that unlike some other Thais who took advantage of tourists, he was straight. He accompanied me to an open air restaurant - a few tarpaulin-covered frames and some folding tables - where local women prepared meals.

Pawn ordered a round of beer and as we talked he kept topping up my glass. I wasn't concerned because he clearly couldn't handle his drink and whatever scam he had in mind he was already too pissed to pull it off. Sure enough, when I asked for the bill he stepped in telling me it was 700 bhat.

"For four beers? Bollocks!"

I left him swaying on his stool and asked the woman in charge how much.

"Two-hundred-eighty."

I quickly paid and left Pawn to ponder how he could improve his technique.

Kau-San Road throbbed to the sound of the latest reggae, soul and techno beats. Cool bars, restaurants and cafes overflowed onto the pavements with hip young travellers from around the world, while market stalls did a roaring trade in Celtic tattooing, illegally copied CDs, sarongs and leather goods. Sipping a milkshake, I sheltered from the brief, steamy evening deluge before catching a *tuk-tuk* to the Thai boxing stadium.

A low tuk-tuk fare means your driver will probably get you to look in a couple of shops along the way, jewellers or tailors, so he can get a voucher from the owner. I stood in a tailors shop, totally disinterested. It was already our third stop and I wondered if I'd ever get to the stadium.

"Can I help you sir, nice suit?" asked the tailor. "We make for you here."

The tuk-tuk driver grinned through the window as if to say, 'Everything OK?'

"I don't want anything from your shop," I told him, exasperated. "I just want to see the boxing."

Suddenly the tailor got really angry. "You no buy? Then piss off back to Kau-San Road!"

tuk-tuk - funny open top three wheel taxi that makes a loud 'tuk-tuk' sound.

I left as the driver filed in to collect his voucher, but I guess he didn't get one because we sped off and he dumped me half way across town in some deserted district. Eventually I found another tuk-tuk and climbed aboard, insisting on paying the full fare. Barely had we reached the end of the street when the traffic ahead stopped sharply. Crunch!…and we slammed into the back of a stationary car.

The cops arrived and made me wait for ages until they found an interpreter to take my statement. Finally a third tuk-tuk got me to the boxing stadium just as the last bout finished and the spectators began to leave.

* * *

Having finally got through to Boris, the German guy I met in Masai Mara, we arranged to meet at his office one evening. I was curious to see if he really was who he said he was – self made business tycoon or just an over imaginative office clerk.

I duly arrived to find that everything he'd told me about his life was true. Boris ran his own computer consultancy from a plush office suite above Succumvit Road in the financial centre. Annual turnover around $2 million.

He'd been badly hit by the collapse of the Asian economy a few months earlier but since then his company had gone from strength to strength, winning important deals with Siemens and SAP, plus a major contract on the new overhead railway project for the city centre.

Our conversation was interrupted by a tall slim woman in a smart blue suit, who discussed a job applicant waiting in the next room with Boris.

"She's perfect," announced the manageress. "but she wants forty thousand."

"No, no, no," Boris shouted, infuriated. "What am I, a charity?"

He rose stern faced and walked with the young manageress to the next room. A few moments later out came the new employee beaming a glowing smile and got straight on her mobile phone to tell her family she had accepted 35,000 bhat per month.

At 8.30pm we finally left the office and the pile of CVs from unsuccessful job applicants on Boris's desk. It was a ten minute walk to his flat.

"Leck, my girlfriend used to be a barmaid. You'll be meeting her at the apartment. I don't think she's made anything to eat so we'll go out for dinner. I hope you brought your swimming trunks."

I asked Boris if he'd ever dated his manageress but he was horrified at the suggestion.

"That would never work. The relationship lasts three months, she leaves, then her lawyers come and take my business. Thai intellectuals are not allowed to marry below their class and we *farangs* are definitely below their class. This woman was educated with the King of Thailand's daughter. Her parents are extremely wealthy and if anything happened between me and her they would put a contract on my life. I'm serious!"

By the same token, Boris explained he could not afford to be seen in town with Leck.

"If I'm seen anywhere with her by my staff I can close up my company tomorrow. I would lose face and it would cease to function."

I was shocked. "Bangkok may be a big city but sooner or later you're going to bump into one of your colleagues when your out with Leck."

"If it happens tonight I tell them she is with you," he said with a grin.

"Oh…OK," I replied, not sure how well I'd carry off the

farang - foreigner of low standing.

119

pretence.

"...But you're right," he said, thoughtfully. "It's bound to happen sooner or later."

Leck greeted us in the small modern apartment, hugs and kisses for Boris, big warm smiles for me. She was tiny with plain features and a rounded face. Leck showed me photos of herself and Boris on holiday in Chang Mai, northern Thailand, while he changed into swimming shorts.

Relaxing in the roof-top swimming pool Leck was in a playful mood clinging to Boris's neck as he swam, but when she moved out of ear shot he whispered,

"Don't talk about Masai Mara. I told her I was on a business trip and she thinks Masai Mara is in Germany. She's been with me nine months now, that's the longest I've spent with a girl in Thailand. Maybe it's time I found myself a new one."

We dined in a German owned restaurant because it was convenient and they served Weitz beer, then a taxi took us to the pulsing red-light area and obligatory girlie bars. We sat on stools right by the podium while the girls flounced above us to seedy music. If I looked up, I got an eyeful of shaven fanny and frankly, it was embarrassing. It was early morning and I was knackered so I said goodbye to Boris and Leck and took a cab back to the youth hostel.

RURAL THAILAND

Having taken the bus an hour's journey north to Ayutthaiya, ancient capital of Thailand, I rented a bicycle from the Ayutthaiya guest house and 'did some temples'. They stood in neat rows on a grid plan with crumbling red brickwork, looking like giant bishop's hats. At the time the place didn't feel very holy, the only visitors being tourists, backpackers and Japanese couples with enormous SLR cameras, but in its day it was a hugely important religious centre.

In the sweltering heat of mid-afternoon I stopped for a break in the night market. The place was slow at this time of day so I waited patiently while a young lad completed a large food order. When he'd finished I tried to explain what I wanted, pointing to the food in the display cabinet.

"Pork and duck."

"Pook?…dup?" he repeated, hopelessly confused.

Frustrated and hungry I muttered under my breath as the young man started serving another customer. Clearly I wasn't worth the effort.

"Oh well, fuck it then!"

He snapped round, face stiffened in anger. 'Oops'. I had more success at the next stall and a couple of middle aged women wearing conical straw sun hats quickly stir-fried some noodles and meat for me. Chatting as they worked, they sounded like cats meowing melodically. In Thai, tone rises and falls within each word, unlike European languages where it varies along the whole sentence. It seemed as if everyone was singing. I ate my meal while watching rafts of water hyacinth drift down the Pa Sak river. "Hey, that stuff looks familiar," I thought, as I remembered the great swathes of it I'd seen covering Lake Victoria.

With daylight fading I sat outside the guesthouse sipping beer with the other residents. Two large packs of mongrel dogs fought over ownership of the street and pavements. They were half wild, none wore collars and the weaker ones were starved to the bone.

The guesthouse manager recommended some places of interest, so early next morning I set off for Khau-Yai National Park. Stepping off the train a couple of hours later at the busy little town of Pak-Chong, I was immediately pounced on by a short squat woman in her late forties, touting for her guesthouse, Jungle View Lodge. She clung to me like a limpet, grabbing at my arm and repeating the name again and again. Tired, hot and hungry from the uncomfortable train ride I stopped in the nearest restaurant, but she plonked herself down beside me and cackled on about how great her place was, giving the best guided tours of Khau-Yai.

She'd given such a bad impression now, wild elephants couldn't have dragged me to her sodding guesthouse so I pulled on my rucksack and quickly walked away, almost tripping over a smallish balding European guy in his fifties. By incredible luck he turned out to be the manager of Khau-Yai Garden Lodge, so I jumped into his waiting minibus and escaped.

Klause, my rescuer told me the crazy woman didn't have a tourist licence and had been in trouble with the police for operating illegally.

"She changed the name recently because of a bad write up in the guide books but her lodge is in the middle of Pak-Chong, six miles from Khau-Yai National Park. How can she call it 'Jungle View?'"

As soon as I had dumped my bags and showered I joined a group of guests on a guided tour. First stop was a marble factory where huge chunks of the quarried blue stone were sliced into slabs by enormous power saws before being shaped into tables, tiles and all manor of artefacts.

Next we visited a Buddhist temple a few kilometres away. Outside, a small number of animals were kept in cramped filthy cages and we gathered around a sad looking gibbon. Nang, our guide, wouldn't go near it, telling us a few days earlier she had gone to help some local kids who'd been bitten after tormenting it, and it tore her hair. I held out my hand to him, despite Nang's protests, and he took it gently. His hands were so similar to mine with wrinkles, lines and fingernails and his face was deeply sad, frowning, questioning.

Late that afternoon we set off in a canvas backed truck to visit a bat cave deep in the heart of the national park. It was a short, desperately steep climb up slippery, algae covered rocks to the site. We made ourselves comfortable on a ledge, half-way up the near vertical cliff, looking out over a rainforest valley. As the sun dipped behind the opposite ridge, the sky began to burn brighter and brighter until our cliff face glowed with a fiery orange sheen.

The group from Garden View had got there before us and their guide, sporting a little pony tail, had abandoned the rest of his group to chat up two French girls, encouraging them right into the mouth of the cave where they could get the best views - and cause the maximum disturbance. Nang asked him to observe the rule of silence before the bats exit but he ignored her, his loud voice piercing the silence, and the faint hubbub from within the cave fell silent.

More than an hour late the nightly ritual finally began. The first few brave scouts became a trickle that slowly grew to a torrent of tiny flapping, chirping dark shapes flowing around the mountainside like a black river, to feed on insects in the forest below.

Now the tourists broke ranks, some moving right into the cave mouth, flashing their cameras directly into the midst - they must have that all-important shot no matter what the cost - but with every camera flash the bats were startled and the flow stopped.

"It's OK," yelled pony tail. "they come back!"
Nang was clearly upset and pleaded with them to stop. Two other Garden Lodge guests and I jumped down to lend support and reluctantly, 'my little pony' and his group withdrew.

A great bat hawk, probably already gorged, flew menacingly through the river of tiny bodies creating a halo of space. The astonishing spectacle would continue for several hours but it was dark now and time for us to leave.

At the start of our jungle trek the following day Nang was clearly in her element, pointing out creatures and plants we would otherwise have overlooked. Magnificent greater hornbills flew into mahogany trees towering above us, the slow beat of their great wings making a loud, wow-wow-wow sound, and gibbons shrieked and whooped as we approached before making off into the forest to hide.

The jungle humidity was saturating, leaves constantly dripping heavy drops of moisture. Moving stealthily along the slippery mulch trail we stopped frequently to remove leeches from our gaiters. Our ears slowly became accustomed to the silence and we tuned in to rustling sounds from the undergrowth, perhaps a snake or a shrew. The jungle creatures were shy and hard to spot and a faint sound or movement of leaves were often the only things to give away their presence.

Plants were thinly spread on the forest floor. Light filtering through the different canopy layers was never more than a dappled green gloom, so most low lying shrubs were shaded out and never took hold. Those with huge umbrella leaves or multiple fronds like palms and ferns did well, collecting as much as possible from the poor light. Parasitic bromeliads thrived where there was no soil at all, adorning upper canopy branches and the crowns of small trees. We even saw them suspended from liana vines where they filtered rain water that collected in their heart. Saplings were everywhere and usually grew little taller than a man before they ran out of steam and died. Their only chance to mature came when a grand old tree succumbed to age or disease and crashed to the ground, creating a clearing.

Now and again there was a pungent smell of rotting vegetation and decay. Fallen tree trunks once tall and proud now crumbled to the touch, seething with termites and covered in great tiers of orange fungus. Often the termites didn't even wait for a tree to die, making their way to the uppermost branches hidden from predators inside tunnels of secreted pulp like varicose veins. New growth had its own smell too like raw runner beans or freshly mown grass and if you shut your eyes and placed your head close to certain plants, you could smell their greenness.

Nang placed her fingers over a honey badger's claw marks in the bark of a tree, to show us how it stretched and exercised like a cat. She explained how the strangling fig took on its incredible shape, twisted gnarled root systems large enough to walk through, choking out the host tree that had long since rotted away.

After a couple of hours we heard voices, growing louder and louder. Who on earth could be making such a racket, scaring away the timid wildlife? Who else but, 'my little pony'. He swaggered past at the head of a very large strung out group, singing at the top of his voice and swinging his sweat shirt around his head. His followers seemed completely bored and oblivious to their surroundings. It was as if he didn't want them to see anything.

The following morning I set off into the forest on my own, wading across a waist high river and up the opposite bank. Alarmed by my presence, a troop of gibbons defended their territory from up in the treetops, charging over and throwing down nuts and bits of branch to intimidate me. They moved back, regrouped and then repeated the performance several times. When I moved on they howled excitedly, victorious! "Ouww-Oooow...Eee-Oouww. Woooo-up. Woooo-up – Wup."

There was a small number of tigers in the park and the thought that one could easily creep up to within pouncing distance kept me on edge as I walked the narrow trail. Suddenly a large deer sounded the alarm like a dog's bark and my heart jumped as it stamped off into the forest. Resting by a stream I watched a black and white wading bird search the rocks for insects, while giant squirrels chattered loudly all around. By late afternoon I made it to the ranger station and hitched a lift back to Garden Lodge. People were mostly very friendly and hitching was easy in rural Thailand.

BRIDGE ENCOUNTER

Catching a train to Kanchanaburi two hours west of Bangkok, I moved into the popular Jolly Frog guesthouse overlooking broad, tranquil Kwai Yai river and went straight away to pay my respects at the beautifully maintained Allied War Cemetery.

More than sixty thousand allies were taken prisoner when they surrendered at Singapore in 1942. A disaster caused by grossly overestimating the size of the Japanese force and poor leadership. By the end of the war sixteen thousand of them and over one hundred thousand Burmese, Malaysian and Chinese had been worked, starved, tortured and beaten to death.

Most of the soldiers died in their early 20s. Young men from ten different regiments with a broad mixture of backgrounds, brought together by war. I imagined them standing there in uniform, rifles slung, smiling, chatting, smoking a cigarette…and at work, in the camps, on the infamous 'Death Railway'.

At a shrine where the names of cremated POW's were engraved the inscription read:

'I will make you a name and a praise among all people of the earth when I turn back your captivity before your eyes, saith the Lord.'

A kid of about thirteen had been following a few paces behind me, fidgeting nervously as he watched my every move. I walked away but sensed he was close by. Suddenly I felt a tap on my arm and wheeled round to see him holding his stiff little dick in his hand.

"Piss off you dirty little bastard," I told him, outraged at being flashed and at his assumption that I was a pervert, but he just stood there, expectantly.

"Go on," I shouted. "Piss off!"

He wandered off a little way then stood and stared, a wounded expression on his face.

"Go on. Fuck off!" I yelled and then felt ashamed for shattering the peace of the soldier's resting place.

"Why me?"

Hiring a bike that afternoon I cycled to Kwai-Yai Bridge, 'The Bridge Over the River Kwai'. Two of the original locomotives stood on display and nearby an old gentleman carefully studied the rusting relic of a small shunt loco. I thought, "He's just old enough...I wonder if..."

"Excuse me. You weren't one of the POW's were you?"

"Yes," he said with a far away look, "I worked on the railway," then he turned back to the engine. I was bursting with questions now, but I had to be careful. He wasn't just going to blurt out his painful story to any stranger. His wife, standing nearby, read the anguish in my expression.

"Can you recommend a book about the railway?" I asked her, carefully inviting conversation.

"My husband has written a book about it."

"Your husband? What's it called?"

"The Railwayman."

It clicked! She'd called him Eric, earlier. On the very day I'd come to visit the bridge over the river Kwai, symbol of the notorious Thai – Burma railway, I had met Eric Lomax, author of one of the most famous books on the subject. We talked some more and I had my photograph taken in front of Kwai-Yai - 'Death Railway Bridge' with Mr Lomax, by an Australian newspaper photographer. Mrs Lomax added,

"If an old Japanese turns up it's probably Nagasi Takashi. They're due to meet here today."

I had read, 'The Railwayman' only the previous year. Nagasi Takashi was an ex-prison guard who not only repented for his war crimes but dedicated his life trying to make atonement and their extraordinary, emotionally charged reunion ten years earlier was beautifully depicted in Mr Lomax's book.

* * *

Bright and early the following morning I teamed up with a young woman called Jo whom I'd met in the Jolly Frog restaurant and we visited beautiful waterfalls at Erawan National Park, an hour's bus ride from Kanchanaburi.

The falls consisted of seven distinct stages, each with its own pool, and we clambered up a steep trail littered with tree roots and slippery rocks in the hot, humid air. Shoals of fish swam lazily in the pools as emerald and ruby dragonflies flitted around us. A large monitor lizard basked on a rock while macaque monkeys played in the trees overhead. Our steam bath walk was finally rewarded as we bathed in a luxurious natural jacuzzi pool just above the seventh level.

Most women love jewellery shopping and Jo was no exception, so the following day we set off for the opal processing workshops of Ba-Phang. The two of us sat astride a tiny rented scooter for the two hour journey under menacing storm clouds. We stopped along the way to watch mahouts washing a group of six elephants in the nearby river. The elephants seemed to enjoy having their backs and behind their ears scrubbed with a stiff brush as they stood in brown water up to their shoulders.

It rained for most of the journey and by the time we arrived late in the afternoon the place was shut. Cold and drenched in our T-shirts and shorts, we warmed up in a nearby restaurant with a pot of tea and some biscuits, then Jo had the brilliant idea of making waterproofs from bin liners. Using four large plastic bags from a nearby shop, she tore a big hole in one for a dress and a small hole in another for a top, but no arm holes.

"You'll never reach the handlebars like that," I joked.

"I don't want my arms to get cold," she said.

Copying her design but tearing holes for my arms, my own over-suit worked surprisingly well.

Our first stop on the way back was to investigate a safari park we had passed earlier. The park was closed but around the back we came across an elephant compound containing two juveniles and four adults, including two mothers with babies. The adults and juveniles were chained to posts supporting a corrugated iron roof while the babies played freely between the great grey pillars of their mothers' legs.

A young mahout came out from a neighbouring house and invited us to touch the little ones. Jo and I knelt down between the two baby elephants so they could see our faces and the moment they decided we were harmless they began exploring every inch of us with their tiny trunks, like a child's arm. They sucked at our plastic bag suits and ruffled our hair, carefully checking all the new smells. Jo and I were in complete rapture hugging their little wrinkly bodies covered with sparse wiry hair and milked every drop from the precious encounter.

Our next stop was a large covered market, and as we pottered in on the scooter the locals giggled and pointed at the two sodden westerners wrapped in bin liners. On display was a fantastic variety of fresh vegetables, pulses, herbs, fruit and fish. Vivid colours and marvellous fragrances. Items were weighed on brass scales, prices bargained in sing-song language and money exchanged. With darkness drawing in we didn't stay long and made our way back to Kanchanaburi.

Next morning I shared a minibus with Jo heading for the port of Surat Thani, eight hours south of Bangkok. She woke me about half way, gave me a massive hug and went her separate way.

ISLAND LIFE

The island of Ko Phangan lies about 110 kilometres north-east of Surat Thani in the Gulf of Thailand. It was late in the afternoon when my ferry pulled up alongside the single jetty. Stepping off, I rented a scooter and rode along the coast road for an hour taking in cloudless pale blue skies, beaches of golden sand and crystal clear sea. The last remnants of jungle peeped out between plantations of coconut palm billowing on a gentle breeze. Passing through small clusters of wooden houses, children played and goats and chickens strayed across the quiet road. On the fringes of each settlement open rubbish tips with huge piles of empty plastic water bottles and burnt coconut husks marred the scenery. Arriving at sleepy Wattan Bay resort where around a dozen thatched beach huts stood on stilts between shady palm trees, I swam in the warm shallow water as the sun dipped towards the horizon.

I was up early next morning and went scuba diving with a young English couple and a student called Emma. Nick, our diving instructor in his late forties, ran Chalokam Divers from the neighbouring village and he took the four of us to a reef off a tiny island twenty minutes away by boat.

Emma was an excellent dive buddy, staying close and making frequent air and equipment checks. She glided past sleek as a dolphin and I swam above her, through the swirl of shimmering bubbles when she exhaled. We reached a narrow tunnel in a massive wall of rock, flipped over on our backs to protect our tank valves and gently finned our way through. It was a weird feeling, upside down and weightless, watching bubbles dance like silvery pools of mercury trapped in air pockets in the rocks above.

Out on the other side the reef followed a trench shaped like a ship's keel and we were lulled by the constant clicking sound of myriads of shrimps. Coral formations in vivid shades of purple, red and orange attracted exquisitely coloured angelfish and striped sergeant fish while tiny orange and white clown fish played safely among stinging anemones. Many of the jagged antler-coral tips were bleached white indicating that it had died recently and I felt sick at the thought that pollution and El Niño were destroying this magnificent underwater garden.

That evening I relaxed on a hammock slung between two palm trees, watching the sun slowly dip below the sea.

Haad Rin, largest town on the south-eastern tip of Ko Phangan looked out over a pristine azure sea. Out of season the sprawling hippie resort wasn't nearly as horrid as I'd been led to believe and its shimmering horseshoe beach was pretty and inviting, strewn with oiled bronzed bodies. It was lunch time and far too hot for my pale English body so I sat in the shade sipping a cool, delicious banana milk shake. This wouldn't be hard to get used to. I found a cheap room and somewhere safe to leave the bike and began unwinding into the island way of life.

Despite large numbers of beach huts sprouting up along the coastline and roads bulldozed straight through the jungle, Ko Phangan was still very beautiful. I spent the afternoon exploring the island's west coast on my rented scooter. Its indestructible motor hauled me up desperately steep gradients over bumps and berms where the mud road had been washed away, and eventually brought me out at Aow Thong Nai Pan beach resort, a collection of rustic bamboo huts that clung to the steep sides of a tiny horseshoe bay. Sheltered from the stiff breeze, a handful of dedicated hedonist visitors soaked up sunshine on the fine sandy beach or lazed in hammocks slung under palm trees.

Back at Haad Rin that evening the bars and restaurants all had at least one large screen TV showing illegally copied films long before general release, so I settled down to watch yet another violent American movie.

By midnight, hundreds of revellers overflowed from the Cactus Bar with its booming garage music and crowded onto the beach like a noisy seal colony, mixing and talking. Squid boats in the bay and the mountains beyond were silhouetted by distant lightning flashes while on the beach, pot smoke and conversation filled the air.

After breakfast the following day, I boarded a small speed-ferry for Ko Samui island and went aft to check out her twin turbocharged V10 diesels. The engines fired up with a roar in a cloud of grey smoke as the deck hands uncoupled our fuel line and cast off. Without forward speed the rudder was useless and in a heavy swell and strong cross wind it took some skilful juggling back and forth to manoeuvre us out of the narrow quay entrance. Almost immediately we ran into big waves swamping those unwise enough to be on deck in a deluge of warm seawater.

Ko Samui was the antithesis of Ko Phangan and a perfect example of how overdevelopment can spoil an island. The bars of its largest town, Chaweng, rocked and endless lines of street stalls sold everything a tourist could possibly want. There were some excellent art galleries where diligent young artists meticulously copied paintings by Dali, Vermeer and other western painters. The island attracted short stay European tourists with plenty of money, pushing up prices and encouraging outrageous hotel construction; virtually all native forest had been replaced by neat rows of coconut and banana palms.

After a couple of days I'd seen enough and caught an old wooden sleeper ferry back to the mainland. The passenger deck had a very low ceiling and sleeping mats were laid out herring bone fashion either side of a central compartment stuffed with life jackets. The boat's nauseous, lurching progress made it difficult to sleep and passengers shivered in the chill sea air with cockroaches scampering over our faces. We docked before sunrise and an hour or so later a minibus arrived to take us to Hat Yai, last big city before the Malaysian border.

Stopping at a petrol station just outside Hat Yai, our surly driver told us we had to pay him 20 bhat each otherwise we'd have to walk the last two kilometres to the border. It wasn't much, but I'd already spent every last cent on food and obligingly got off when ordered. The minibus sped away and as I rounded a corner sweating in the afternoon heat under my heavy rucksack, the shimmering road stretched away into the distance with the border nowhere in sight. Why hadn't I toughed it out on the bus? What was he going to do, drag me off? Call the police and tell them I hadn't paid my bribe money?

Before I had walked very far a plush new saloon car driven by a middle-aged Malaysian with a young woman in the passenger seat drew alongside.

"I take you to border," said the friendly driver.

"Oh thanks mate. You're a life saver."

"Where you from?" he asked as we drove off.

"London. England."

"You spend long time in Thailand? Where you stay?"

"Well, I flew into Bangkok and then went to..."

"Ah, Bangkok," he interrupted. "Many prostitute in Bangkok."

"Oh, really?"

"I from Malaysia. Come to Hat Yai for weekend, for prostitute."

"Hmm, that's nice. She's very pretty," I said nodding towards the young woman beside him.

"She not prostitute!" he exclaimed, much affronted. "She my daughter!"

"Oh shit, sorry mate," I offered, as we approached customs.

My benevolent sex tourist driver shoved me out to walk the last few steps and I was relieved to find my fellow bus passengers. We walked through passport control and back onto the minibus where I stared daggers at our driver through his rear view mirror.

Arriving at Butterworth late in the afternoon, the remaining passengers caught a ferry to Georgetown on the island port of Penang, where we moved into the Bazaar hostel.

Away from the ugly commercial docks, Georgetown consisted of neat rows of two storey terraced houses, shops and markets. Mobile food stalls were very popular and it was possible to fill up quite cheaply with tasty snacks: duck and spring onion in thin pancakes with plum sauce, king prawns in satay sauce or pork with delicious black bean sauce.

My plan was to travel on through Indonesia home to some of the most fascinating but endangered wildlife and rainforest in the world, wildly different volcanic terrain and an unusual culture. Only a month earlier, however, the newspapers had warned of an upsurge of violence between different religious and political groups and the British consulate advised people not to go there at all.

Rising early next morning I made my way apprehensively to the ferry terminal and joined a queue of passengers for the 200 kilometre crossing to Medan, Sumatra. Inside the large twin keel hydrofoil the air conditioning was set to freezing. She lurched heavily in the swell and Asian passengers sat shivering in dumfounded silence watching Mr Bean on TV, as he staggered about with an enormous turkey stuck on his head.

INDONESIA

INDONESIA

After around four hours we docked at Medan and immediately the hassles and hustles started. My heart raced as natives were segregated from tourists and herded against metal barricades into an austere customs building by police, shouting and wielding long battens. They weren't afraid to use them and lashed out at stragglers, some of whom had a genuine look of fear. My first instinct was to turn and run back onto the boat. What on earth had we got ourselves into?

"Today is holiday," shouted the police captain to the small group of westerners. "All banks closed, best rate here at money exchange. Change money now!" he ordered.

The rate was 16,000 rupias to the pound. A fellow passenger told me she got 22,000 back in Penang but it was far too risky to wait for a better deal. I changed up 100 $US and was given 1,200,000 rupias in an unexpectedly massive wad of notes. Quickly stuffing bundles of cash into socks pockets and underpants it was clear Indonesian money was going to be difficult to deal with, let alone carry.

Escaping swarms of noisy touts I took a minibus through sprawling shanty suburbs to the tourist office. The staff spoke no English and didn't seem to know very much about tourism so I put on a bold face and made my way to Bukit Lawan village, on the eastern border of Leuser National Park.

The tourist minibus cost about £1.25 for the two hour journey but the public bus was a mere fraction of that, and given my low budget there didn't seem to be any point spending more than I had to. I discovered a meal cost less than a Mars Bar back home and a room was around £1. If I could stay out of trouble, exploring Indonesia was going to be incredibly cheap.

The public bus was very uncomfortable and slow, stopping at every tiny village along the way. I stood for the first hour because the knackered old vehicle was jammed so full, bodies compacted into the aisle like anchovies in a jar. I was terrified because they insisted my rucksack went behind the back row of seats where I couldn't see it but thankfully it was still there when the passengers thinned out, so I found a painfully narrow seat and jammed it under my feet.

We passed endless fruit and palm oil plantations. Small houses by the roadside had front yards with goats and chickens and there were swarms of children everywhere: walking home from school in uniform, playing by the road in rags, clamouring after the bus holding up bananas and nuts for sale, or simply begging.

Seeing a free space, a lad in his late teens left his own seat to join me.

"Where you from? Where you go?"

After giving the obligatory name, rank and serial number I asked him about his country and politics.

"So who did you vote for in the last election?"

"I not vote," he said complacently. "Government all the same. They all no good."

"But if you don't vote," I reasoned, "how can you ever change anything in your country, make things better?"

"It not make better, all government the same. What work you do?" he asked, changing the subject abruptly.

"I fix washing machines," I told him. Then it occurred to me he had probably never seen a washing machine in his life and even if I could explain the concept, I would never be able to explain why people would want to squander such a huge sum of money on a machine when there was so much surplus labour around to do the job for free.

"How much money you make?"

That was a bit awkward. If I told him the truth he might think I was some wealthy aristocrat and it may cause resentment.

"In a month or a year?" I asked, stalling while I worked out the arithmetic.

"Month," he said.

His friend was now listening intently leaning on the back of our seat and made me feel quite nervous.

"Probably more than you because my country has a stronger economy," I told him, and refused to answer any more questions about wages, money, or my country's investment in the destruction of his rainforest. The lads became irritated at this and I was a little relieved when they got off at a small village.

Bukit Lawan was a line of rustic wood and bamboo guest houses, restaurants, general stores and grocers, stretched out along the eastern bank of a broad, fast-flowing river. A bridge had been swept away leaving a tall wooden tower on the opposite bank and fearless children clambered up to leap into the river below with a loud splash. A single pathway ran the length of the village leading to a sharp bend in the river, where a narrow dugout ferry was hauled across by local lads or park rangers using a rope fixed at both banks. They didn't charge for this but usually waited until there was a large enough group of visitors to make the crossing worthwhile. Clambering out of the ferry, one entered Leuser National Park and to the right, the orang-utan rehabilitation centre. Having found a guesthouse with a balcony overlooking the river, I dumped my bag and walked back down to the visitors' centre on the edge of town, to arrange a guided trek into the forest.

Sinar, a park ranger and professional guide, offered to take me on a ten day jungle trek for around £70. Small but tough looking, quiet spoken Sinar had an exceptional knowledge of the forest, unlike the numerous unofficial guides who touted for business in the restaurants and cafes along the river; all acoustic guitars, pony tails and bullshit.

Even in Leuser, Sinar told me, you now had to walk more than ten kilometres into the interior to find primary forest. Elsewhere, the larger hardwood trees had been felled and dragged out years ago. Our trek would take us to the fringes of the last unspoiled area of rainforest but beyond this, the jungle was just too dense to penetrate.

"You not ready for that," said Sinar with a grin.

When I got up to leave early next morning my head throbbed and the room shuddered. Every movement was a tremendous effort and when I finally dragged myself out of bed I found to my horror, I had completely lost my sense of balance. A sachet of re-hydration salts mixed with water gave me enough energy to start walking towards the ranger station, but with every step the horizon bounced and I felt like one of those dolls whose eyes roll up and down on a pivot. After only a short distance the picture blacked out altogether and a moment later I found myself upside down in the trackside hedge, facing the wrong way. When I'd picked myself up I continued on my way, passing one of the volunteers from the orang-utan rehab centre.

"Could be dengue fever," she suggested, grimly.

"Great! What does that mean? Is it terminal?"

Unable to start my trek, I made my apologies to Sinar before struggling up a narrow winding track to the feeding post on the edge of the forest. Sharon, a rehab volunteer from Sheffield, explained that recently released orang-utans could visit twice a day to supplement their jungle diet of leaves and fruit with bananas and sugared milk. The handouts were deliberately mundane to encourage the orangs to use their jungle food store. Volunteers paid for the food themselves and for medication when animals arrived sick or malnourished, which was often.

"Two of our orphans were donated from the head of park's private collection," she explained.

"You're kidding. If the guy in charge has so little respect for wildlife, what hope is there? How did you get him to part with them?"

Sharon filled shallow containers with sweetened milk from a five gallon drum and handed them over the wooden fence to a ranger.

"They were spotted by volunteers who went to investigate. The volunteers made it very uncomfortable for him by making sure everybody knew about it."

Twigs and branches cracked and fell to the ground as a large adolescent male made his way to the platform. Slowly swaying like a pendulum in the top of a small tree he reached out to grab a branch from its neighbour, hauled himself onto it and swayed again to reach the next. At the platform he took a plastic beaker of milk from the ranger and drank it down. A female carrying a tiny baby in one arm drew close on a neighbouring tree but was intimidated by the male's presence and refused to come down while he was there.

Trudging back down the track I felt weak and nauseous and rested outside a holiday chalet. Pongos, a luxurious complex of private apartments, stood right next to the rehab centre on national park land. It was a crazy situation undermining the painstaking work of the volunteers, as recently released orang-utans often came down from the jungle for handouts, human contact and shelter.

After a mandi wash and some food back at the guesthouse my mysterious illness slowly subsided. Next morning I figured, if I took it steady I should be able to begin my trek.

R H I N O !

On the day of the trek Sinar substituted his younger brother Aman as my guide, just before we were due to set off. Aman had never been to school and his English was lousy, which meant I wouldn't be able to learn as much from the experience as I'd hoped.

"What's that, Aman?" I asked, pointing to a massive tree with a smooth parallel trunk rising up from thick tangled roots.

"Resin tree," he replied, showing me a spot where the bark was damaged and resin had bled out to protect the wound from insects and infection.

"And this one?" I continued, slapping a solid narrow buttress root that extended up the trunk to head height.

"Also resin tree."

Now I'm no botanist, but these two trees clearly had very different root systems. Perhaps one could argue both produced resin, but that didn't help me much. For all that, Aman was clearly a skilful guide with an intimate knowledge of the jungle and its inhabitants. Dressed in beige ranger shorts and shirt he was barely half my size, lean and fit, but he moderated his pace to help me keep up.

We walked for a good six hours that day. Aman pointed out a greater hornbill as big as a goose in the treetops high above us. It hopped further up into the crown when it spotted us, showing off an impressive black and white barred tail. Lower down a black squirrel ran around a bough until it was upside down, staring directly at us.

We heard birdcalls and spotted a black rhinoceros hornbill. With my binoculars I could clearly see its nest marked by a slit, high up in the trunk of a large tree. Long tail feathers were built into the adobe wall enclosing the chicks. The entrance was just wide enough to admit a beak bearing food but hopefully narrow enough to keep out snakes and prying monkey hands. The male arrived and using its massive bright yellow bill with the dexterity of a brain surgeon wielding a scalpel, carefully fed a lizard to the chicks inside.

The trail cut straight up steep ridges and down to countless streams, tributaries of the same broad meandering river that fed into Bukit Lawan. Late in the afternoon we reached camp set on a sandbank in the river gorge. Our home for the night was a large tarpaulin spread over a frame of wooden poles, open side facing the river. A group of guides had arrived before us with two tall Dutch lads and were huddled round a fire smoking rollups. I went for a swim in powerful rapids that swirled me around and dumped me at the riverbank. Small brown dippers with white collars screeched on the opposite bank, occasionally diving into the fast flowing water in search of fly larvae. There were butterflies as big as bats, and bats flitted and swooped past catching insects on the wing.

Huge trees towered above us on the steep mountainside and all around as dusk drew in, amazing jungle plant shapes were silhouetted against the purple sky, the whole scene dimly lit by a full moon reflected in the river. Bamboo stems thick as a drainpipe stretched higher than a two storey house before bending into the water under their own weight. Parasitic plants flourished on the boughs and trunks of living trees or dangled from liana vines like massive hanging baskets.

Just before dawn I was jolted awake by a nightmare. I glanced at the others, afraid I might have called out, but they slept on peacefully and slowly the shelter, river and jungle materialised through the still mist and gloom.

Aman and I left camp after a late breakfast. It was already hot as we climbed almost vertically for long stretches. Tangled roots held fragile soil and loose rocks in place and we used them to haul ourselves up. The humidity was unbelievable. My clothes were drenched in sweat and as perspiration drained out it was vital to keep topping up with water. Aman told me this was the 'dry season', but close to gullies or streams the ground was a slippery mulch underfoot.

At the top of a sharp ridge as he scrabbled over high buttress tree roots in the middle of the trail, Aman recognised Yanti, a rehabilitated female orang-utan up in a nearby tree. Now heavily pregnant, she bitterly resented our intrusion. Breaking off branches, she threw them down at us and made the characteristic smacking alarm sound with her lips. Waiting for the right moment we ran underneath her while she rearmed, sliding and stumbling down the other side of the ridge.

We reached camp by mid afternoon to find Aman's friend and fellow guide, Alohu, waiting for us. Alohu wore casual clothes and was of similar height and build to Aman with a big rounded face and dark heavy eyebrows.

While the others prepared food I went for a swim to cool down and take in my surroundings. The rushing river cut a meandering path through steep hills cloaked with emerald rainforest. At a bend upstream, a tributary fed in via a waterfall and sheltered pool. Wading over to investigate I knelt in cool water up to my chin and occasionally felt small fish sucking at my skin. The pool was ultimate relaxation, rejuvenating my body and mind from the day's punishing walk.

Aman called from the opposite bank waking me from my thoughts. Supper was ready, plain but delicious hot chilli fish with rice. When we'd finished and the plates were scrubbed it was time for a brew and a smoke of fresh local weed. It was still only late afternoon and seeing I was restless, Aman constructed a puzzle from bamboo and twine to keep me entertained.

Next morning the three of us continued up-river crossing a dozen times from one overgrown riverbank to the other before cutting straight up through the jungle. The younger men made steady progress on the steep ascent hauling themselves up by exposed roots, vines and bamboo stems, digging in footholds where they could. I cursed quietly to myself nicknaming the hill 'heartbreak ridge'. It was brutal!

Despite regular meals and constantly topping up with water, I could feel myself losing weight. Back home I hovered around 12 ¾ stones. In Bangkok when I weighed myself I was down to 12. Now, in the jungle powerhouse steam bath, I'd be surprised if I was more than 11, but it was all muscle.

Mile blended into mile, day into day. The terrain looked similar but there was always something unusual and interesting over the next hill. Scaling one steep ridge there was a defined animal trail strewn with large, fresh pats of dung.

"Elephant," said Aman authoritatively.

"No way!"

"In jungle, elephant climb too," he continued, unperturbed. I stared in disbelief. Climb maybe, but they weren't sodding mountain goats. We had trouble scrabbling up here, let alone one-and-a-half tonnes of Asian elephant. I looked down the ridge trail and back at the dung pats. Those nearest had sprouted tiny mushrooms and were covered in a downy layer of mould indicating they were around a month old. Further up the trail some were fresher, maybe only three days. Well it wasn't bird shit, and there really wasn't any other way it could have got there. Asian climbing elephants! To clinch it, Aman placed a hand in one of several faint depressions in the soft humus. He was right of course. Elephant spoor.

By day four we were passing through noticeably denser patches of jungle and there were more hazards: Long broad leaves with razor-sharp serrated edges, rattan like thick steel cables covered in lethal spines and tree sap of waxy poison, contact with which causes an extremely irritating rash or fever. Then there were the insects. Disease carrying mosquitoes were worst near streams or stagnant pools. Scorpions and biting centipedes lurked under every root and fallen tree, while soldier ants as big as your thumb had to be avoided at all cost. The sound of a thousand cicadas seared the mind like tinnitus, hour after hour and bloodsucking leeches found their way into our boots. The rainforest's intense heat and humidity made it an ideal breeding ground for bacteria. All it took was an embedded rattan spine or seemingly insignificant insect bite and the tiniest cut or wound could rapidly become a major problem as infections you'd never even heard of raged out of control.

Strangely, I wouldn't rather have been anywhere else in the world. I relished the hardships, the sense of achievement from pushing oneself to the limit and being able to thrive using the bare minimum of tools and equipment. The uniqueness of what we were doing felt incredibly special and the rainforest constantly reminded us it was alive, with every sound, every smell and every creature such a contrast to life back in the man-made world.

Our meals became more exotic and as stocks of rice, biltong and dried fish grew low, we ate on the move. Aman carried our billycan filled with hot coals and the flow of air as we walked kept them glowing. Alohu fashioned a sort of giant lollipop from the stalk and narrow leaves of a palm branch. He coated the broad business end with sticky tree sap and walked along more open sections of trail with it raised above his head. All manner of insects stuck to the palm mat, which he pulled off and handed to Aman for grilling. Succulent locusts and juicy praying mantis taste surprisingly good when crispy.

The jungle closed in, becoming impossibly tangled and dense. We made good progress on day six following wild pig trails, although the interminable gloom and constant stooping to avoid low foliage was a great strain. I figured we had reached the region Sinar told me about when we were forced to turn back from two such trails because they simply disappeared after some time into impenetrable jungle or dense drainpipe stands of bamboo. A third trail proved more reliable so we followed it for an hour until it bisected a steam.

We had walked less than two hundred metres upstream when Alohu, who'd been scouting on ahead, returned very excitedly. He whispered anxiously to Aman and motioned for me to follow. Rounding a bend, the stream opened up into a muddy clay pool. Alohu stopped abruptly, motionless, and Aman and I instinctively froze. Alohu crouched, hand held back imploring us to stay put. There was a splashing sound up ahead. Whatever it was, was leaving. Alohu waved us on again and continued around the wallow's edge.

When I reached the spot, wet clay still dripped from leaves up to chest height. It was big! Aman stood in near darkness waving frantically for me to keep up and my nerves frayed as he disappeared through a tunnel in the wall of green. I felt light-headed from a racing heart and from severely regulating my breathing so as not to make a sound. Here and there new tunnels crossed our trail but I could clearly see which way the great beast had gone as I brushed fresh clay from my arms.

Where the hell were Alohu and Aman? Wildly irrational thoughts entered my head and I shivered with fear.

"They've abandoned me. This is their sport, their kick. Take the dumb tourist into the jungle and lose him! How many ever return from this green oblivion," I wondered. "The rainforest must be littered with the mummified corpses of Alohu and Aman's victims…"

"Huh!"

Too late, I recognised the massive shape ahead of me and let out the loud, involuntary exclamation. The rhino's huge horned head and periscope ears lurched in my direction and in the next nanosecond it thundered up the track towards me with horrifying speed.

I ran like hell, instinctively dropping my day-sack in the mud, branches and creepers whipping my face. Bang, I slammed into an overhanging tree trunk and bounced back, but my legs were still running and I kept on. At the entrance to the muddy pool, I snatched a lungful of air and threw myself in headlong.

Scrabbling in thick sludge I grabbed hold of a root and pulled myself under. There was a pounding splash and thrashing sound as if all the water would be thrown out and I'd be left exposed.

Just as I ran out of air and my lungs felt as if they would burst, the thrashing stopped. Silence. I rolled back my head, breaking the surface and gulped for breath. Opening my eyes, I saw my attacker had made off leaving the undergrowth dripping with brown water.

I must have stood there for several minutes, disconnected, peering down that black tunnel until the sound of voices coming closer brought me back from my trance. Aman and Alohu gasped when they saw me.

"Am I a ghost?" I thought, looking down at my body covered in brown slime. Moments later Alohu burst out laughing and Aman joined him in uncontrollable hysterics.

We moved out an hour's walk to where the jungle thinned, made camp and slung hammocks. The two guides, normally shy and quiet spoken, couldn't stop babbling about the incident. Aman kept smiling and patting my back.

"This very special Andy. This I tell to grandchildren long, long time!"

I felt honoured, acutely aware that I might be one of the very last people ever to see a Sumatran rhino. I was also deeply shell-shocked and floated in a state of unreality, tired from adrenalin burn out and sensory overload. Slowly I drifted asleep to the band saw screech of cicadas and the barking of sambar deer.

Before full light we began our three day march towards our western camp. My shoulder ached and the welts on my face, legs and arms stung like mad, but inside I felt terrific. I'd survived a rhino attack - how many people could say that? - and the little anger I felt toward my guides for losing me had vanished. They kept making such a fuss: "Was I OK? Were they walking too fast?" Anyway, it had been as much my fault for not keeping up.

Illness and daily exertion had worn me down and the raft trip back to Bukit Lawan was like a reward for our efforts. Aman and Alohu assembled the simple raft, lashing together three truck inner tubes that had been left on a previous visit. Our gear was bagged up and strapped down, Aman cut rafting poles and we were off.

They weren't major rapids but we were bounced around enough to get a thorough soaking. After an hour or so we pulled over to the bank.

"Why are we stopping?"

Aman, sitting behind me, pointed to a small brown snake that had dropped onto his lap from an overhanging branch. When it slithered onto the raft he took the opportunity to slide off. Coaxing it onto a stick, he laid it in a bush and we continued. A monitor lizard basked on a rock in the sunshine and another, much larger, foraged by a smouldering campfire. We rounded a bend and there, on a steep bank by the water's edge was a young orang-utan, from its size around three years old.

When I described her reaction during supper back at Bukit Lawan, - folding her arms and shyly looking away - sanctuary volunteers Andy and Sharon immediately identify her as Rasi. Recently released, she was intimidated by some of the larger orang-utans and hadn't been seen at the feeding post for several days. The sighting was a great relief for Sharon who would be leaving soon and had taken a special interest in Rasi.

ENVIRONMENTALISTS' MEETING

Andy and Sharon were going to Medan early to investigate a tip off about a baby orang-utan held illegally in a crocodile farm. I wanted to visit the offices of Leuser Development Project concerned with conservation of the national park, and joined them. Organisations were set in place to rehabilitate the apes but I was determined to find out who, if anyone, was protecting the shrinking rainforest.

When we arrived at the crocodile farm there were no other visitors. Two very large crocs festered in their own mess in concrete pens so small their tails were permanently bent at right angles. Nearby in a muddy ditch, around a dozen young crocs waited patiently for their next meal. It wasn't long before Andy spotted our target, a male orang-utan of about eighteen months. He seemed to be in good condition, well fed, no skin problems, bright and alert. Andy carefully questioned a keeper who joined us. How old was the animal? How long had they had him? What did they call him? Assuming we were ordinary tourists she brought 'Peach' out of his tiny cage and handed him to Andy.

Peach was a little beauty, lively, playful and despite his tiny prison, apparently well adjusted. He'd clearly been well looked after but that didn't change our feelings for a second. Sharon was quite prepared to 'do a runner' with the infant but Andy was determined to return Peach to the wild lawfully, with official support.

Peach took turns at playing with each of us. Initially I held back - surely human contact would make rehabilitation more difficult - but Sharon told me the kindest thing at his age, having been torn from his natural mother, was not to deny him surrogate contact.

149

My turn came and I held him in my arms. He stretched and squirmed and hugged me tight. I held his little hands and he stared into my eyes.

"Who are you? Have you come to take me home? Where's my real mother?"

The manager heard we were asking a lot of questions and came out to see what was going on. We introduced ourselves and shook hands but when Andy suggested the young orang-utan might be better off in the wild, he cursed and stormed off in a rage.

Some tourists showed up. A fairly typical back-packer couple in their late twenties, open-minded and inquisitive, and then an extended family of westerners with twelve kids between them, dressed in smart but dour 1950's style clothes. The men looked like identical twins, short and balding. The women, slightly taller, wore plain ankle length dresses and small head scarves. They made a beeline for Peach who was promptly dragged out of his cage again for them to play with. The youngest of the children screamed when Peach was thrust in front of him and was immediately scooped up and pampered by his mother.

No interest was shown in the other 'boring' animals at the croc farm menagerie: a beautifully spotted and striped civet cat, a porcupine with torturous looking quills, an adorable bush baby with wide staring eyes and a thoroughly depressed-looking gibbon. The crocodiles themselves were incidental.

The back packers left, promising Sharon and Andy they would visit the rehab centre bringing fruit, vegetables and much needed medical supplies and we followed them to the gate.

"Before I leave Indonesia," said Andy, with a look of absolute determination, "that baby is going back into the wild!"

Our next stop was Medan zoo where Andy and Sharon hoped to meet dynamic young Canadian biologist, Chris Sheppard. Chris visited the zoo several years ago when it was in an utterly disgraceful condition. He'd never seen animals so ill treated before and decided on the spot to stay and help improve conditions. Now a respected conservation consultant, Chris had re-stocked the zoo with animals rescued from private collections and deforested areas. He was out when we arrived so we took a look around by ourselves.

Andy pointed out several significant improvements Chris had made: larger enclosures, better sanitation and regular cleaning.

"In a way it's lucky he's not here. He always ends up finding jobs for us when we come. Last time he had me scraping the inside of the tiger pen clean."

The male Sumatran tiger moaned softly as he paced the cage bars. He stopped occasionally to fix one of us with the most penetrating stare. In his environment, caught in that gaze, it would be the last thing you ever saw. The tigers were truly awesome, more than two metres from nose to the base of the tail and weighing over ninety kilograms. Their coat had a reddish orange hue (unlike their Indian cousins), with broad dark stripes running down to a cream belly.

"If we allow these to disappear life won't be worth living any more!"

Andy and Sharon nodded in agreement. Two Indonesian lads sat on a railing facing the adjacent side of the cage throwing lighted cigarette butts inside, so we asked them to stop.

Andy told us Chris rescued the female two years ago when he got word a tiger had been caught on the outskirts of the forest, and went to check it out. She lost half a paw in the snare and was in dreadful shape, stressed out, dehydrated and badly beaten by the poachers. Chris arranged transport back to the zoo but when she arrived she'd gone completely berserk and had to be sedated. The driver had hacked off her tail with a machete for a souvenir.

She gave birth to three beautiful cubs a year later but one of them died. Tigers regularly spray urine on trees to mark their territory but in the pen it dried and built up a hard layer of concentrated ammonia. The cubs often licked the walls and that's what killed the little one. Chris and Andy scraped the walls clean, sterilising the enclosure. Since then the two remaining cubs had almost doubled in size and were doing well playing close to their mother.

I left Sharon and Andy and took a cab to the office of Leuser Development Project. The manager was away on important business but I was invited to meet his second in command. Yarrow Robertson offered me a chair in his office, politely explaining that he couldn't spare much time.

"After all," he said, "While we talk, trees are coming down."

"What, inside the park?"

"Yes, up on the north-west coast for example," and he gestured to the map of Sumatra on the wall. "A large timber consortium moved in here recently and cut down a lot of hardwood trees."

"Isn't there anyone to police the park boundaries and prosecute companies that fell trees illegally?"

"It wasn't illegal. The forestry department granted logging concessions inside the park and rights for a palm oil plantation."

Yarrow explained that whilst the head of forestry agreed with conservation, some of his superiors had a vested interest in the timber companies. I thought of the garden furniture on sale back home in all the DIY and superstores proudly labelled as hardwood, yet none of it bearing the Forest Stewardship Council mark.

Leuser Development Project was founded in 1995 when the United Nations agreed the area was of special scientific interest because of its incredibly rich diversity of flora and fauna. They knew that if the rainforest was destroyed, the streams and rivers that feed the lowland plains and irrigate crops would dry up.

"Leuser National Park is the last refuge for critically endangered species like the Sumatran tiger and rhino," Yarrow continued. "Trees are being felled at such a rate that in ten years' time there will be no rainforest left outside the park boundaries."

Yarrow told me there were somewhere around 300 Sumatran rhinos and less than 500 Sumatran tigers left in the world. He added that the total population of Javan rhinos was estimated at a little under 70 and they were in even worse shape because the groups were fragmented in various parks, and the enormity of his words hit home. Three of the most amazing land mammals that ever lived were on the verge of extinction, right here, right now in Indonesia. Couldn't we have made space for these amazing creatures? Couldn't we have done better than this?

I thought it best not to mention my near fatal encounter a few days earlier. He probably wouldn't be too impressed that we had put ourselves in extreme danger and caused the animal unnecessary stress, so I left him to continue the work of protecting the national park.

Note: Following the Tsunami disaster of 2004 over £3 billion was raised to help the survivors rebuild their lives in a wonderful humanitarian effort. Indonesia is one of the worlds most overcrowded archipelagos and the human population (as is the case in many of the poorest, most vulnerable countries of the world) is still rising exponentially.

As far as I know there has been no increase in funds to protect Indonesia's dwindling rainforest or support the valiant efforts of NGOs and the Indonesian rangers to save the Sumatran rhino, Sumatran tiger and Javan rhino from extinction. See Epilogue.

EXPLORING SUMATRA

It was a wonderful surprise to find Stephane, a French Canadian backpacker I'd met in Penang, eating breakfast in a restaurant overlooking the river. After catching up on one another's news we agreed to travel together for a while and took the next minibus south to Berastagi.

We arrived early in the afternoon at the quiet drive-through town with its broad empty boulevard. My illness was back again - listless, bouncing vision, the runs - but I went for a brief walk around town to get my bearings. Away from the main street shops on a small cultivated allotment, I caught my first sight of a traditional Indonesian longhouse. Standing well off the ground on stout wooden stilts the front leaned heavily outwards while the roof tapered upwards pointing to the sky. Secured to the top was a massive pair of buffalo horns, symbol of strength and fertility.

Despite feeling pretty rough next morning I set off early with Stephane to scale the lower of two nearby volcanoes, Gunung Sibayak. Our trail connected with a broad unmade road, bulldozed through young pine forest almost all the way to the top where it terminated at a large ugly construction site. Beyond the next ridge was a deep crater the size of a football pitch, with impressive superheated steam vents and yellow sulphur trails. The site below was going to be a natural energy power station, hopefully replacing the town's monstrous diesel generators that howled day and night.

The next day Stephane and I took a minibus to Lake Toba, at 72 kilometres in length the largest lake in Sumatra. We approached with spectacular views of naked green hillsides leading down to a gorge where a waterfall high in the cliff face fed the lake's northern shore.

In a volcanic holocaust sixty thousand years ago, an entire mountain range blasted into the atmosphere leaving the gigantic crater and creating a cloud of ash that blocked out the sun around the world. Natural food sources were devastated and the world's human (Neanderthal) population crashed from around three million to an estimated three hundred thousand.

Stephane and I bought tickets to Tuk-tuk peninsula on Pulau Samosir island in the middle of the great lake and wandered around market stalls of exotic fruit, vegetables and fish, while we waited for the ferry. I tried a durian, munching on the soft creamy inner fruit with its texture a cross between avocado and chewing-gum but eventually its scent of rotting meat filled me with revulsion and I gave up. Unrecognisable pieces of goat, buffalo and who knows what else were displayed in the sun with attendant swarms of flies, while in the centre a large stall did a brisk trade in freshly barbecued chickens. I drew closer to satisfy a morbid curiosity.

When an order was placed the stall owner removed a victim from one of several cramped bamboo cages and cruelly dispatched it, partially severing its neck with a rusty sickle. He threw the flapping creature into a basket, placing the lid on top so it couldn't escape. When the next order was received, he took the chicken from the basket - occasionally still flapping - and placed it in the automatic chicken plucker. This device consisted of a heavy steel drum lined with rubber flails the thickness and length of an index finger. In the centre was a rotating core, also bristling with flails, that whipped round at a furious rate removing all but the most stubborn feathers. Finally the bird was gutted, impaled on a spit and roasted in front of a gas powered grill.

After a while a small, top heavy wooden ferry arrived to take us across the placid lake. One of the young touts on board pestered Stephane and myself, asking us over and over,

"Where you stay? How much you pay? How much money you have?"

He followed us off the ferry. No amount of persuasion, reasoning, or threats deterred him and he only quit when we turned off the main street into a guest house.

In Rumba Home-stay we took a double room each at an astonishing 75 pence per night. There were nicer places to stay on the peninsula; squawking yelling kids woke us early in the morning and the makeshift rock and boulder jetty made swimming impossible, but Rumba was the coolest place around and it was just too much effort to move.

Hiring a pair of scooters we set off at lunchtime following the coastal road anticlockwise. The sun was warm and welcoming as we passed Buddhist temples and a Christian shrine standing starkly against a perfect clear sky and the still, blue lake. The landscape was green and fertile with rice paddies flanked by clusters of palm trees and conifers. We rode through villages of impressive wooden longhouses set back from the road, roof beams ornately carved and pointing upwards like the prow of a sailing ship. In one village we stopped to watch a group of dancers dressed in sarongs and tunics of bright red, green and gold, perform to the rhythmic beat of goatskin drums and a large wooden xylophone.

We'd barely made it half-way round when I was hit by a wave of dizziness and nausea, for a while completely losing my sense of balance - not the best thing when you're riding a scooter - and when the dizziness subsided we gingerly made our way back to the guesthouse.

Stephane had a pale complexion and wispy white hair. I enjoyed his relaxed companionship and smiled at his goatee beard and comic antics. He was a talented musician and after supper, borrowing the proprietor's acoustic guitar, serenaded appreciative guests with White Snake, U2 and whatever else came into his head.

As darkness drew in, more tourists arrived to spend the evening at Rumba. Stephane took a bow and handed the guitar to local maestros huddled in a corner at the back of the restaurant. Everyone gathered in close to watch and listen as they played from a selection of their own melodies. The lead guitarist had a severely withered right hand, yet the sound he produced from the simple guitar was a joy to hear. We sat enthralled as the sweet sound of guitar and vocal harmonies drifted on the warm evening air.

Early next morning Stephane and I set off, determined to ride the clockwise circuit of Pulao Samosir, some 80 kilometres. After about an hour, having climbed the hills at the northern tip of the island, I stopped to take in the hauntingly beautiful view. Looking out over a carpet of gorse and giant ferns, a great expanse of calm blue water reflected wispy clouds and beyond this, the green hills and forests of the mainland folded into the distance. Unaware that Stephane had come back to look for me I carried on, assuming he was still out in front and disappointingly, we never met up again on the bike ride.

We spent the following day lurching and swaying around endless curves, in the stifling humidity of a minibus heading for Bukittinggi. I began to wonder if there were any straight roads in Indonesia and we seemed to drive for hours without really getting anywhere. Sadly, it was time to part company with Stephane as he had different plans and time constraints. He'd become a real friend and we had shared many good times.

Bukittinggi was a midsize town with a population of around forty thousand. Its central streets were lined with two storey houses from the colonial Dutch era, a number of which had been converted into guesthouses. Mostly now in disrepair, their wrought iron balconies and shuttered windows spoke of a former elegance. The main street lay at the bottom of a gorge that cut through the centre of town, spanned by a sturdy steel suspension bridge with wooden walk boards.

The lad at reception in my guesthouse was friendly enough, occasionally asking me to help out with his English studies, but on the whole people in Sumatra seemed to treat foreigners with suspicion. Shop owners were often unhelpful and bus touts seemed to enjoy giving visitors the run-around. Kids in school uniform constantly yelled out when I passed,

"Elloh friend, where you go? Where you from? Elloh friend, you come here!"

When they were in groups they giggled to one another, holding their noses and complaining about the foul smell coming from tourists or mocking the funny way we dressed.

Indonesian language was often a babble with sounds like, 'bing, bang, boingy' and lots of 'prr' sounds. The written word was even stranger with strings of characters resembling 'p's, 'q's and lopsided 'n's. Altogether it could be quite daunting to find your way around and a good guide book was essential.

* * *

Travellers described Bukittinggi zoo as a disgrace so I decided to go and see for myself. Near the entrance were a pair of Asian elephants. The unpredictable male let me come close and then lurched for the wide spaced bars with his powerful trunk, but the female was more docile and enjoyed a good scratch under her chin. They looked so sad inside their tiny enclosure.

The zoo's gibbons had two terrific howling sessions at around 8 and 10 o'clock every morning. A lone brown male displayed schizophrenic behaviour, stretching an arm through holes in the fine mesh cage. He was immensely strong and when I was within reach, grabbed my fingers with both hands, pulling me towards gnashing, bared teeth. Next door lived a young female who, in sharp contrast seemed desperate for any contact, even human. She offered her hand and I held it gently for a while.

An inquisitive teenager followed me around the zoo asking lots of questions about life back in the UK. Goreng told me he wanted to improve his spoken English before going to university. He had never heard of Leuser National Park but was fascinated by my visit there and the tale of my rhino encounter. When he left to pray at the local mosque, he told me he would find out all he could about the national park and tell his friends and family.

Heading south again early that afternoon, the country bus snaked steeply down a series of forty-four hairpin bends to lake Maninjau. Mist rose slowly off the still water above a line of palm trees forming wispy cotton wool clouds.

After lunch, when I'd recovered from another dizzy spell, I rented a scooter and rode around the lake in pouring rain. The road was appalling and I bounced and skidded over boulders and potholes, passing a brave Frenchman who was covering the 24 kilometre route by bicycle.

It seems crazy looking back, but I was already planning to move on again next morning. My only neighbour at Febby's Home-stay, an English woman in her mid-twenties, joined me for a breakfast of banana and chocolate pancakes.

"You've come here to one of the most beautiful, relaxing places on earth and already you're thinking of leaving? You've got to learn to unwind!"

She was like a mother hen admonishing her wandering chicks but I could see her point and when she left for her batik course that afternoon I wandered into the village to buy some fishing tackle. Having dug up some unfortunate worms, I borrowed our host's wobbly dugout canoe and paddled out a little way onto the still lake. Rigging my gear to a makeshift bamboo rod, I arranged myself in the boat so I could keep an eye on the float, sat back and chilled out.

A couple of hours later there hadn't been a single bite and I was pretty well cooked by the sun. The relaxation had done me good though and to cool off I swam in the magical soothing waters of Lake Maninjau. Now fully unwound, it was time to find the waterfall my neighbour had told me about at breakfast.

After the usual misunderstanding and misdirection I found the trail, opposite a domed Mosque with a fountain and arches that stood in a shallow tiled pool. The trail wound up through rice paddies and forest following a babbling stream. Occasionally stream and path merged and I hopped from boulder to boulder trying to keep my boots dry. Clambering under fallen tree trunks and steeply uphill the jungle became more lush and beautiful the higher I went. Reaching a near vertical section I hauled myself up by tree roots and vines, carefully testing footholds in soft crumbling soil before committing my weight. Beyond the ridge the river split into two cascading waterfalls. To my right, water danced over a series of steps worn in the rock while ahead of me, the main body of water poured over a sheer rock face. As I stood peering up through sparkling droplets falling in slow motion, the spray made a rainbow in the dappled jungle light and a cloud of mist rose from boulders pounded smooth below.

Leeches and mosquitoes were a nuisance on the walk back down to the road but I felt terrific. Turning down towards Febby's Home-stay the sky and mountains started to glow fiery red, reflected in the mirror lake. Above, thousands of giant fruit bats completely filled the air in an amazing spectacle, slowly making their way to the forest. They flew with three or four powerful wing beats and then a glide. Much lower, their tiny cousins the pipistrelles flitted and darted among the coconut palms. Later that evening, my neighbour and I sat by the lakeshore under a bright full moon eating grilled fish from our host's captive nets and I felt so glad I had taken her advice.

The following evening I left Lake Maninjau taking a minibus to Mount Kerinci, a dormant volcano roughly halfway down the island. At around one o-clock in the morning I was jolted awake when we pulled up outside Subandi Home-stay in the tiny village of Kersik Tua. I cringed with embarrassment as my driver hammered on the door until it rattled open, but good natured Mr Sabandi welcomed me in and showed me to a tiny room with hardboard partition walls and a firm but creaky bed.

Kersik Tua was little more than a handful of modest bungalows by the side of a quiet road. Chickens and ducks wandered between gardens of sun flowers, runner beans and exotic fruit. In the distance Mount Kerinci, with deceptively gentle tapering sides, towered over flat cultivated surrounding landscape. The only remaining forest lay like a mantle around the upper half of the mountain and a single cloud hung above it like a halo. Huge smoke plumes rose in the humid air from clearance fires steadily eating away at the tree line.

I got on straight away with the other guests, Sharon from Australia and Tracy from the UK and we agreed to do some exploring together. Sharon, in her late twenties, was a seasoned traveller with a warm personality. In conversation she told me she'd given up trying to find her ideal partner and was getting ready to go it alone as a single mother with the support of her family.

"I take it you'll be leaving the conception until you get back to Adelaide?"

She looked me up and down for a moment. "Yeah!"

Tracey was tall with long blonde hair. She'd worked as an English teacher for a year in Japan and more recently, as an escort in the more lucrative karaoke clubs.

"Japanese businessmen are such perverts," she told us matter-of-factly. "The more you abuse them, the more they like it. They can't understand the concept of escorting and always think we're going to have sex with them at the end of the evening."

In the afternoon we visited the bustling market of Sungai Penu, a twenty minute bus ride away. A covering of tarpaulins and polythene hadn't stopped the rain getting through and we squelched over rotting wooden floor slats between stalls overflowing with chillies, mangoes, beans, pulses, poultry and fish. Aromas alternated abruptly from sweet and savoury to the pungent warm smell of rotting fruit. Outside a few ancient motor vehicles struggled through the milling crowds, but two-seater wooden carriages drawn by ponies with decorative bridles and canvas pooh-catchers strapped to their hind quarters were a favourite means of transport.

That night as we binged on fresh fruit salad smothered in chocolate syrup, Tracy told us more about her adventures in Japan and for some reason I found my mind wandering.

"Your having a laugh aren't you? You're not really called Sharon and Tracy."

"Pardon?" said Sharon frowning deeply.

Tracy's mouth dropped open and she glowered at me. "Oops."

Next morning I shared a small taxi van with Sharon back to Sungai Penu. She needed to do some shopping and I wanted to visit the offices of the World Wildlife Fund and Kerinci Seblat National Park to find out about conservation of the mountain forest. As we stepped on-board a middle-aged woman complained bitterly to her young son about the stench from the westerners, fanning the air with her hand, pinching her nose and edging as close as she could to the front. Surely we didn't smell that bad?

Inside the WWF office I was introduced to Mr Masud, director of operations, a small balding man in his late fifties dressed in a light grey suit. Mr Masud talked about improving the productivity and efficiency of local farms so that farmers would be less tempted to clear new areas of forest, but as Indonesia's population continued to grow exponentially the long-term future of the national park looked pretty bleak.

After our brief chat I thanked Mr Masud for his time and went next door to the office of Kerinci Seblat National Park where I talked to Mr Alip, works supervisor, in his early thirties. Mr Alip told me anti-poaching units operated in the national park and that they often caught poachers, but the mild punitive measures were a weak deterrent. It seemed that if action wasn't taken soon internationally at government level, the rainforest and all its treasures would be lost for ever.

Around mid afternoon the uniformed office staff of KSNP assembled in the courtyard for a parade. When the silly giggling and falling about was almost under control, a quick salute was given to the boss and everyone went home. Disappointingly, there was little current information on the condition of wildlife in the park so I made my way back to the guesthouse.

After breakfast the following morning I set off to climb Danau Tujuh about five kilometres away, a small volcano with its own crater lake. I splashed across streams and waded through marshes to an area where the cinnamon I'd seen bundled up for sale in the village had been stripped from young trees. On the forest fringes I spotted a bush baby, a small furry round-faced animal curled up like a cat in the fork of a sapling, but it saw me and hopped onto another tree out of sight.

Further up the trail the forest closed in and suddenly I was dazzled by a whirlwind of brightly coloured birds, chattering and singing all around me. There must have been around twenty of them ranging from tiny tree creepers pecking insects from tree trunks, to a jay sized bird that plucked berries from nearby bushes. It was astonishing to see such close cooperation between the different species as they swirled around the forest in a communal group. Safety in numbers perhaps, or exploiting different fruit, insects and grubs exposed by each other's efforts. When they moved on, the forest fell eerily silent again,

The morning's steady drizzle became a downpour and around lunchtime I splashed and stumbled the last few paces to the crater's summit. Looking out through the trees, Lake Tujuh appeared majestic and foreboding in the rain. A steep slippery trail led down to the water's edge and from there it was a short walk towards the roaring sound of a waterfall. The crater rim had eroded in a narrow cleft and the noise from the river thundering over the edge to crash more than thirty metres below, was deafening. A large tree with undermined roots had fallen over to form a natural bridge across the top of the falls and its fresh branches rose vertically like railings. I ventured half way across and peered down. The first stage falls were followed by two others, trailing off into the forest far below.

Another tree had fallen headlong into the water. Its trunk leaned heavily against my bridge causing it to shudder rhythmically with the movement of water and the whole lot could have gone at any moment. I could see the newspaper headline, 'Washing Machine Man Washed Away' and moved back to a safer position.

Late the following afternoon Sharon and I said goodbye to Tracy, making her way north to Medan. We were heading for the town of Banko via winding country roads, from where we could catch a fast coach all the way to Jakarta, Java.

The medium size country bus was designed to carry twenty very small passengers with bums of leather, but with more than thirty on board the touts still jammed children in beside us to fill up any gaps. The hard steel seat frame poked through lumpy foam padding and my backside and knees were in agony before we even got going.

Immediately we set off our driver cranked up the jingly-jangly music booming from two fridge size speaker boxes to an ear-splitting level, but I'd come prepared and rammed toilet paper into my ears to limit the damage. As the road started to twist and wind up and down we lurched and swayed on our uncomfortable seats in the hot, humid evening air. Our guts churned and I had a pounding headache. I pleaded for our driver to reduce the volume but instead he made it even louder.

A fundamental requirement on mid size Indonesian buses is that everyone must smoke. Now we really felt sick. As darkness closed in I watched the guys in front and to the side of me draw the last from their smouldering stubs. Just as they finished and I felt a false sense of relief, others sparked up in a sort of unbearable, chain-smoke-reaction.

I was getting ready to chuck up everything I'd eaten in the last week and tried desperately not to think of the tasty cake slices a couple of nights before; thick as your thumb and cut neatly into small squares. A brown layer like dates sandwiched between a white creamy substance and a yellow layer covered in bobbles, like carpet loops. I took a large bite and munched on it.

"Yuck. Cow's intestines!"

Yes, best not to think about that, or the filthy scrapings-from-the-bottom-of-the-pan burnt gristle curry I had with Stephane while out on the bikes at Pulau Samosir. Meat was clearly in short supply but with the astonishing abundance and variety of fresh vegetables, fish and fruit we saw in the markets, why was it the food in Indonesia always ended up tasting so awful?

All of a sudden, a kid at the front of the bus threw up over some baggage in the aisle. The smell wafted down the bus and one by one, others joined in. So that's what the little squares of paper hanging from a string above our heads were for. Incredibly, the distraction of seeing others in distress cooled my bubbling guts. Sharon and I managed to hang on to our suppers and we arrived in Banko late at night.

The travel office clerk assured us a luxury air-conditioned coach would be going through to Jakarta at around 1am but in actual fact, the next bus with two available spaces came through at 4.30am…a day later.

Having spent the best part of two nights on hard wooden waiting room seats we were both in a pretty evil mood but now to add insult to injury, my 'luxury' coach seat turned out to be bolt-upright, sandwiched between two fellow passengers adjacent to the toilet, making sleep impossible. Sharon fared little better three rows up with her broken seat back resting on the knees of the passenger behind. She refused to inflict such suffering on the poor guy and curled up between the toilet door - which was constantly on the go - and the stairwell. This was intolerable and I put my vast engineering skills to work, wedging a rubbish bin between her seat back and the armrest of the seat behind.

We reached the town of Lahat, Sharon's stop, at about two in the afternoon and she kissed me goodbye. Befriended by my neighbours, 29 year old Sony and his aunt, the time passed a little more easily. Despite the regular clatter of the toilet door I managed to snatch desperately needed sleep curled up on the floor until at some unholy hour, the bus touts woke everyone for the two hour ferry crossing to Java.

JAVA

By mid morning we reached the outskirts of Jakarta to find the sprawling grey low rise city already clogged with smoking traffic. I moved into shabby, but comfortable, Wisema Delima guesthouse on Jalan Jaksar and had my first real shower in several days. Maybe the locals had been right about the smell?

Hopping on a bicycle taxi I made my way to Sunda Kelapa (Jakarta harbour) where magnificent wooden Buginese Macassar schooners were moored side by side, stretching along the quay for over a kilometre. Each vessel had a tall wooden bridge, low broad beamed cargo deck and distinctive curved prow and bowsprit pointing towards to the sky. The cargo of hardwood from the last of Indonesia's rain forest was loaded entirely by hand. Fat taskmasters strutted about occasionally giving orders, pointing here, a nod there, while slim gaunt figures sweated and slaved all day under a baking sun, carrying heavy beams up narrow gangplanks, trapped for ever in a cycle of poverty.

One of the boats was nearly ready to sail, deck piled high with timber. It sat way down in the water, gunwales barely a metre above the surface. What would she be like rolling in rough seas, with the bilge pumps working flat out day and night?

On the minibus to Pandangaran, a tourist town midway along the south coast, I chatted with my neighbour, an elegant, quiet spoken English teacher in her late fifties. Some thirty years ago when President Suharto began a birth control campaign in Indonesia, she and her husband agreed to limit themselves to having only one child. The campaign was never properly backed or enforced and failed miserably but she told me she had never regretted having only one son.

Late in the evening the bus stopped a couple of miles from Pandangaran but apparently this was the end of the line. I walked the rest of the way guided by a full moon and followed by a rickshaw driver who seemed quite offended that I didn't use his overpriced services. The place was a ghost town, there were no other visitors and the eerie quiet was broken only by a stiff sea breeze rustling palm fronds and slamming a loose window shutter back and forth. Lanterns swung casting a crazy orange light over welcome signs in the empty bars and restaurants.

As I finished my meal a lone visitor walked past, squabbling with the rickshaw driver who had harassed her all the way from the bus stop. Chivalrous bloke that I am, I left my table and went to offer support. She didn't really need it, but we were alone there and a storm was coming.

Late next morning the new guest and I hired a small motorbike for next to nothing, rode up the coast a while and took a walk along the shore under boiling grey skies. The sea looked beautiful and inviting but we dared not swim because the coastline was jagged limestone covered in spiny urchins and the currents were deadly.

I was glad to be leaving the spooky deserted tourist spot and early next morning a minibus whisked me off to a small wooden ferry with canvas sun roof, moored in a broad river estuary. The boat chugged slowly along past mangrove and reed beds, home to egrets, herons and basking crocodiles. An hour or so up river fellow traveller John, a lawyer from New York and I transferred to an air-conditioned bus, reaching the outskirts of Yogyakarta city late in the afternoon.

YOGYAKARTA INCIDENT

Sitting in a cafe eating breakfast I was joined by a young woman from Amsterdam.

"It seems silly to sit alone with just the two of us here," she said.

Tosca was blond and of medium height. Her father gave her that name after falling madly in love with Puccini's opera and her Italian friends loved the idea. She was travelling alone with an air of confidence and independence that would normally see her through most countries, but right now in Indonesia there was a tension building and a frightening unease. Deep-seated religious divisions fuelled by a corrupt brutal regime were set to explode and the handful of travellers who ventured there during the recent lull in the violence could now sense real danger.

"I'm getting funny looks wherever I go," she said, poking disinterestedly at the omelette on her plate.

"I'm sure whatever it is will blow over in a few days," I told her, trying to make out it wasn't really so bad. "I haven't had any trouble here."

"Yes but haven't you heard the news lately?" she continued, suddenly more animated. "The high court got a...how do you say it?...a warrant to arrest Suharto on corruption charges. They say he simply paid off the judges and now his militia have been burning mosques in the Christian sector."

I'd heard the rumour that this act of vandalism had been instigated by Suharto to distract from his own appalling mismanagement and the national state of economic collapse. Trouble was, there was no way to prove it. It was a real mishmash of hostilities. The Moslems hated the minority Christians. The Christians mistrusted and hated the Moslems. Enough believed the wild rumours circulated by Suharto's agents, that Christian extremists were behind the recent violations. It seemed astonishing that in the meantime his army found the energy to buy sophisticated weapons from Britain and the west, invade neighbouring islands and commit genocide.

John, my companion from the ferryboat arrived and joined us.

"Look," he said, "if its gonna kick off there's not a lot we can do about it. Best thing is just to stay sharp and listen out for trouble. I came here to explore this place and I don't see any benefit running home like frightened rabbits until we know what's really going on."

Tosca and I agreed. In a crazy sort of way this sense of danger was one of the attractions of Indonesia, heightening the experience. You always imagined that nothing really bad could ever happen and if you listened to enough rumours from people who had never actually been, you could talk yourself right out of going to a place.

Tosca went back to her guesthouse to change while John and I waited in the café. We both stood to leave when she returned and, oh my word, what *was* she wearing? The shortest little denim dress I'd ever seen, showing off long tanned legs. John and I glanced at each other in disbelief. Tosca had travelled enough to know what was right for her but, considering where we were, her dress code seemed a bit wacky. If we made an issue of it she'd simply go her own way and aside from enjoying her company, solidarity and a bold front were our best weapons of defence.

"You look nice," I threw in casually as we walked off.

"Thanks."

The moment you turn out of the tourist guesthouse and restaurant area you are assailed by the sights and sounds of bustling Yogyakarta. Market stalls lined the pavement in front of the high street shops, trailing off into the distance. John and I, being head and shoulders taller than the average Indonesian, had to keep ducking under awnings and made awkward progress through the milling crowds. Tosca though, was on a present-buying mission. She knew exactly what she wanted and how much to spend. Ploughing on ahead, ignoring frowns and looks of distaste from passers by, she paused occasionally to allow John and myself to catch up.

"I like this one," she declared, holding up a T-shirt emblazoned with the Buddhist all-seeing third eye.

"Yeah, cool," I agreed, trying to appear unconcerned but flicking occasional glances up and down the row of jostling heads to keep an eye out for trouble. John was checking some elegant twisted wire candelabras hung from the adjacent shop front.

A police siren shattered the chaotic order among busy shoppers, then another and another, screaming down the high street. Suddenly the crowd was like a herd of antelope alerted to the presence of a leopard. Startled looks all around, young men broke into a jog heading in the direction of the sirens and simply barged people out of the way. My neck hairs bristled, whatever was happening was just a couple of blocks away and I looked at John and Tosca as if expecting them to know what to do next.

BOOM!

A dull thud from down the street and the sound of shattering glass gave way to screams and a ringing burglar alarm. My heart dropped into the pit of my stomach and I felt the sickening surge of adrenalin. Instinctively I moved toward Tosca and firmly shepherded her to where John was standing by the shop front. More young men ran past and we looked on helplessly as an old lady was toppled to the ground ahead of us.

The sound of screaming and shouting intensified. Riot and plain clothed police appeared from behind us moving quickly down the street in broken ranks, lashing out viciously with long heavy batons at anyone who came within range. Pop, pop - smoke grenades landed among the crowd ahead, causing hysteria. BANG! I winced as one exploded close by.

171

Suddenly the men who'd been running towards the trouble turned and ran back our way. Stones and bottles flew through clouds of tear gas and hordes of protestors wielding clubs and sticks stampeded towards the approaching police. John battered on the shop door but the owner, standing right behind it, refused to let us in.

In the last instant I think I saw something hurtling towards us from the corner of my eye and ducked instinctively as John was hit squarely on the back of the head by a rock. He fell against the shop door and slumped to his knees. That was it! Tosca and I grabbed him under the arms, dragged him to the neighbouring shop where the owner and his wife were helping in an elderly couple, and hauled him inside. Through the window I saw vicious hand-to-hand fighting between cops and rioters, some wearing balaclavas or neckerchiefs over their faces to disguise themselves from the secret police.

Back inside the makeshift hospital that in peacetime had been a fabric shop, Tosca had already bandaged John's scalp wound and propped him, semi-conscious, against a wall behind the counter. Several other people had taken refuge and the owner's family cowered in a far corner.

The raging battle moved away as the police drew back, heavily outnumbered and the looting began. Not a single shop window was left unbroken and soon it was our turn. A chair was thrown, and on the second attempt the glass burst inwards. Looters, all fired up and seeing there were foreigners inside, rushed at the window frame but the brave shopkeeper picked up the chair and used it as a battering ram to fend them off. Two men who'd taken shelter lashed out at the mob with anything they could get their hands on and I joined them, jabbing at our attackers with a metal pole from a fabric hanger. For a few terrifying moments the fighting was desperate but with nothing worth stealing inside and no support, the looters gave up and moved on.

Sporadic running battles continued for a while until the military arrived in large numbers and the street cleared. Any stragglers were beaten mercilessly to the ground, then, with wrists and ankles cable-tied together, they were dragged off for further torment.

By mid-afternoon most of the soldiers had left and civilians ventured nervously back onto the streets. Severely rattled, we thanked the shop owner and his wife for giving us shelter and, supporting John on either side began making our way back home. The scene outside was utter chaos; debris strewn everywhere, market stalls and shop fronts smashed to pieces. Battered and bewildered locals rummaged through the wreckage for their belongings, taking little notice of us.

We reached a junction and were about to turn down our street when a soldier yelled at us to stop, and calling his mate to join him, they jogged over to us. The first shouted something in Indonesian, pointing an automatic rifle at our bellies. He focused his attention on John's injury, trying to make out he'd been involved in the riot and grabbed at John's arm. I think he was hoping Tosca and I would bottle out and leave him when the second 'soldier', rifle slung over his shoulder, began screaming at us, waving a pistol around like it was a toy.

I was shit scared. The two were completely out of control and getting more wound up by the second. As the yelling and screaming reached a deadly crescendo I thought, "These fuckin' maniacs are goin' to shoot us right in the middle of the street!"

Of all things, an old stooping lady hobbled over, and incredibly began tugging at the rifleman's sleeve. When he turned to deal with her she let rip with a wailing tirade of abuse. He shouted back but she was joined by a middle-aged man I took to be her son. Others, hearing the commotion, wandered over until a small group of witnesses had gathered round us. The soldiers held their ground for a while trying to save face but it was too much for them, and putting up their weapons, they turned and ran down the road to catch up with their comrades.

There was no applause, no jeering after the thugs in uniform. The people had simply had enough of poverty, corruption, and violence. As the group dispersed we thanked the old woman profusely. She may well have saved our lives!

BALI

We lay low for two days not daring to venture beyond our suburb. It might have seemed wise to get the hell out of Indonesia but there were no more signs of trouble and newly arrived travellers confirmed that the violence had not been widespread. A local nurse dealt with John's head injury and when we were sure it was safe we went our separate ways, John and Tosca heading north for Jakarta. I boarded a coach going all the way to Denpasar, Bali and figured that if things hotted up again I could jump on the next plane to Australia.

I remember thinking as I stepped onto the coach, "That gap under the seats is almost big enough for someone to crawl under." The vehicle was only half full, which seemed a little too good to be true after my other cramped experiences on Indonesian buses, and why did the driver and touts need such a large closed compartment at the rear? My money belt was saturated in sweat and unbearably uncomfortable so, ignoring my instincts, I placed it in my day-sack and curled up to sleep on a spare double seat.

It wasn't until the following morning aboard a minibus heading for the centre of town, that I realised I'd been robbed. During the night someone had crept under the seats and gone through the western passenger's bags. Several cameras had been stolen and I lost all my loose cash plus £1,000 worth of traveller's cheques. Everyone reckoned it was an inside job and the bus company staff were involved. I was broke but Karina, my neighbour and another passenger kindly lent me enough money to survive until I could replace the stolen cheques.

Kuta, Bali had a wild party atmosphere, especially in the high street restaurants and bars which vied for popularity every evening as tourists emerged from their guesthouses in the maze of adjacent alleyways. In one such alley I watched a puppet show with a large gathering of locals, still an important means of spreading news and political views in a land where TV was beyond the reach of most people. The island was a shopping Mecca of designer label copies and a huge favourite among Aussie short-stay tourists, European ex-pats and honeymoon couples.

The breakers on Kuta beach were massive and one afternoon I saw three rented surf boards broken clean in half by the pounding surf. Sunsets were breathtakingly beautiful and watching them was a spectator sport but the binge drinking, partying, hung-over scene just didn't interest me any more. I knew there was so much to explore on the island, so I met up with Karina and we prepared to move on.

The roads in and out of Ubud tourist town and many of the villages north of Kuta were lined with neat rows of wooden carvings, from tiny figurines to six foot tall giraffes. Bali didn't have any of its own hardwood left however, and all the materials were ransacked from endangered rainforest elsewhere in Indonesia, Borneo, Sulawesi and East Timor. The process was catastrophic for native jungle tribes and wildlife, and ultimately an important contributor to global warming.

That evening we watched some very impressive Balinese dancing. Characters in elaborate caricatured costumes included a monkey, a lion and a storyteller who actually took part in the plot, while two young princes dressed in sarongs and smart purple tunics fought over a pretty girl. When one of the princes was killed his demon spirit attacked the assailant but then it all got hopelessly muddled.

After breakfast next morning Karina and I drove by minibus up the mantle of Batur volcano. Staring down into the massive crater more than six kilometres across, Lake Batur lay on the right hand side and on the left stood three younger volcanic peaks ascending in height. A massive column of steam jetted from the lowest of these forming a rolling, twisting cloud. The vent mouth glowed brilliant orange and could be clearly seen from almost anywhere in the crater.

Touts huddled round us the moment we arrived at our lakeside guesthouse asking for $50 each to guide us over the three volcanic peaks, a six hour walk. It was more than the average Indonesian's wages for a month but people paid because, "You have to see the sunrise from up on the volcano" and you wouldn't want to be stumbling about up there on your own in the dark.

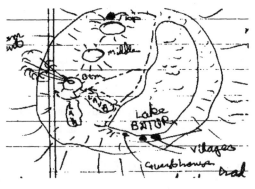

Lake Batur

Our young minibus driver was unusually big and muscular by Balinese standards. Good looking with the obligatory ponytail, he sat himself down between Karina and myself, repeatedly interrupting our conversation and on finishing his meal of chilli fish and rice, thrust the plate of leftovers at me.

"You like feesh?" he asked grinning broadly.

"No thanks, I can buy my own."

"Take, take!" he persisted.

He made innuendos about 'my wife' and seemed to be looking for a fight, but Karina was neither my wife nor partner and seeing him as no threat the situation cooled again.

After lunch I set off alone on the volcano walk. The locals wouldn't tell me where the trail started and giggled to one another as I wandered down the road. For two exhausting, shin scraping, ankle twisting hours I clambered over horridly uneven lava flow, ridges and deep potholes camouflaged by thick vegetation. Eventually I spotted a guided group up ahead, found the official trail and followed them up the south face of the lower peak.

I crouched on a fine ash slope just a few paces from the vent mouth of glowing molten rock, wide as a car. Superheated steam roared like a rocket engine in a mighty pillar as tall as a five storey building, before condensing into cloud. The cloud billowed and churned hypnotically as if alive, drifting over the taller peaks behind in an awesome spectacle against the gigantic crater backdrop.

The volcano had moods just like a child and spluttered petulantly emitting wisps of sulphurous steam from cracks in the rock. Every now and then there was a lull before the vent erupted with an earth-trembling, whoomph! I had an overwhelming feeling of insignificance and not being in control, knowing that if Batur's mood swung just a little too far, I would cease to exist.

Behind the steam vent and a little higher lay the peak's own jagged crater rim, roughly fifty metres across. Wisps of vapour escaped through the scree slope forming brilliant yellow and orange sulphur trails. By late afternoon I reached the top of the middle peak but had neither the time nor energy to scale the third, so I made my way back before darkness.

The following day Karina and I left Mount Batur for Lovina, a pretty fishing village on the north coast, popular with tourists who came to view dolphins in the warm fertile waters.

With my onward flight looming closer I said goodbye to Karina early next morning and hired a boat and skipper to go dolphin watching. More than a dozen trimarans laden with excited tourists were already out on the clear blue water, chasing their prey. A single pod of around seven small blue-grey porpoises with black flanks sped like torpedoes darting left and right as they hunted sardines. Glistening bodies broke the still surface and dived again leaving us wondering where they would come up next. We got fairly close but the animals were fed up with humans trailing their every move and soon after they headed out to sea.

Back on Kuta beach that afternoon, massive breakers spun me until I didn't know which way was up, pounding me against the sand. You have to take a deep breath when one of these monsters swallows you because it can be some time before you surface again. Waiting for the right moment I swam under the waves to where the water was relatively calm, but there was little time to relax before I noticed the buildings on the shore line rapidly getting smaller as a surging current dragged me out to sea. Fighting back frenzied panic I swam with all my might to escape the pull and just as my last drop of energy was about to run out and I felt the fiery warning of imminent muscle cramp, made it back through the breakers. Exhausted, I collapsed on the beach thinking how easy it was to end up a one-liner on the news.

Had I known there was an airport tax in Bali of just over £3, I wouldn't have spent my last rupias on a new leather belt just before my flight. Airport customs were adamant that I couldn't board without paying and even my police report stating that all my traveller's cheques were stolen only a week before, made no difference. It was almost boarding time when a kindly British couple heard the commotion and gave me the money I needed.

Now I discovered I'd lost the immigration form I was given on entering Indonesia. The customs staff wanted a 'financial contribution' in order to allow me through so I asked to see the supervisor. The supervisor took a sharp intake of breath and suggested it could be a very expensive problem. I was having none of it so he took me to the manager who mercifully okayed a new form before I missed my flight altogether.

Back again at the customs kiosk the young woman in front of me had also lost her immigration form.

"Don't give them a penny," I whispered, "it's a scam."

In the departure lounge she told me she'd booked the holiday with her Mum, intending to stay for three weeks, but her terminal liver condition flared up and she passed out on the beach after only a couple of days. At twenty two years old, this was the first time she'd been away from Australia. The bright young woman explained that as her condition deteriorated she would soon be forced to give up work. She didn't know how long she had.

AUSTRALIA

PERTH

Landing in Perth, I got straight on the shuttle bus and headed for Northbridge Youth Hostel near the city centre. I marvelled at ergonomic stainless steel fittings, solid engineering and comfortable patterned velour seats with masses of leg room. The bus glided with air cushioned suspension on smooth tarmac roads, past tidy fences and neatly mown lawns.

Sitting beside me was Grim (Graham) from Stewart Island, New Zealand. A year older than me, this was also his first long trip away from home. Grim was a fisherman by trade with long straggly blond hair, thick moustache and hands coarse as sandstone and big as clams.

The modern glass-fronted tower blocks of central Perth stood out as monuments to capitalism and commerce. Neighbouring streets had Scottish names and less imposing five storey terraced buildings with Victorian facades. My first impression was of a thriving, multi-racial community living harmoniously in a litter-free environment.

Northbridge Backpackers had a busy impersonal feel and most of the guests were young international students with whom I had little in common. Grim and I were handed fresh sheets and squeezed into a tiny dorm with six others.

The following morning Grim and I hopped on a plush modern train - part of the region's multi-million dollar new rail network - for the boating and fishing suburb of Fremantle further down the coast, to check out the work situation.

Grim was looking for a job in mining, construction or welding. With his skills and a favourable work exchange agreement between New Zealand and Australia, he wouldn't have to search for long. I on the other hand, was ten years over the age limit for a working visa and without one, most jobs were off limits. Suddenly facing a 'real world' cost of living and with my resources running low, I felt an outcast under Australia's work and immigration laws.

The new Northbridge underpass a few blocks from the youth hostel, was like an enormous badger's set excavated beneath the freeway and seemed like a good place to start my job hunt. The site foreman however, zealously defending Australian jobs for Australians, took great satisfaction telling me,

"You've got a bloody nerve. I've got a letter here from the department of trade saying it's a criminal offence to employ someone without a work permit!"

I walked to the Portakabin door and was about to leave but something made me turn and face him.

"If a job needs doing and I'm prepared to do it, what does it matter where I come from?"

"Go on, piss off ya bloody pom!" he yelled as the door swung shut behind me.

* * *

Indigo Lodge on Aberdeen Street was a tastefully converted bungalow, bright and airy with a wonderfully relaxed atmosphere, a welcome change from stuffy, boarding school-like Northbridge Backpackers. There was a large courtyard at the back to unwind in and a front garden overlooking wild west style, 'The Good The Bad and The Ugly' bar and its owner's enormous pink Cadillac parked out front. Most of the twenty or so residents had lived there for some time and were really welcoming. It felt more like home than a hostel and despite a lack of irritating rules and regulations, everyone made just enough effort to keep the place clean and safe.

The manager of Indigo Lodge put me in touch with a local paraglider pilot called Mike. Mike's paragliding club was having a tree planting day in gratitude for the use of local farms as flying sites, so one morning we drove out to a huge ranch two hours south of Perth. Broad rolling hills with a smattering of trees resembled the Lake District, only everything was much bigger. Crows talked to one another in that distinctive way you hear in Aussie soaps. 'W-h-a-a...W-o-a-h...' The sound is a constant feature of temperate Australian countryside. After brief introductions Patrick, a pilot and local farmer in his early forties, explained,

"This whole area used to be covered in forest but in the fifties the government ordered one million acres to be cleared each year for agriculture."

I was horrified. "How on earth did they do that?"

"Two bloody great bulldozers, three times the size of anything you'd see in Europe, dragging a chain and massive steel ball between them.

With the trees gone the water table rose, bringing up salt from below. That killed off crops and even more trees, turning the land into salt marsh. The story's the same over much of Australia. We're hoping the saltbush we plant today will reduce the water level and firm up the soil in one really bad spot."

Salt-bush apparently has deep roots and a high tolerance of salinity. Working in pairs we planted the young shrubs in a small boggy paddock between two hills and when we'd finished, we drove up to some high ground where the farmer's wife had laid on beer and sandwiches for the paraglider pilots and a local group of clay pigeon shooters.

Shooting resumed as we finish eating. The paragliding club secretary hove into view with his paramotor, a motorised propeller strapped to the back of his harness, and it looked for all the world as if they were shooting at him. Bang, bang, bang!

Bit of a hostile landing site. He'd flown over from his bungalow perched on a hill, just visible in the distance. The motor had cut and the prop spun slowly in the headwind as he glided in gracefully for a textbook landing. Wandering over we saw that the retaining nut had come off the prop shaft during flight, allowing it to move forwards and slip the drive belt.

"More technology, more to go wrong," said Mike reticently.

At the nearby flying site a stiff breeze created a zone of lift above and in front of the west-facing ridge. Mike lent me his spare canopy, an old medium size Edel Apollo, which by modern standards flew like a sack of washing.

Patrick and some other pilots were already up, 'gale-hanging' in the marginal conditions, as I laid out the Apollo well behind the ridge. My attempts to bring the canopy quickly above my head failed each time, with the wind dragging me back, out of control. Mike joined me to discuss the situation. Even if I did get airborne there was a real danger of being pushed back behind the ridge into *rotor*, as the poor old Apollo lacked the speed to penetrate forwards. It just wasn't worth the risk.

Back at Indigo Lodge that evening we had a barbecue in the front garden and I met Steve from Essex. At thirty, Steve wasn't allowed a working visa either, but friends in pubs, clubs and backpackers helped him out with regular work and odd jobs.

"I've been working here for ten months, on and off," he told me.

"What will you do if they catch you?"

"I don't give a toss really, I've had a good time here. If they catch me they'll send me back, but I'll be goin' home soon anyway. I'll probably get some shit at the airport but they can't do anythin'."

rotor - swirling, broken air currents that occur behind a windward ridge.

Warren, in his mid twenties, came from Oxford although he spoke with a strong north London accent. He'd heard about a painting contract on a new estate, twenty minutes drive south along the coast. Evan, an amiable young Kiwi surfer, was also interested, so Steve drove us all down to the site in his van. Aside from Steve, who couldn't work with us because he had too many other commitments, Evan was the only one who had ever swung a paintbrush in anger, and we walked apprehensively towards the site office.

Warren refused to don one of Evan's dirty work overalls emblazoned with the logo 'B 'n K painters', claiming it would cramp his style, instead sporting dark sunglasses, gaudy wristwatch and his loudest designer shirt. The site foreman naturally took him for the boss asking work related questions to which Warren was clueless. Evan dived in to save the situation as Warren floundered and the foreman, a burly Italian, smiled and shook his head.

We took a look around one of the huge, very expensive-looking bungalows. The job was clearly way over our heads but we priced it up all the same and approached the office.

"Ten days work... We'll do it for 3,500 dollars. You supply the materials."

The foreman scoffed and pulled out a folder of business cards.

"This guy here...Otto...quoted 2,300, materials included!"

We looked at each other in disbelief. The site bulldog contemptuously pressed a length of boxwood he'd been chewing against my leg and it gave way with a sharp crack! Why were all Australian dogs built like oversize wombats with teeth? We couldn't match Otto's price but we offered to go to $2,000 with materials supplied. Now the site foreman knew we were desperate. Steve took us home and we talked ourselves out of the job.

* * *

With my own transport I figured I'd stand more chance of finding work. I started feeling rough on the bus out to the suburbs to view a camper van and by the time I got there, the dengue fever that had first struck in Sumatra was back with a vengeance. Tunnel vision, nausea, sense of balance shot to hell. The worried owner must have thought I was some junkie-weirdo, but I just had to lie down on her porch before I fell down.

In a little surgery on Frith Street the following morning the doctor prodded and quizzed me.

"Did you feel any discomfort in your ears during the flight out here?"

"No."

"Well you should have done!" he exclaimed. "That's the worst inner ear infection I've seen for quite some time."

"What, no dengue fever?" I asked, almost disappointed. "Is that why I keep falling over?"

"Yep."

He put me on a course of serious looking horse tablets and I made an appointment for a follow-up examination in ten days. "Phew!" I must have picked the bug up while swimming in Thailand. The locals probably crapped upstream and goodness knows how many others had been infected; a bunch of whacked out tourists wandering about, falling over a lot...and they weren't even pissed!

KL, the Malaysian-born manager of Aberdeen Lodge across the road from Indigo, offered me free accommodation in return for some light cleaning work. KL was almost like a father to his long-term guests and couldn't understand why backpackers preferred other hostels, even though he charged the lowest rates in town.

Aberdeen Lodge was an old semidetached bungalow knocked into one building, with rotten window frames and fittings, battered doors and loose locks. The place was regularly cleaned but the carpets were worn out, covered in ugly stains, all surfaces had a thick coating of grime and worst of all, the kitchen was infested with baby cockroaches that scuttled away when the lights were switched on. Two push-button TVs dating from the seventies stood in opposite lounges to help keep peace among the Lodge's more rowdy occupants, and the cupboards, chairs and sofas looked as if they'd been rescued from a skip. I tried tactfully to tell KL that people were turned away by the appearance of the place but he argued that if he spent any money on refurbishment, the residents would only wreck it again. I shared a room with a Japanese lad who cleaned the kitchen, showers and toilets - rather him than me - and a young Glaswegian called Malcolm with short curly yellow hair, who looked after the office.

Taking a huge gamble, I blew most of my remaining cash on a Mitsubishi L300 van (like a small Transit), from a painter and decorator. Basically sound but rusty, the interior was covered in multicoloured paint splodges, the tyres were bald and she steered heavily to the left. I had her checked out at a local garage before parting with $950 (around £400), then I bought five used tyres, third party insurance, a complete ventilation unit from a breakers yard - the previous owner had ripped the L300's out - and a few other bits and bobs.

Not having to shell out for lodgings took a lot of pressure off and I'd been settling in to the new routine when, late one night there was a loud persistent knock at our room. I opened the door to a thick-set Polynesian looking guy. He seemed to know the Japanese lad and they talked for some time, so I went back to sleep.

Malcolm arrived at daybreak, clambering into the bunk above mine, thoroughly pissed and a little while later I took a quick shower before starting work. It was funny, my instincts told me to take my pants and wallet with me but for some reason I left them behind.

Back in the room I quickly checked my wallet to find one hundred and fifty bucks, three crispy yellow fifty dollar bills that I'd changed up the previous day, were gone. For some curious reason the thief left $45 behind and had time to replace the wallet in my trouser pocket, roll the trousers up again and replace them by my bed.

I felt certain it was Malcolm and when he heard me telling KL later he pushed open the door and leant up on his elbows.

"Is that me gettin' accused eh this?" he asked in his broad Glaswegian accent. "When ye told me yer money was gone I had sympathy for ye, but now I couldnae give a fuck!"

That was great. I'd been robbed and now I was the one in the wrong. If Malcolm was innocent I had made an enemy and I was no closer to finding the culprit, or my money.

Everyone, including KL, said stealing was completely out of his character and over the next few days I'd been slowly patching things up with Malcolm. The Polynesian guy had probably taken my money and it was my fault for letting him in. At around seven o-clock one morning Malcolm arrived shitfaced with drink - as he often did - and staggered up to his bunk. KL had gone to Malaysia on business but Malcolm had assured him he would look after the office.

A young couple wanted to leave early and I needed to give them back their key deposit, but Malcolm had the office keys. I tried shaking him awake but he was comatose.

"That's damp," I thought, touching his clothing. "Bugger me, he's wet himself!"

Sure enough his jeans, shirt and mattress were wringing wet and guess what, it had gone straight through and drenched my sleeping bag on the bunk below. I got him awake enough to find the keys and the tirade of abuse he gave me was frightful. Outraged, I went about telling everyone in Aberdeen Lodge what had happened and when I'd done that, I went across the road to Indigo Lodge and told them too.

When I got back that afternoon Malcolm called out from the office.

"Andy. Uh need tae huv a worrd with ye."

"Ah, an apology," I thought.

Malcolm faced me in the corridor, away from the others.

"Did ye huv tae tell everybody what happened?"

"Hey, wait a minute," I thought, "I'm the one who's sleeping bag got pissed on. I'm the injured party here."

"I didn't tell everybody," I said, rapidly starting to feel ashamed.

"Aye, well everybody knows. That makes you a *big* man, Andy!" and he stormed off back to the office.

After finishing my chores next morning I sat on the front steps of Aberdeen Lodge in brilliant sunshine with a young hippie called Lee. Lee was a good listener and had a gentle, positive nature. He was slim and in his mid-twenties but his long red hair and goatee beard made him look much older.

"There's a moment before you open your mouth to gossip," he said, "when your inner voice tells you, 'You don't have to do this'."

We chatted for a while and he made me feel a lot better about myself. Lee was also low on cash and with the fruit picking season about to start, agreed to travel south with me in search of work.

That afternoon I bought tools, oil and an oil filter from a motor accessories shop out of town and was driving back to Perth when the van's back end started to wobble unnervingly. Suddenly the rear left corner dropped down, there was an horrendous graunching noise and I found myself staring up at the clear blue sky. Fighting the steering, I guided the L300 into a lay-by where she ground to a halt at an alarming tilt and I watched bewildered as my left rear wheel bounced up the kerb and continued on down the pavement.

Thank Christ it was a rear wheel and I hadn't been on the freeway doing 70mph. I remembered watching the guy in the tyre fitting shop replacing my wheels with a knackered old air tool. His real trade back in the UK, he told me, was a shoe repairer - much like the job he did on my van. Cobblers! I wondered how many of his other customers survived to tell the tale.

The following day a friend from Idigo Lodge told me there were jobs at the Perth Royal Show and by late afternoon I was there selling game tickets. Peel back the windows and match any one of five numbers on your ticket with a number on the winning board to win a large cuddly toy. We stood like dummies hour after hour, fanning handfuls of tickets at the passing crowds.

The show was an enormous, multimillion dollar business. Hundreds of fairground rides and stalls, ranging from hooking plastic ducks out of a paddling pool to the most vomit-inducing roller coaster, covered the entire area within a horse racing track fifteen minutes' train ride from central Perth. An estimated thirty thousand people visited each day from the city and outlying farming communities in a sort of annual pilgrimage. An Irish girl on the same stall told me,

"Don't look so miserable Andy, think of the money."
I was. Nine bucks an hour! Still, it was cash, no messing about and I was desperate.

I was absolutely terrified of speaking over the PA system to call out winning numbers and bring in the crowds but it wasn't long before everyone else's voice had packed up. When things settled down after the mad weekend rush there were just too many of us and sooner or later the boss would have to send someone home, so I had to make myself indispensable.

One night when it was pretty quiet I borrowed the mike, jumped up on stage and gave it a go. The stage and screen behind were covered with large furry toys: shocking pink panthers, grizzly bears, bulldogs with vicious looking teeth and my favourite, a mean looking purple Tasmanian devil. To my amazement, when I got used to the sound of my own voice it was actually quite fun. You could say whatever you liked and have a laugh with the punters and other staff...

"Oi you, don't be so mean to your kids, come over here! Where d'you think you're going? I didn't give you permission to leave!"

...so the time passed a little more easily. The bosses, Jo and Tanya, liked what I was doing so they kept me on the mike and at the end of the first day I had shouted myself hoarse, just as Jo said I would.

I fully expected Jo and Tanya to be tyrannical, unpleaseable task masters, but instead they were totally fair with everyone who worked for them, full of praise and encouragement. They did very well for themselves but it was only through desperately long hours and extremely hard work.

It was a blazing hot afternoon and after a particularly long session on the mike a little girl ran in front of the stage in floods of tears, pursued by her distressed mother.

"Oi, you can't do that," I yelled. "We don't allow crying at this stall!"

"You can stop taking the piss out of me daughter," shouted the irate mother. "I've just spent thirty bucks here and she hasn't won a bloody thing!"

"Woops!"

There was only one bad apple among the bosses, a rather plump indignant woman who worked in the caravan office counting the piles of cash we brought in. Gasping with thirst I trooped off to the office and as I filled my canteen from a large inverted water tank the plump boss poked her head round the door.

"What d'you think you're doing?"

"Getting some water, it's hot out there."

"Well that water's intended for the staff and there's not much left."

"I'm staff!" I said indignantly as I continued filling. No tea supply was bad enough, but this was absurd.

"We paid for that water and if you want some I suggest you buy your own!"

I couldn't believe it. "We're out there shouting ourselves hoarse for you lot and you can't even spare a drop of water!"

"Well you've had your drop. Now leave!"

Pay day finally arrived, the show wound down for another year and we gathered round the office to collect our wages. My turn came and Tanya slipped me an extra forty bucks.

"Don't tell the others," she whispered. "We'll be in Queensland in a couple of months. If you're over that way and you need work, give us a call."

The money I had left after celebrating paid for a job lot of second-hand camping gear. Vehicles and equipment were constantly advertised on backpacker notice boards and prices came down daily as flight dates loomed and travellers became increasingly desperate to sell. If you timed it right and weren't too choosy, some incredible deals could be had.

A young brother and sister from Lichtenstein moved into Aberdeen Lodge having driven up east, across the top and down the west coast to Perth. Wherever Bea and Sanil went everyone asked in chorus,

"Lichtenstein? Where the hell's that?"

We spent some time together with two young Israelis, Raz and Udi, who had followed the same route across the Northern Territory. The nights were warm and we cruised the cafes observing Perth's throbbing nightlife. Bars and clubs overflowed with locals and backpackers getting drunk and

R&R, Ko Phangan

Cutie on the bus to
Bangkok

Bangkok Royal Palace

Standing with Eric Lomax, author of 'The Railwayman' in front of
Kwai Yai "Death Railway" bridge

Utterly adorable baby elephants - there are still small groups of wild
elephants in some of Thailand's national parks

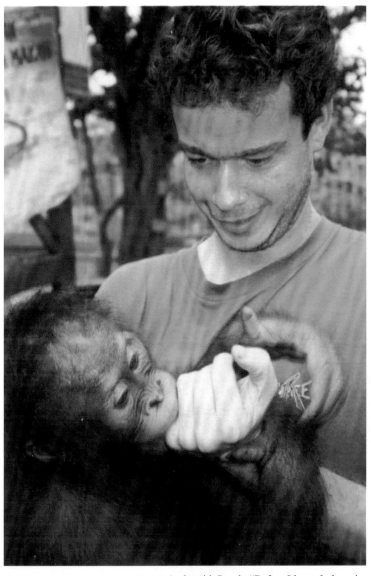

Andy with Peech, "Before I leave Indonesia,
that baby is going back
into the wild."

Sharon comforts a
female orang-utan,
Medan Zoo.

Family transport,
Kersik Tua

Automatic
chicken plucker

Fattest dog in Indonesia?
Tuk Tuk Peninsula

Alohu (left) and Aman (white shirt) chat with fellow guides shortly before our rhino encounter

Breathtaking views, Lake Toba

Lake Toba

Skies on fire, Lake Maninjau

Lake Maninjau

Loading schooners with the last of the rainforest, Sunda Kelapa, Jakarta harbour

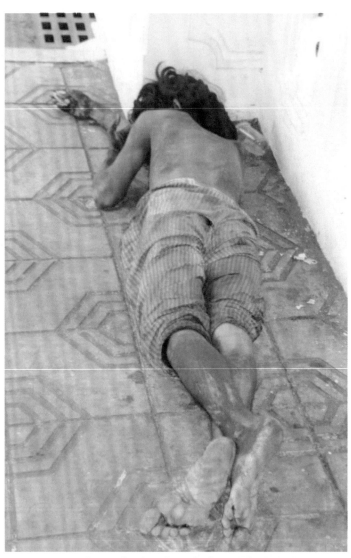

A tourist paradise, but all was far from perfect in Bali

partying, but for me the novelty was wearing thin. There had to be more to see in Australia and I was still desperately short of cash so I prepared to head south to look for farm work. Bea gave me a fluffy bumble bee to hang from the van's rear view mirror as a going away present.

"It's your lucky bee," she said.

Just before I left I received an e-mail from John, my companion from Java. His head injury had healed really well and he was lording it up somewhere in Thailand.

"It can't be that difficult," he wrote, "sitting around all day drinking with your friends, picking the occasional berry."

WORK

The sky was ominously grey as we made our way south past endless sandy beaches and broad stands of gum trees. Lee had hitchhiked around much of the world living by his wits, accepting kindness from strangers in return for his labour. Often he found himself alone, hungry and penniless but he said he was never discouraged, so I asked him where he found his unshakeable inner strength.

"From Jesus!" was the reply, "and it may be that I was sent here to help you."

I wasn't too alarmed at this announcement. I enjoyed Lee's company and wanted to know more about Christianity anyway.

"I can't just blindly believe without proof," I told him.

"How much proof do you need? The essence of faith is trusting without physical proof. Remember the Roman centurion who asked Jesus for help when his servant was dying."

"Yeah, yeah, I know the story. But how do I become like that centurion? How do I find faith like that? What makes you believe without question?"

"Oh, I have questions alright," Lee confided, "I just don't let them stand in the way. If God wants to reveal himself to me, he does. Sometimes he doesn't answer me at all. I can see that God is working in you Andy. I believe he has great plans for you."

Great plans for me? Who was I to deserve special attention? I ignored the curious remark.

We rolled into the quiet little town of Edgerton late that afternoon with its broad deserted streets and bungalows set behind long gardens. It looked like the kind of place you would drive through unless you definitely had business there. A guy from Aberdeen Lodge had given Lee a possible work contact and the name of some people we could stay with but unfortunately we only had part of the address.

A couple of cops wearing beige uniforms and holstered pistols had pulled someone over in a Ford Falcon and one of them saw me slip on my seatbelt as we passed. Coming back a few minutes later with fresh directions we passed them again.

"Oops, better put my seat belt on. You too Lee."

Too late! They flagged us down and one stayed in the patrol car while the other came over to my window.

"That's twice I've seen you driving in town without your seat belt."

"I think I was wearing it the first time," I mumbled weakly.

"No you weren't. You started to put it on when you saw me."

"I normally always wear a seat belt. We have the same laws in the UK and..."

"Drivers licence?" The cop demanded, cutting me off.

"It was stolen in Kenya," I told him in a shaky voice. "I'm travelling round the world and it was stolen in Kenya with a load of other stuff."

The cop took out his ticket book.

"Are you going to give me a ticket for not wearing a seat belt?"

"That's right, and I'm going to give you another fifty dollar fine for not producing a valid drivers licence."

"But I told you, it was stolen when I was in Kenya. My brother back in England is getting me a replacement. It should be here any day now."

"Do you have any form of ID with you?"

I handed him my PADI diver's card.

"Are you guys on commission or something? Back in the UK they usually give us a verbal warning first."

"You're not in the UK now."

"I'd have a lot more respect if you'd give me a verbal warning," I said in desperation.

"I'm not looking for your respect."

He gave Lee a $150 seat belt fine as well and while I muttered obscenities, his mate got out of the patrol car and started snooping round the van.

"Go on, take a good look. You won't bloody find anything wrong with it."

Lee caught my arm and steered me away. This had already been expensive enough.

"And we can fine you fifty dollars for that too!" exclaimed the second cop, pointing to my not-so-lucky bumble bee hanging from the rear view mirror.

For weeks the TV had been full of the rising crime rate and the latest craze in south-west Australia, 'bikie wars' (motorcycle gang wars), but this pair preferred to stay out of danger handing out parking fines and speeding tickets.

We found the address we'd been given and a surprised looking woman in her mid-thirties answered the door. Mania came from Slovenia. She was tall and slim with dark piercing eyes, heavy eyebrows and wavy jet black shoulder length hair, and even if she hadn't spoken with a strong accent I would have guessed she came from around that part of the world. She said she hadn't been expecting us but if we wanted we could stay there for thirty bucks each per week. Mania rented the bungalow with her boyfriend Tony and the little extra cash would help.

The weather was appalling. Drizzle, rain and perpetual gloom cast a shadow over our first week in Edgerton, then Lee found a couple of books on a shelf by some anti-Christian author. He decided he didn't like the situation and made up his mind to leave before he'd even given it a chance.

"There's something demonic about people who read books like that. I have a bad feeling about this place."

I didn't share his view. Whatever Tony and Mania wanted to read was their business and didn't concern me. This was where everyone said the work was and I had to stick it out and wait for the weather to clear up or I'd be broke within a month.

Work

Lee's decision was disappointing, I would miss him and what ever happened to, "It may be that I was sent here to help you, Andy." Maybe he had already.

I wandered out of Cole's supermarket one lunchtime in a daydream, thoroughly depressed. The work I was counting on hadn't materialised because of the weather and I withdrew into my shell, switching off to everything around me.

"Excuse me brother, you look like a traveller."

The voice came from a smallish man beaming a broad smile who, from his dark skin and jet black curly hair, had to be at least part Aborigine.

"I'm not your brother." I thought to myself. "What the heck do you want?"

"I could tell you're not from round here. You look lost. Where are you from?"

He introduced himself as George, shaking my hand vigorously and I gave the cursory name, rank and serial number.

"Do you believe in the word of the Lord brother?"

George's sudden launch into religion took me by surprise. Under normal circumstances, coming from a complete stranger this would have been fatal, but George continued and I didn't have the energy to stop him. The sky blackened, suddenly bursting in a torrential downpour. I fumed. In the ten minutes George had been rambling I could have made it back to Tony and Mania's bungalow nice and dry, so he gave me a lift in his fat old Holden coupé.

Over the next few days the weather cleared a little and I went to work with Tony and Mania's crew. About twenty of us converged on nearby Doolin's farm to plant vine cuttings or 'sticks', in raised soil rows. The sticks were planted five centimetres apart and would be left for nine months to grow roots before replanting. Each stick was worth a dollar and our contract was to plant one million of them.

If you could manage one thousand per hour you got $17 before tax, a pretty fair deal and as far as I knew no other employer in the district paid more for farm labour. We were expected to plant at least eight hundred sticks per hour which seemed really easy at first. Then the muscles in your back and legs started to burn.

Collecting fresh bundles of sticks gave us a moment to straighten our tortured bodies and check our surroundings. Acres of rolling furrowed soil led to an inviting lake and beyond this stood an isolated forest of magnificent karri trees, some twice as tall as an old English oak, with smooth parallel trunks and huge lollipop canopies. A chainsaw buzzed and screamed all day long. The chainsaw stopped, there was an eerie pause, then the earth shook with a resounding crash, marking the death of another grand old tree.

It was a hot sunny day and the race was on to plant vine sticks as fast as we possibly could. I cursed quietly each time a big tree crashed down in the distance but rough and ready local lads, Jimbo and Garry expressed a difference of opinion as we edged up our rows, plunging sticks into the soil.

"Fuck the trees!" said Jimbo. "Fuckin' greenies comin' da'n from the city where they've cut da'n all their own trees, tellin' us how to manage our forest."

"It doesn't matter where you come from," panted Gary. "You don't have to be from the country to care about the countryside."

On we went, planting bundle after bundle as the days grew hotter. The skin on my shoulders, neck and calves seared under the blazing sun while my lower back and thigh muscles burned like fire from maintaining a crouched position, legs astride the planting furrow hour after hour. Despite the discomfort I was getting stronger, rediscovering muscles I hadn't used for a decade, and the rest of the group were good company.

Jimbo's mate Wozza was driving the tractor, handing out bundles of sticks. He hadn't come to work the previous day because he'd been entertaining the police down at the station after getting involved in a pub brawl. His mates, who jumped in when it got out of hand, had talked about nothing else all morning. From today, he told us, he'd been barred... from all the pubs in the area! It was official, he had it in writing.

"Fuckin' wankers!" scruffy Nick exclaimed. "They're all just jealous that we was havin' a good time, but!"

Despite his fierce, rowdy reputation I found Wozza to be remarkably civil, courteous and conscientious, only giving a sharp reply when his mates gave him lip.

After a hard day's work at the vineyard we sat in Dave's car while he bought a new battery from the local garage. Contract manager Dave and his second in command John were rugged characters, having worked on farms all their lives. John was heavily built and covered in tattoos. His matted brown hair receded at the front and was tied in a pony tail at the back.

"They're cutting down a lot of forest around the vineyard," I said to John, cautiously inviting his views.

"All of it!" was the terse reply. "It's state owned forest. At the rate they're goin' it'll all be gone soon."

"What do you think about that?"

John turned to face me from the front passenger seat.

"I think it's a bloody disgrace! Some a' them trees are over four hundred years old and the forest has been there longer than the Aborigines. But there isn't a family round here that doesn't depend on the timber industry one way or another. Its difficult to conserve the forest when your jobs in timber and you've got a family to feed."

John explained that CALM - the department of Conservation And Land Management - had been appointed by the government to 'manage' all state owned forest, but CALM had unhealthy connections with the timber company, Bunnings and the giant farming monopoly, Wesfarmers. In some areas they were replanting, but only with straight rows of fast growing conifers for timber and wood chip or, as in our case, grape vines.

* * *

Israelis weren't allowed working visas at all in Australia, possibly something to do with their country's civil rights record. I knew Udi and Raz were desperate so I phoned them at Aberdeen Lodge and suggested they came down to Edgerton right away. Two days later they arrived and tried to get on the vine sticks team but their strong accents alerted Dave and he asked to see their work permits. Stirred up, he now drove around the vineyard asking all the foreign workers if they had a work visa.

It was exhausting work. Young Aussie, Steve and I were planting finished vine sticks along steel guide wires. There were acres of them to be done and it was even hotter than previous days. Any area of exposed skin burned within minutes and anything that could have offered shade had been cut down and bulldozed into huge piles, trunks, roots and all, still smouldering on the hillside.

All of a sudden Dave pulled up at the bottom of our row.

"Have you got a working visa?" he shouted.

I was stumped. What should I do, come clean and hope he'd be merciful?

"I have a *tax file number*," I told him feebly.

"That's not what I asked. Do you have a working visa?"

If I said yes, what would I do if he asked to see it? If I said no, he might order me straight off the farm. I paused for so long that if he hadn't known already, he certainly knew now.

"Yes!" I shouted.

---

tax file number - equivalent to national insurance number.

Dave laughed. "That's all I wanted to hear!" he called back as the *ute* pulled away.

It was ironic. Australia relied on migrant labour to plant and pick most of its crops. A hefty tax was deducted from our wages yet the regime treated us like thieves, undesirable aliens. Now and again they caught someone working illegally and how they loved to make an example, throwing them out of the country.

We worked nine gruelling days straight, then Dave ran out of sticks and we took a break. Everybody moaned but it gave me a chance to build a false wooden floor up to the wheel arches of my van and cupboards for storage space. I bolted struts across the roof bars to make a proper roof rack, hung curtains inside and painted over the worst areas of rust. Then I visited the local dump and scavenged the battered components to make a bicycle from a heap of rusting frames for an incredible, five bucks (although new tyres, inner tubes and the obligatory crash helmet later added a bit more to the cost). To finish off I made a cycle rack from an old metal chair frame, painted it and *tech-screwed* it to the rear door.

Raz, Udi and I moved into a caravan with a large annexe in Edgerton Caravan Park, while Tony and Mania rented a very smart caravan nearby. The park owner kept a semi-tame grey kangaroo called Skippy in his back yard, whom I met while he rummaged around for our door key. Skippy didn't want to make friends with strangers and dipped her head, making alarming clicking noises as I edged closer. Almost everyone has seen kangaroos before in the zoo and in Australia they're so numerous some people even regard them as a pest, but the hair stood up on the back of my neck as I knelt closer still. Skippy

ute - utility vehicle or pickup truck.
tech-screw - hexagonal headed self-drilling and tapping screw for wood or sheet metal.

had the face and head of a deer, but she stood and hopped around on huge back legs and an overdeveloped tail. She kept her babies in a pouch, for goodness' sake. All at once it hit me; this was a land so ancient and strange that evolution itself had taken a completely different path from everything I was used to. Suddenly Skippy lunged forwards hissing with anger and I bolted for the gate, slamming it shut just in the nick of time.

Early in the season there were times when Dave didn't have work for us and on those quiet days it was really nice to have company. In the evenings we listened to Genesis, Pink Floyd and a curious mixture of Israeli rock that sounded like Klingon, on Raz's tiny Walkman speakers.

One afternoon the whole sky turned a filthy orange grey and it started to rain spots of soft grey ash that covered everything in sight. The rain continued all night and through the following day until the wind changed direction. They were burning the forest to the west of us.

Mike, a local farmer, offered Udi, Raz and myself a job in his apricot orchard. The money was low but he promised consistent work through to January once the season got underway. It was our best chance and we made a start.

For the first two days we followed two Welsh guys pruning rows of young trees, painting the myriad cuts they made with white fungicide paint; by the end of the second day I was seeing white spots in my sleep.

The orchard was as big as three football pitches laid end to end. Neat rows of healthy green-leafed trees, supported by an irrigation system of plastic sprinkler pipes, were surrounded by a broad dusty firebreak and tall dry gum forest. There should have been plenty of work to do but another spell of shitty weather made the apricots slow to ripen and we seemed to spend more time at home then at work. It started to drizzle and once again Mike decided to send us home early.

I was on autopilot, functioning on thirty percent of my brain and failed to notice how thoroughly pissed off Mike himself was with the situation. Mike and his eldest son were busy loading the ute with pallets of early fruit, keen to get them into town before the apricot lorry left.

"Do you think it'll start to pick up soon?" I droned in a whinge-full tone. "We can't go on like this."

Mike boiled over and dropped what he was doing.

"You've asked me that same bloody question every day you've been here."

Now we were glaring at each other and all the pickers stopped to listen.

"I've gone out of my way to help you and put myself at considerable risk, so if you feel like that you'd better find another job. But whatever you do, don't fuck me around when we get busy!"

"Whoa, bit of an over reaction there", I thought. Suddenly I didn't even know why I was whingeing any more. As I turned and walked away I felt ashamed for being such a pain in the arse but wished he hadn't bawled me out in front of his son.

* * *

During his many visits to our caravan I discovered that George was an extremely jovial and positive fellow. Most backpackers passing through Edgerton Caravan Park sooner or later encountered him spreading the word and nicknamed him Jesus George. One chilly evening George and his friend Butch the butcher invited Udi, Raz and myself to go roo shooting with them on a nearby farm. The thought of Religion, guns and needlessly killing a creature tall enough to look me in the face and only slightly less intelligent than myself was pretty unappealing, so I politely declined.

When they returned late that night Raz told me the guys had killed two kangaroos, both females, both with young in the pouch. Feeling guilty, they had dropped the babies off at the home of a lady who ran a wildlife orphanage. She seemed depressingly used to this sort of thing and didn't question their lack of motive. After butchering the roos at Butch's house - apparently a filthy, gruesome business - Raz and Udi returned home with a roo's arse and tail.

Every outback Australian I had met raved about how good a roo's tail was. Well, this one was as tough as old boots, all gristle, bone and sinew. For hours we tried to tenderise it with cooking until our gas cylinder ran out and we gave up. I felt sorry for the poor animal that after all, hadn't done us any harm and knew I could never again look Skippy in the eye.

We were joined in the apricot orchard by Australians, John and Gloria. The couple in their late forties, had sold up back east and spent the last two years travelling the length and breadth of Australia in a solid looking 70's Toyota Landcruiser.

John was a rugged cheerful character, always cracking jokes. Tall and slim, he wore cowboy boots and a traditional fawn coloured leather bush hat. He took Nobby (Nobuhiro), a young Japanese arrival, under his wing and immediately began teaching him some useful Australian phrases:

When buying petrol, "Fill 'er up, slime bucket, I'm gonna' get some cold piss."

Or to the staff in a fast food restaurant, "What's your grub like, shithouse?"

Nobby, was a good humoured, likeable little character. Neal and Louise from Yorkshire, delighted in teaching him new swear words and learning their equivalent in Japanese. Nobby couldn't pronounce his l's, using r instead, so they teased him while we plucked apricots from the trees.

"So what route is it yer takin' across Australia, Nobbeh?" asked Neal.

"Aw, yes...*Nurrabor*."

"Nurrabor?" quizzed Loise. "I don't think I've heard a that wun Nobbeh."

Later, in the back of Mike's ute screaming into town at 80mph Nobby jumped up in the breeze like a dog sticking its head out the window.

"This very exciting. In Japan, this irregal!"

"In Australia it's bloody irregal an' all!" shouted Neal. "Get your bloody head down ya daft twat!"

A few days into the picking season Udi left us to go back to Perth. He planned to sell his Ford Falcon, fly to Lichtenstein and meet up with Bea, whom he'd fallen in love with. With perfect timing that same afternoon, likeable blond-haired windsurfing wizard Marcel from Holland introduced himself and moved into our caravan.

Marcel had been travelling around OZ for nine months in a Toyota van and knew the ropes. He'd been working in an orchard in Victoria when immigration officials raided the place and chased two French lads who had overstayed. For the onlookers it was like a scene from a Buster Keaton movie as the two bolted like rabbits for the bush with the law in hot pursuit. They were caught, ordered to leave Australia and forbidden to return for five years.

Over the next few days Mike and I quickly patched our differences, the weather rapidly improved and the apricots began to ripen.

* * *

Nullabor - southern coast road across Australia.

People said Edgerton was boring. Sure there wasn't much to do in town with only a handful of shops, a bank and a post office. There was one incredibly raucous pub where *skimpies* served behind the bar while local lager louts, stripped to the waist, shouted and drank until they fell over in the beer and vomit they slopped on the floor. Just a short trip into the surrounding countryside on my junk bike brought great rewards, however. A bewildering variety of crops from avocado to grapefruit lay between stands of pine and gum trees on the gently undulating landscape. In one small copse a family of kestrels lived high in the branches of an old Scots pine. Two juveniles screeched as they performed aerial stunts, trying to coax food from their parents.

It was another beautiful day in south-west Australia. I'd spent most of it baking hot up an apricot tree, so for once I forewent the customary after work beer session on Mike's lawn and raced home in glorious sunshine. Behind Edgerton lawn cemetery I came across a pair of beautifully coloured parakeets in a bush by the track-side. Scarlet body, blue wings, green cap, with orange bars across the head and tail.

A kookaburra kept watch from the top of a telegraph pole as I reached the end of the road and entered a paddock of tall, gently billowing golden grass. High overhead, wispy patches of cirrus cloud stretched northwards to the distant horizon where farmhouses peeped out from between forest fringes. Behind me Cyclone Billy reached ominously southwards, drawing all surrounding cloud rippling towards itself like a vacuum cleaner and forming a gigantic ship's keel shape, resting on the earth. "Wow, what an amazing land!" I thought to myself.

skimpie - bar girl dressed only in bra and panties. A popular bar game is tossing a $2 coin. If the punter loses the call the skimpie keeps the coin, if he wins the skimpie flashes her breasts.

Back at the 'van' as we prepared food that evening, Marcel told us about his exasperating day in the orchard.

"Suzan (Mike's girlfriend) played her car stereo full blast all afternoon from the packing yard. It's thirty degrees, I'm picking apricots and she's playing Bing Crosby's 'White Christmas!'"

The weather reached a stifling thirty-four degrees centigrade that December, the days were long and life was good. I took my bike out every evening for a one hour circuit and on rare days off, rode all day exploring the countryside.

As we worked our tree together one hot afternoon, Raz told me how he and Udi had been astonished at the brilliant colours and incredible beauty of northern Australia.

"Andy, you have no idea," he said with a passion. "In spring and early summer it's so beautiful. Everywhere is covered in flowers. So many different types, I used up ten rolls of film!"

We went for a walk in the small woodland at the back of the caravan park and sure enough, the area was awash with colour. Most startling was the way flowers completely covered bushes and trees. Brilliant purple, yellow, red and white vine blooms adorned tree trunks as high as a two storey house, and this was the start of the dry season.

Our evenings were spent putting the world to rights, sharing views, thoughts and emotions. I couldn't have wished for better company and it was a pleasure to smoke a bong with Marcel, unwind and slowly drift into a harmless state of contentment.

Before we knew it the 25th of December was on us, although it didn't really feel like Christmas in Edgerton. We only had the one day off and most of the time it was a dusty, sweltering, thirty degrees with thunderstorms occasionally bringing saturating humidity. Mike and Suzan organised a barbeque for the pickers with masses to eat and drink. Suzan's stereo pumped out a cool mix of contemporary music while everyone got thoroughly pissed and had a really good time, before getting up for work again, dehydrated and hung over next morning.

In pairs and small groups the picking crew had already started to disband, heading for Margaret River, 200 kilometres away on the coast. Mike said it was one of the worst years for that, leaving him desperately short staffed. Raz and I worked right up until December 31st as we'd promised but by that stage there was only enough work for six of the original crew plus Mike's family.

We finished work on New Year's Eve, quickly packed and headed for Margaret River. Marcel led the way speeding through vast Kalimatta forest, whipping up a dust storm in his battered Toyota van. A gleaming golden sun set over Australia's unique western landscape of gum forest and dry bush country as Raz and I hit the beer, and our spirits rose through the roof as we rolled into Traveller's Tavern car park singing Nick Cave's 'Straight To You' at the top of our lungs.

All the picking crew were there plus a few of the vine planters, including Tony and Mania. Marcel, Raz and I slipped next door to the function room where a live rock band was giving it all they'd got. Then it was back to the Tavern and as the clock struck twelve to signal the end of 1998, a great cheer went up and everyone hugged and kissed like old friends.

Mania was one of few people well enough to be up and about next morning so we had a coffee together in a nearby restaurant. When the others finally surfaced we drove the short distance to Prevelley Point, a local beauty spot right on the Indian ocean.

A powerful breeze kicked in later that morning and Marcel the flying Dutchman donned his brightly coloured wetsuit, slapped on a thick layer of sun block and made his way like a gladiator going into battle, down to the roaring surf. We watched the unassuming expert from our vantage point on the cliff top as he guided his windsurf board and sail through a narrow channel in the rocks, occasionally swamped by pounding breakers. When he was clear he lifted the boom slightly into wind and was off like a rocket! Mast leaned hard over against the wind, head and back clipping wave tops, he joined the rest of the pack several miles out. Their turns were so fast and tight on the glistening ocean, they almost went unnoticed as they suddenly hurtled back to shore on the same tack. The fun board he'd sold me was disabled with a broken downhaul pulley. A good excuse to leave it to the pros.

The following day Raz and I found the apricot pickers sunbathing down on the beach, sheltered from the sea breeze behind a platform of rock. It was incredibly beautiful. Piercing blue sky met endless ocean on the blinding white horizon while roaring breakers pounded fine white sand and large outcrops of granite.

We said our farewells to Marcel and the others. I was choked and Raz, normally cheerful and upbeat, was clearly upset. We'd worked with these guys for several months and become very close. Who could tell if we'd ever see them again. All Raz could manage as we walked up from the beach was, "I hate goodbyes."

Making our way down the coast to Jewel Cave the road wound through a section of jarrah forest. Perfectly straight and smooth barked, these ancient trees towered over their neighbours. A uniformed park ranger guided us and a small group of Japanese around the cave network. Jewel was not just one but a series of vast, interconnecting limestone caves dating from around five hundred thousand years ago. The first cavern, almost forty metres from floor to ceiling, had been eroded by underground streams making their way to the ocean, carrying tiny particles of rock.

Thousands of years ago a massive jarrah tree pushed its spiralling root down into the void in search of moisture. Eventually it died and completely rotted away leaving a narrow spiral entrance. Delicately marbled stalactites and stalagmites, some as big as a house, grew from the ceiling and floor while curious calcified formations of spiky straws, furrowed curtains and tissue-thin fans peeked out from nooks and grottos. In one low-roofed opening lay the skeleton of a possum that had fallen through the root entrance hundreds of years ago. The partially mummified body of a Tasmanian tiger or thylacine, dating from around 25,000 BC, was found in another. The Tasmanian tiger, a wolf-like marsupial with striped hind quarters and an ungainly long muzzle, was wiped out by European settlers in the early twenties. When our guide turned out the light so we could experience the feeling of utter darkness my thoughts ran wild and I imagined its baleful howls injured from the fall, plunged into total blindness and infinite silence.

From Jewel we drove further south through the small tourist town of Augusta with its popular camping grounds and guest houses, reaching Cape Leuwin lighthouse, the most south-westerly point of Australia by early evening. Staring out across the vast expanse of ocean gave me an awesome feeling of space and isolation and I felt acutely aware of how much I needed people around me.

Here the Indian and Southern Oceans met, huge breakers rolling in from east and west colliding in a chaos of spray more than three kilometres off shore. A white plume of spray. "Wait a minute," I thought, "is that what I think it is?" By the time I had my binoculars to hand the spray was drifting off and I started to question what I'd seen.

Raz and I scoured the waves for another twenty minutes and were about to jump in the van when something drew me back for one last look. Bingo! My heart raced as four separate whale spouts appeared in close succession, several kilometres off shore. Even though the great beasts were so far away our first ever whale sighting felt very precious and strangely emotional. It was a special treat when one animal rolled on its side, raising a great fin and smacked it down on the water. A moment later the pod dived and was gone.

Making our way back to Edgerton to pick the last of the apricot harvest, a huge full moon hovered above the trees shining pure gold. As I shook myself awake once again, something large and white leapt out from the trees and started across the road just up ahead. I slammed on the brakes, we skidded, and hit it full on with a loud, donk!

Had it been a roo it would have been all over for my van, but the much smaller wallaby's head and back struck a stout cross member behind the bumper, doing little damage. I walked back to make sure the animal wasn't suffering and pulled it to the roadside, fuming with myself. What a pointless waste.

* * *

The last of the apricots were picked on January 3rd and those of us who were left sat on Mike's lawn to enjoy champagne, cheese and biscuits. A perfectly ripe apricot dropped into the glass gives champagne a wonderful flavour, and the apricot an exquisite taste. The banter started to flow, John and Gloria in great form, and some of Mike's neighbours showed up from nearby farms.

Suzan told us the story of how she and Mike first met in the orchard two years earlier. Mike had been prowling the grounds one morning checking for slackers as he often did, and overheard a conversation between Suzan and another picker. He listened for a while and then stopped by Suzan's ladder.

"You're actually quite intelligent aren't you," he told her.

"And you're actually quite a condescending bastard, aren't you!" she replied, quick as a flash. They got to know one another but it's amazing the clangers even the most level headed bloke will drop when love turns his brain to jelly. A few weeks later Suzan confided with Mike,

"I'm a bit concerned about my weight. I think I'm too fat." Desperately searching for a complement while trying to show concern Mike told her,

"You're not fat. Look, I'm a farmer. I can tell the weight of a heifer from twenty paces!"

"Even in calf!" added John.

Mike and Suzan made up and their wedding date was set for early May.

My plan had been to return to Margaret River and find more work but Mike invited Raz and I to stay and mind the farm while the family took a well earned break on the coast. TV, hi-fi, hot shower, swimming hole and comfortable beds were things a backpacker could normally only dream about. There were also fruit trees laden with succulent peaches and plums, our own bush-land and a quad bike to explore it with.

One evening Raz and I drove to the local tourist attraction, a giant karri tree at the centre of a few acres of protected forest, one of only two this size remaining in south-west Australia. As we approached the base it was clear this tree was something special. The grand old tree had perfectly smooth grey bark around its barely tapering trunk. There were no branches for almost three quarters of its height but at the crown the boughs were massive, home to a myriad of birds, possums and lizards.

Steel spikes had been driven in around the trunk forming a spiral staircase, but inadvertently this had opened the way for infection which would ultimately destroy it. Even with its top replaced by a ridiculous wooden shelter the enormous tree towered high above its nearest neighbours, giving us a chance to look out over the top of the forest and surrounding countryside with a bird's eye view. The sun blazed its last golden rays before vanishing and the clouds began to glow fiery red across the horizon. Squawking cockatiels swooped and dived around us and we made our way back down as a breeze caused the tree house to sway unnervingly.

We found work on a nearby vineyard removing unwanted leaves and training the young branches to follow horizontal wires. Another of those important but incredibly tedious little backpacker jobs. The rows were a kilometre long and with only six of us to cover the entire vineyard we hardly saw a living soul all day long. Eerie dust devils occasionally whooshed past keeping us uneasy company under the baking sun.

The time had come for Raz to leave. He'd booked a seat on the lunchtime bus for Perth and from there he planned to fly to New Zealand. I had been dreading the moment. We hugged, wished each other all the best and he stepped up onto the bus.

Needing a distraction I visited the hostel in Edgerton caravan park, known locally as 'the barracks', to try and find a companion for a rodeo over on the coast at Bunbury. Just as I was about to walk away unsuccessful, two young women returned from a shopping trip and after a brief introduction Lana, in her early twenties, grabbed some cash and off we went.

Arriving two hours later the main events were just starting. Unfortunately the only available seats were downwind of the corral and a strong breeze blew dust into our panda faces every time a rider went by.

An audience of about five hundred sat in tiered rows around the small arena. Starting with barrel racing, young ladies powered their horses round impossibly tight obstacles, then came calf chasing, steer lassoing and the bucking broncos. The riders took an incredible pounding and just as the thought entered my head, that sooner or later someone was going to get hurt, a bronco reared up inside the pen slewing the rider half off its back. There was no way to shut the gate now and as the horse forced its way out, the rider clearly had his hand caught in the rein and was being dragged. The rodeo clowns were straight on the scene preventing the animal from breaking into a gallop, swiftly bringing it under control while avoiding viciously flailing hooves.

The bulls were next. A thousand kilos of snorting, slavering muscle and horn. Names like Sun Dance and Silver Shadow belied their true nature of meanness and aggression. As the first were let out, tossing their riders like rag dolls, Lana and I whooped and cheered with glee. They twisted and turned their massive hind quarters in mid air with astonishing agility and then, having failed to connect with flailing hooves, turned on a sixpence, horns down, charging forwards for the gore. The skilful clowns were there in a flash, running in front of the turning bull and distracting its attention from the fallen rider. The show ended with a triumphant ride-past by all the courageous participants and the tally of injuries became clear from strapped up arms, legs, ribs and a bandaged foot.

CALM AND WATTLE

The vineyard office told me it would take ten days to process my wage cheque. In the meantime I decided to explore the south east coast and visit a forest protest camp I'd learned about from posters on backpacker notice boards.

A few kilometres out of town I passed a young man with a Mohican hairstyle and a bulky canvas swag bag slung over his shoulder. He put out his thumb and I pulled over to give him a lift. The hitchhiker wore clumping great army boots, long green shorts and a black vest that showed off muscular, tattooed biceps. He said his name was Wayne and he was on his way to the forest protest camp at a place called Wattle. I asked him about the movement but he wasn't very talkative so I didn't push it.

Echidna camp on the edge of Wattle forest was marked with brightly coloured banners and flags. A camper van and a couple of utes stood on the sloped dirt road entrance in front of a battered blue caravan. There was a well presented information bay with before and after photographs of devastated forest pinned to a board, and a pile of information leaflets from a group calling themselves the Western Australian Forest Alliance. Tarpaulins stretched from the rear of the caravan's roof supported by wooden posts to make a communal shelter. I parked my van across the road and joined some of the group as they sat on logs and car seats around the camp fire.

The atmosphere was very relaxed. Long-stay residents wore a mixture of hippy rags, torn baggy woollen jumpers and army trousers, some skinhead, others with dreadlocks. I wanted to find out what was going on but everyone seemed very wary of strangers.

Marcus, in his early forties with weathered skin and a tough appearance, gave me the benefit of the doubt and a warm welcome. He'd traded sex, drugs and rock-'n-roll for protecting the forest and the most important thing in his life, bringing up his fourteen year old son, Eli. Marcus wore a leather waistcoat showing off muscular arms and a six-pack stomach, and with his long wavy blond hair and thin moustache he looked like a Viking. I wasn't surprised when he told me he used to ride with the Club Deros, Australia's equivalent of the Hell's Angels.

From the look of his smart city clothes, James was clearly not a permanent resident. He said he was a photographer on a short visit from Perth and offered to take me on a guided tour of the *clear fell* area. We followed the logging road through a forest of enormous, smooth barked karri trees with towering parallel trunks leading to a crown of massive spreading branches and deceptively small, rounded leaves. Tall as a ten storey block of flats and as wide as a large saloon car at the base, the elegant giants stood wide apart with kookaburras and parakeets chattering from dense undergrowth and a variety of smaller trees in between. There must have been some mistake. They weren't really going to destroy all of this, were they? I was concentrating on what James told me, staring down at the dirt road, when suddenly he fell silent and I looked up to see why.

"Fuck!"

The lush forest came to an abrupt end and stretching into the distance was a sea of smashed, mangled branches, huge tree stumps and baked mud.

"That's most people's reaction," he said sympathetically, but I was too shocked to respond.

After collecting my thoughts I took some photographs, otherwise no one would ever believe me when I tried to describe how it was and we made our way back to camp.

clear fell - area where all trees and undergrowth are cut down.

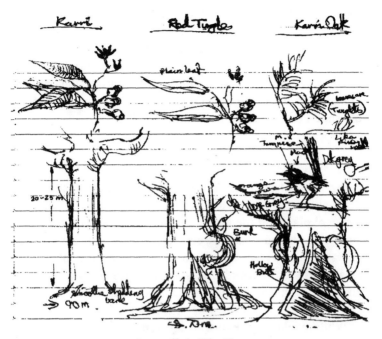

Australia's Big Trees

The following day a local man turned up with a truckload of supplies for the camp. In his seventies, he'd been a farmer all his life and said he wanted to give something back by helping to save the forest. We offloaded rope, tarpaulins, tools and stacks of tinned and dried food.

All of a sudden there was a terrific commotion and a fight erupted between two members of the group. As the rest of us looked on stunned, the two cart-wheeled over seats and cooking pots, smashing through a wooden barrier. Like a scene from a wild west movie, the fighters rolled around in the dirt punching gouging and biting, until one of them ended up with his back in the smouldering camp fire. He let out a yelp of pain and I caught a glimpse of his face. It was Marcus. I wanted to help but was paralysed with fear and Marcus's opponent, a blonde skin-head by the name of Darren, was dragged off by some of the group. Shaking himself free he spat foul abuse.

"You're all a fuckin' bunch a soft-cocks!" he yelled and stormed out of camp, alone. It didn't seem appropriate to point out that this was an oxymoron. I looked at Marcus, the only one who had trusted me and given me a warm welcome, then stared at my shoes, deeply ashamed for not helping.

* * *

Leaving the protest camp I headed south along deserted country roads towards the coastal town of Albany. Albany looked like a pretty cool place but the locals weren't too keen on scruffy DIY campers. A broad main street lined with attractive shops, restaurants and cafes led down to the coastline of official caravan parks and fenced off sandy beaches. In the evening I skulked off to find a woody lay-by to spend the night.

While cooking breakfast in my van next morning, looking out at the huge glassy bay from Emu Point, there came a smack...smack... sound from the narrow estuary. Large, grey, bottlenose dolphins! It was only a fleeting glimpse as the glistening grey forms, as big as a man, leapt from the water, but they were supremely beautiful and close enough to send a shiver of excitement up my spine. The next instant they submerged and were gone.

At a boat chandler in town the assistant repaired my windsurfer's mast foot and I was finally able to rig the sail. The wind was blowing strongly onto shore so that afternoon I drove along the coast to a large deserted bay and went sailing. The water was only knee deep for a long way out and the board's tail fin trawled heavy weeds or dug into the sand, but when I managed to get her aquaplaning she fairly flew along. Leaning right back against the boom I dipped my bum and hair in the water.

Whale World, a popular tourist attraction further west, might have been more aptly named, 'The Whaling Museum'. For all that, the place was a source of essential information about the barbaric trade still practised by a handful of countries today. I learned a new word: flensing-deck. This was where the whales had their skin torn off before being ripped apart, the pieces pushed into boiling vats below. A giant steam-powered saw, now a rusting hulk, was used to cut off the head and then cut it in two. When the whole station was up and running it must have looked like a scene from Dante's Inferno; furnace spitting flames and sparks, smokestack belching steam and choking black smoke, the whole place awash with blood, reeking of rancid whale fat and death.

Whaling finally ceased in the area in 1978. Not because of public pressure - although anti-whaling protests played a crucial role in raising public awareness - but for financial reasons. The price of whale oil plummeted as synthetic alternatives became cheaper and more readily available, while the decrepit fleet of three whaling ships needed replacing at a cost of two million dollars each. It simply wasn't viable.

My route back to Edgerton took me past Wattle forest again and I decided to stay for a couple of days to see if I could help out. Around mid morning a small group of us followed a young man called Simon to a spot in Wattle forest block III, to dig *lock-on* trenches. Simon was slim, about five feet ten with crew cut hair and wore a threadbare army style combat jacket and pants. The others called him Simon Two-Dogs because wherever he went his two pet mongrels were always with him. There were no leaders as such in the group but some, like Simon, had a great deal of experience and people listened to what they said.

---

lock-on - to padlock oneself to an object and create an obstruction. A blockade, obstruction or person locking on.

The trenches needed to be long and deep enough to lie in. The idea was to dig as many as we could in a threatened area of forest. When the loggers came, protestors would lie in the holes and chain their wrists inside a metal tube set in the bottom of each trench. Apparently it could stop logging work for hours, even days. Blisters quickly formed from wielding the pickaxe but my workmate and I had our trench dug by the time Simon returned from helping the others. Lunch was ready when we returned to camp. Rice, veggies and a salmon large enough to feed everyone donated by an ex-logger, of all people.

Around mid-afternoon I joined the others skinny-dipping in the dam at nearby Shannon forest. The dam was in a particularly beautiful spot surrounded by tall trees, bush and wildflowers. Sitting on a large floating tree trunk, watching the others playing in the cool dark water, I began to feel a real admiration for them. They cared about the same things as me but they had turned their backs on the materialistic rat race, committing their time and energy to defending the environment.

Back at Echidna a meeting was held to discuss an important action scheduled for the following morning. A retired couple who had done a lot for the visitors' centre and publicity side spoke about the 'disgraceful appearance' of camp and the poor impression it gave visitors. There were sniggers and comments from the guys behind me while someone else suggested holding anti-swearing and non-violence workshops.

"You'll never get me on one of those, 'cos they're just a load of fuckin' bullshit, aye," yelled one of the young men. Paul was born and bred in the country, wild and raucous with a scruffy hillbilly appearance, but he was also intelligent and innovative and a strong character to have on your side.

The chairperson was Jess Two-Fins, so called because of two prominent, bright orange fins at the top and sides of her otherwise crew cut head. A bihecan, I wondered? Jess quickly resumed order, reinforcing the need for actions to stay peaceful. Even swearing could inflame a situation and it gave a bad impression to potential new supporters. The need to get short-stay visitors actively involved was discussed and Paul butted in again.

"Most a' them are lazy cunts that just sit around camp all day and do fuck all!"

There was uproar. Mike, aged nineteen, hair in long matted dreadlocks, hauled himself up on crutches and spoke to the group.

"I hoped this meeting was going to be about discussing strategy but we seem to be stuck on issues like, whether it's OK to smoke dope in camp, and 'fly-bys', who are only here to appease their conscience and justify their existence."

It was a kick in the guts. I may have only meant to stay a short while but my intentions and commitment were totally genuine. Sure, these guys were doing all the work, making the sacrifices and taking the risks, but hard core protestors alone wouldn't stop the logging of old growth forest.

Sleeping under the stars with the others that night there was a soothing smell of pine and bracken, owls hooted and kangaroos skulked about occasionally rustling leaves or cracking twigs.

Next morning there was quite a buzz as everyone assembled ready to move out and occupy CALM's office in the village of Walpole, a half hour's drive away. Banners were finished and assembled, plans rehearsed and as part of some strange ritual the men donned women's clothing.

"Where's your frock, Andy?" yelled a young woman as she walked over to the black converted Transit ambulance she shared with her husband and baby daughter.

"I didn't think you were serious about that."

"Better get something around your waist," she cajoled. "Frock on Friday!"

"Must be out of your bloody minds," I muttered as I ransacked my van, searching vainly for any suitable piece of material. The protest was to have a determined but cheerful, non-aggressive emphasis and all the guys had to wear a dress or sarong. I borrowed one with a pretty yellow kangaroo print and slipped it round my waist.

The first wave entered quickly, moving into the central office and Jess Two-Fins immediately put forward our statement.

"We're here to peacefully occupy the CALM office of Walpole and we will continue to carry out similar actions until we're granted a moratorium on Wattle Block III and the clear-fell logging of Western Australia's old growth forest."

While the rest of us filed into the building, a smaller group clambered onto the roof to hang a large banner, 'WOODCHIPS OR WILDERNESS?'

A third group set up an information desk outside with photographs of the devastated areas, leaflets and contact details. It all went very smoothly. We were asked to leave but of course we stayed and at one point there was some spontaneous singing. A man in his late forties came in and the big chap who seemed to be in charge of the office told him,

"No Bill, it's probably not a good time to visit at the moment, but if you've got any questions I'll try and answer them later."

It was too much of a temptation and I blurted out,

"…but if you have any questions you'd like to ask us, we'll be happy to answer them now."

"Do you mind not interrupting me when I'm trying to talk to a member of the public!" barked the CALM official in my face.

"Yeah, I know what I'd like to do to you lot!" spat Bill as he wheeled round and stormed out of the office. Pulling a knife from his pocket he waved it around until those nearest the large banner drew back, then he lunged forward and slashed it in three gaping tears.

"Who's gonna stop me?" he raged as people filed out of the building to see what was going on.

The majority of passing motorists were on our side, including a logging truck driver who paused to shout his support. One guy however, cruised past the group in a flashy new Toyota ute and yelled,

"Get yourselves a fuckin' job, ya hippie bastards. Ya bunch a' pig-fuckers!"

I for one, have never fucked a pig in my life but I guessed we couldn't have it all our own way.

On our return to camp the atmosphere was fantastic: jubilant, positive, morale overflowing and there was more great news. Tony Barris, a journalist from the 'Western Australian' newspaper had arrived to do an article on camp life, the cross section of people involved in the movement and to find out why they were there. He wanted to photograph the devastation of clear-fell contrasted with the wonder of areas earmarked for destruction. Fantastic! It was like a reward for all the hard work the protestors had put in over the past months: the digging, the lock-ons, the arrests, long vigils, personal sacrifice, physical and mental pain.

Tony was clearly fascinated and asked lots of questions. The protestors came from all kinds of backgrounds and ages ranged literally from seven to seventy-seven. Camp had been cleaned up, it was now free of drink and drugs and some very switched on people were there, talking freely. We took a stroll down the logging road past smaller Dragonfly camp, and a group photo was taken for the front page with everyone sitting astride CALM's giant log barricade with the devastated area as a backdrop. As the others drifted back to camp I watched in near darkness as a pair of little owls emerged from a pile of dead tree stumps and branches. Their home used to be high up in a tree hollow but now they were forced to live like refugees.

In a light moment around the camp fire, Mike and Paul discussed the morning's occupation of CALM's office.

"I read some of the tourist information books they had for sale in the foyer. They're great," said Mike. "'...we breed loads a' these trees down here at the nursery...and it's just as well 'cos we're really fucking them up at Wattle!'"
Talk turned to a proposed action involving a prominent pro clear-fell state politician called Sid.

"I think we should just slap our dicks out on his leg," joked Mike.

"Yeah," agreed Paul, "with the cameras rollin'."

"...and then when he whacks me out," Mike went on, "I'll be lying there on the floor with me dick out, in front of the camera. 'Hey, this guy's a pervert. He whacks me out and then plays with me dick!'"

"No man, we should just occupy his house!"

"Yeah. Set up a *tripod* in his garden!"

None of this was so far from reality because a few days later in a wonderfully bold publicity stunt, Simon Two-Dogs locked himself on to Sid's car.

Another meeting or 'circle' was convened, the group buzzed with excitement and we were joined by veteran protestors Donna and Tom who lived near Walpole and had nursed the campaign from its infancy. Somehow the couple had lost their impetus and seemed more concerned that we had offended the local community. Why hadn't they been informed about the action which took place on their doorstep? What on earth did we think we were going to achieve by it? Jess kept repeating,

"A moratorium on Wattle, because when we have it in writing that they're not going to log here, it frees us to set up camps in other, more threatened areas and allows more of us to take part in actions."

tripod - simple construction of metal or wooden poles mounted by a protestor to form an obstruction.

"But there's no way they're going to give you that because of what you did today,"

Tom remonstrated.

"We know that, Tom. The purpose was to send a clear message that we'll continue staging actions until we get the moratorium."

The ding-dong debate continued for much too long with Donna and Tom taking turns to pour cold water on the day's action, and another proposed for CALM's tourist trap and cynically named, 'Treetop Walkway - Valley of the Giants'. The latter was a steel framed walkway suspended about twenty metres above the ground, weaving through a small stand of tall trees. When CALM were finished, this sad little Disney-style attraction would be all that was left of the once mighty forest.

"I urge you," pleaded Tom, "whatever you do, stay well away from Valley of the Giants. We've been trying to win over the support of Walpole community for five years. You did so much damage to that support today. You've upset so many people."

The trees were being ground into mulch by machines that could eat ten hectares of forest a day and this pair were worried about 'upsetting' Walpole residents. All four hundred of them! Tom and Donna stayed long enough to demoralise everyone and when they finally left it was agreed to postpone Valley of the Giants action because the couple were convinced they were on the verge of a breakthrough at political level.

Spirits depressed, most of the group wandered off to their various sleeping places, when around midnight two Edgerton boys rolled into camp, pissed.

THE PIG KILLERS

Bill and Tom were timber workers from Edgerton. Both aged twenty, big Bill drove a skidder, a gigantic vehicle like a Volvo earth mover used to push felled trunks to the loading area, while skinny Tom worked in a timber yard. Simon Two-Dogs welcomed the lads to our campfire.

"We don't turn people away even if they're on the other side," he said. It was important to understand the opposition's point of view and this was an ideal opportunity to find common ground and forge new bonds.

From their thick drawling accents to their desert boots, shorts and lumberjack shirts with sleeves torn off at the shoulder, the lads were as far out backwoods as you could get. More surreal than real. Simon chatted to them about their views on the forest before the conversation somehow switched to wild pig hunting. Mat, aged nineteen, was a roguish runt of a character with brown greasy hair and an ugly gold fronted tooth that glinted in the firelight as he beamed a devilish grin. In his drunken state, despite being dwarfed by the two yokels, he thought himself invincible and teased out the Edgi boys just as far as he could without getting himself whacked. Then, just when the rest of us thought he'd gone way too far, he'd pull the conversation back from boiling point.

Mat turned to Bill, twice his size. "You're a fuckin' arsehole mate, 'cos ya chop down trees...but hey, I respect ya!" and he thrust his hand into Bill's, shaking it firmly before Bill could knock out more of his teeth.

"Man, we aint got no feelin's about anything," slurred Tom, brashly. "We could kill four hundred a' them fuckin' pigs and not feel a fuckin' thing. We got no heart!"

There was a brief pause as if for effect, then Mat started again.

"So what d'ya use to shoot the pigs?"

"We don't waste time fuckin' shootin' 'em," scoffed Tom at Mat's ignorance, "...and some a' them is fuckin' big! You can shoot 'em and they'll keep comin' at ya'. We use traps."

"So what kinda traps d'ya use? Spear traps, deadfall traps with spikes down the bottom? Claymores?"

We sniggered, but Tom ignored Mats quip.

"Weld mesh traps. Like a cage, but."

"What's fuckin' weld mesh?"

Concerned looks all around as we struggled to come up with a description of weld mesh for Mat. Criss-cross, heavy duty steel mesh used for barriers and walkways. The strong, springy trap doors overlap and face inwards, allowing a pig to push its way in for the bait - sweet potatoes, apples etc - but not out again. Something like a cray pot.

"...then we lift the lid and hit 'em over the head with an axe."

Mat continued to tease the boys until they left, all three by now thoroughly pissed on the drink the boys had brought with them. That night someone completely wrote off the two donated vehicles parked half a kilometre up the road in the protest information bay. We never knew whether it was pro-logging thugs or the Edgi boys out of sheer dumb spitefulness.

There was a buzz around camp next morning that a nearby forest was in imminent danger. Things were fairly quiet at Wattle and the place was well represented so I headed for Gardener Eight forest block half an hour's drive away, to help set up camp. When I arrived Marcus and Mike were busy with a small chain saw cutting *burls* from huge felled trunks to sell to craftsmen. The money would be used for food and supplies. Bunnings were going to woodchip the lot. They weren't

burl - callus of hard wood with amazing grain pattern that forms around a wound.

interested in sustainable forest use so the burls, some almost an arm span across, were simply left to rot where they lay. We bolted for the bush when the chain saw disturbed a nest of wild bees, one of the countless casualties of clear-fell logging.

Some strangers rocked up in a big blue Mercedes so we stopped work while Mike hobbled over on his crutches to check them out. The visitors were Liz Davenport, popular West Australian fashion designer and her shrimp fishing millionaire husband. Mike returned some time later with a crispy new one hundred dollar bill, donated for supplies.

There was plenty of work to be done. Two hollow-butt lock-ons were planned for the following day involving lots of night time digging, numerous bags of cement, gravel, rocks and water. A hollow-butt is a tree with a large inverted 'v' shaped opening in its base. *Tree fallers* were not allowed to work within a 100 metre radius of a protected tree and there could be several other trees within that radius. Hollow-butts are ideal for this type of work because a lock-on pit can be dug in the soil right in its heart.

Stuart worked feverishly in the darkness, digging deep into the soil at the centre of the two hollow-butts. Tall and slim, his tireless good humour and dedication were an inspiration to us all. We brought him materials and mixed cement on a tarpaulin. The soil he dug out was bagged up and spread further away in the *scrub-roll* to disguise the location of the lock-ons.

A length of metal pipe with chain and padlock connected to the bottom, was lowered into the hole for cementing in position. Work was completed early next morning and we rested back at camp, discussing who would lock-on and who would go black-wallaby.

---

tree faller - lumberjack.
scrub-roll - area where the forest under storey of young trees and bush has been bulldozed and left lying.

Black-wallaby tactics were to camouflage up and sneak in as close as you could to the tree faller without being spotted, then jump up blowing a whistle and shouting so they couldn't ignore you. If you could get within fifty metres they were obliged to stop work. The trees were enormous with huge boughs concentrated high up at the crown. When they fell they literally exploded, sending massive chunks of branch flying in all directions and dead protestors were bad publicity for the logging company. A good number was three or four wallabies because, when the police or CALM were chasing you, your mates could jump up, distract their attention and split the pursuers. I volunteered along with some others and we finally got our heads down. The fallers would be coming in at dawn.

I got little sleep worrying about the coming adventure and was woken a few hours later by the sound of vehicles approaching. More experienced and relaxed, the others dosed on while I went to the edge of the clear fell to take a look. Nothing was happening at the main entrance but when I returned, two police cars and a number of CALM officers had come in through the back road and the whole camp was already being dismantled.

"Are we still going to black-wallaby?" I whispered to people as they loaded gear onto vehicles, but nobody wanted to talk. The police were watching us, looking for ringleaders. One young guy finally spoke, fixing me with a stern look,

"You'll be on your own and if you get caught, you'll be arrested."

Bold images of myself and a couple of experienced comrades running rings round CALM and the police evaporated, but I couldn't bottle out now.

One of the group agreed to drop me off at the edge of the forest and pick me up in my van next morning by the access road. Out of view of the cops I slipped from the van and ran down a gully at the edge of the clear fell, before scrambling through undergrowth on my belly to find a good hideout where I could wait for things to settle down. It was just after 10am.

Silence, and as time went on it began to look as if I might get away without having to take any risks. March flies - large biting horseflies - and mosquitoes were relentless. Then, in the early afternoon two chain saws started howling at opposite ends of the *coop*, followed by the drone of the heavy skidder and *loader*. 'Bugger!'

Working alone meant that the moment I broke cover, all eyes would be searching for me. I was terrified that my lack of fitness and experience would make me an easy target but I had a fair idea what needed to be done and began creeping on all fours over thick scrub-roll, making a wide arc round the source of noise for quick access to the faller and an easy escape route to dense *regen*. By 3pm I was finally in position. My heart raced, paranoia ran wild, but I couldn't postpone any longer. Twelve fine old trees had crashed to the ground since the chain saws started.

I was off, leaping over logs, tangled branches and mangled undergrowth. Short bursts, tree to tree, snapping brush and branches. It didn't matter, I couldn't be heard over the screaming machinery. My target was now in sight. "Should close to fifty metres. Bugger that, I'm close enough!" I stood in full view and blew my whistle as hard as I could. Nine long blasts. Cupping my hands to my mouth I yelled,

"Protestors in the woods. Stop falling trees!"

The faller stopped immediately, put down his chainsaw and glared at me. That was it. I was off like a rabbit running and

coop - small area of woodland.

loader - giant vehicle similar to skidder with enormous three prong pincers for lifting trunks.

regen (regenerated area) After clear felling the scrub rolled area is left completely alone for several years. The resulting new growth forms very densely packed bush.

stumbling, following my route in before turning left and barging my way into the regen.

I stopped to listen. Both chainsaws, the skidder and the loader had stopped working. Blissful Silence. Sweat ran down my face dripping onto my chest and my pulse slowly returned to just fast as I strained my ears. At first I kidded myself my action had stopped everything. I looked at my watch. Three-thirty. Was it knock off time anyway? I guessed I'd never know.

Before long footsteps crunched up and down the dirt track in front of my hiding place, so I sat tight and tried to cover up from viciously biting insects. The flies took it in shifts to torment visitors. Marchies all afternoon, sand flies or midges dusk and dawn, and mosquitoes through the night.

Unbeknown to me, our crew thought I was totally lost and put out a full police missing persons alert. With darkness drawing in I was starting to doze off when someone called my name. Bearded bushman Gary Rabbit and student Jade had come looking for me in Gary's Nissan truck. They told me that my black-wallaby had been a great success but my absence was now causing total hysteria.

In the bungalow home of Peter, a prominent local supporter from nearby Northcliff village, I was greeted like a hero with hugs and kisses. I could get used to this. The press had heard about the tourist lost in the regen, but luckily weren't able to print anything in time. Peter, a well spoken lady in her mid forties, told me it was just as well. The story would have badly damaged tenuous relations with the police as they would have been made to look incompetent.

VERTIGO

The original camp at Gardener Eight was gone. Obliterated. Attention now focused around a gigantic hollow-butt karri nicknamed the cathedral or matriarch tree, because of its cavernous opening and enormous size. That afternoon I was out at the big tree with a tall young man called Gareth and some other crew. Stuart and Gareth had some climbing experience and Stuart had installed a rope that now needed to be moved from the first branch to another, directly above and roughly four metres higher. Gareth explained that the higher you could build your platform, the more difficult it was for the cherry-picker or mobile crane to remove it. Vanessa, a dedicated member of the group, wanted another rope and platform set up a tree in the area where camp had been. Sadly, most of the surrounding trees had been destroyed since camp was removed but Gareth was determined to go ahead anyway, and wandered off to survey the site.

As a youth I'd been an adept tree climber. I figured scaling the cathedral tree was within my ability, it was just a lot bigger than anything I had tackled before.

"Have you ever climbed using prusik ropes?" asked Andrew, a slightly built long term visitor from Los Angeles.

"No...I don't really know what a prusik rope is," I told him, helplessly.

Andrew demonstrated two rope loops whose ends attached to the climbing rope with special knots. These prusik knots locked in position under tension and released, with a bit of coaxing, when tension was released. You climbed by stepping up on one loop and shunting the alternate slack loop a little higher each time. A bit like a caterpillar walking.

The cathedral tree was truly enormous, as wide as a good size living room at its base. Staring to climb towards the mighty bough above me, I began to doubt the wisdom of my original confidence. It was a weird feeling slowly raising oneself out of conversation. I heard voices below and occasionally threw in a comment but the others ignored me or looked up as if I was some alien creature. Climbing higher and higher I began to feel respect for the massive living being that supported and protected me. It might not move or speak as we do but it was very much alive. The tree had a spirit and what was more, I could feel it!

After what seemed ages and with daylight slowly fading, I reached the great branch and hauled myself around it. Sitting astride, my back to the trunk, the cathedral tree exuded overwhelming strength, power and majesty, giving a possum's eye view of the world. My branch stretched out further than I could throw a stone and its surprisingly small, unassuming, willow like leaves stroked the tops of neighbouring trees.

The task hadn't looked that difficult from the ground but up there it was a very different matter. I tried looping about ten metres of rope over my arm, throwing it up over my head. One almighty throw made me overbalance, almost sliding off the branch and I broke into a sweat, heart pounding. Time to try a different approach.

From my vantage point I directed Andrew to a long straight sapling with a right-angled branch near its top, which I hauled up using the main rope. I laid several coils of rope over the offset branch, slowly feeding the sapling above my head. When the coils were level with the upper branch however, the whole lot was so heavy that I swayed precariously like a drunk. I smacked the sapling against the branch again and again trying to knock the rope coils over, but it was hopeless, and it was getting dark.

Gareth returned.

"Better come down now Andy," he called, a tone of seriousness in his voice.

As I dropped the sapling and rope and swung my legs over the branch, I was suddenly gripped with fear.

"OK, but I'm not sure about this branch."

Confused and scared, I started to babble, "I'm not sure…How do I get round the branch? Shouldn't I have a safety harness or something?"

There was alarmed commotion from below, "Isn't he clipped in? what's going on?" and people started shouting up information and orders about karabiners and safety harnesses. Now I was really scared and I could hardly see the ropes in front of me.

"OK everyone, quiet now!" ordered Gareth,
More commotion.

"Everyone shut the fuck up…now!" he screamed.

"…OK Andy, just listen to me! What ropes have you got up there with you?"

"Ehm. I don't know. I've got the main rope…but there's no safety rope!"

"The prusik loops you used to get up there," continued Gareth, "are they still connected to the main rope?"

"Yes!"

"Good! Are you still wearing the harness?"

"Yes!"

"OK, that's good. Now, check that the upper prusik loop is still connected to the karabiner on the safety harness."

I fumbled for the end of the loop and gave it a tug against the karabiner.

"Yes. It's there!"

"He's still connected," I heard Gareth tell the others. "…It's OK. You're still properly connected. You're O-K!"
Sighs of relief and nervous laughter filtered up from below.

Leaving the safety of the branch to drop to the rope tied beneath it was horrid. I had to force myself around but Gareth talked me down, step by step, until I began to regain confidence. By the time I reached the ground, most of my shakiness had gone and it was only left for me to apologise profusely for giving us all heart failure. No one held a grudge though and it was immediately put down to experience and a valuable lesson learned. Drama over, we set our watch alarms for 3am and tried to get some rest.

* * *

It was difficult to get our act together so early in the morning, as Gareth and I made our way to the old camp site. I knew Gareth had been on the go solidly for four days and I'd had little sleep for two. We took a wrong turn and stumbled about in the scrub-roll, illuminated only by the stars. I chatted to try and rouse my brain.

"So what's your background Gareth? What brings you here?"

"Oh, I pulled out of university to do this shit. My father wants me to be a barrister like him... Maybe there'll be a time for that some day. Right now it's more important for me to be here where I can help stop my fellow humans fucking up our planet."

Gareth was around six foot four and slim with it, but I can honestly say I hadn't noticed he was any taller than the rest of us. To me he was just an equal, someone I could trust, with high moral standards despite a wild sense of play. At only twenty-four he possessed astonishing leadership qualities. Not that I idolised him, but I had no trouble at all in following his orders. That was because he made an order sound like a suggestion or something you'd thought of yourself and because everything he said made such perfect sense.

Bleary-eyed, we found the track and retrieved a bow and arrow, torch, rope and line from their hiding place. The spot where camp once stood had been turned into a run-out, an area near the logging road where felled trees were stacked for collection, with only three fine karri trees left standing. The middle tree was an obvious choice because its flat crown would perfectly support a large platform and the lowest of its great branches formed a window for our arrow to pass through.

We took up position and I aimed a weak torch beam up at the branch a good forty metres away. Gareth levelled the bow, a sophisticated device with pulleys, balance arm and a light alloy body, and drew back hard on the string. We had time. Everything was cool.

Release. Zing - Snap!

The reel leapt out of my hand as the arrow sheared the fishing line, disappearing into darkness. "Bugger it!" There must have been a snag in the windings and it was our only arrow. We scoured the scrub-roll on the other side of the tree for over half an hour until Gareth finally said,

"Do you realise what we're doing? We're looking for a stick...in a very big pile of sticks...in the dark."

It might have been funny if it wasn't so depressing. If we couldn't get a rope and climber up one of these trees they could all be gone by the end of the morning. We walked the three kilometres to Vanessa's battered Volkswagen saloon parked at the access road, on the rumour that there might be a second arrow in the boot. Sure enough, we found the banana shaped arrow with its drooping tip weight, a couple of large steel nuts stuck on with duct tape.

Back at the tree time was running out. They'd be coming soon. Andrew joined us, volunteering to climb. Gareth fired a second and third time but the arrow bounced off the tree. The height was OK but too far to the left. She went over but the line snagged and snapped. Then, miraculously on arrow retrieval, Gareth stumbled across our original arrow. As if we needed any more proof that we were on the right side!

Fourteen attempts. We had run out of time and Gareth's fingertips were numb from drawing the bow string. There was no way he could use the bow any more and Andrew didn't have the arm reach.

"OK Gareth, we've got nothing to lose now. Give me the bow."

We quickly swapped gear and Gareth talked me through the procedure.

"Keep breathing, relax. Draw back on the string, elbow at shoulder level. Higher…that's it. Now, raise and point. Aim two metres above your target. Fire!"

She bounced off our branch but I noted - more right next time and a metre higher.

"Draw back…raise…aim - and adjust. Fire!"

W h i r r r r r

Line spun off the reel and kept going as the arrow sailed straight through the gap!

"Second go. God-damn-muvva-fucker…Yes!"

No time at all now. Andrew slipped into the harness ready to climb as soon as the main rope was up. Gareth struggled to attach a length of para-cord to the fishing line. The cord would be used to haul over our heavy climbing rope but as it was played out it became hopelessly tangled. We used what was available, about twenty metres and prayed that the fishing line would take the strain.

All was going well. The climbing rope end was already over our branch and coming back down as I hauled away, then suddenly without warning, the line failed and the whole lot slid back down to Gareth.

"That's it, we're out of here!" he yelled, sick with disappointment.

We stashed the gear safely, made our way to CALM's log barrier roadblock and collapsed on the dirt.

At around 8am spokesperson Jael arrived with Lisa, Mike's girlfriend, and supplies of food and water. Jael had alarming news.

"They're going to continue falling and aside from one person up in the cathedral tree there's no one to stop them!"

Lisa, only eighteen, had already volunteered to wallaby and I knew what was coming. Even if Jael didn't ask, my own conscience would force me to volunteer. I'd told everyone at Wattle I wanted action and instead all I did was eat their food. Butterflies in my stomach, I filled my day-sack with essentials.

Lisa and I walked through the scrub-rolled forest and she found herself a hiding place in the surrounding regen. I sneaked around to the cathedral tree where a young man called Bhakty sat astride the lower branch. Moments later there were footsteps and Bhakty pointed to a CALM officer approaching up the track. He started to run when he saw me. Time to go bush.

The fallers started work at lunchtime so I sneaked around the cathedral tree in a wide arc, heading towards the sound of the chain saw. The flattened scrub-roll gave lousy cover and any movement made a lot of noise. Attack and retreat would have to be fast.

I bolted in, crashing and stumbling, picking myself up out of holes, jumping from branch to broken branch, but I never saw the faller. Before I could get close enough there were three CALM workers standing on a track by a four-wheel drive. Cover blown, I blew my whistle three times then bounded, scrabbled and ran as fast as I could for the regen. (Bhakty told me later it was the funniest thing he'd seen in ages with two cops, three CALM workers and the four-wheel drive in hot pursuit). Hiding in the regen I heard them pacing up and down the access road behind me as the logging continued, so I decided to head straight on through the bush towards the main road and wait for a pick-up.

Back home I'd done quite a lot of walking off trail but I'd never seen anything like this. The further I went the sound of the chainsaws grew fainter and the bush just got thicker and thicker. After a couple of hours I was getting concerned that instead of walking towards the main road, I could actually be walking away from it, heading out into extensive regen. I began cutting left more and more to compensate and doubled back on myself, hopelessly lost.

Here the bush was incredible. Densely packed reeds, shrubs and saplings pressed against my face and body, extending well above my head. Progress was desperately slow and energy-sapping and my food and water were long gone. With every step I had to raise my feet hip high and kick forwards while forcing the brush apart with my arms. It was baking hot and utterly claustrophobic.

After walking for several hours I was completely exhausted, dehydrated and scared. I panicked, gave up on finding the main road and decided to head towards the faint sound of chainsaws, but it was nearly 5pm and they'd be stopping any moment. I hated myself for praying they'd continue. There was nothing to climb for a vantage point. Nothing that could take my weight stood more than two metres tall - the legacy of clear-fell. Suddenly the chainsaws fell silent and I lost it completely, screaming for help until I lost my voice. I blew my whistle as loud as I could but the dense bush deadened all sound. I was terrified.

Another hour went by but it seemed like a lifetime. Clambering up a burnt stump I heard a male voice shouting. Then Jael. Beautiful Jael. I was saved!

"You're safe now Andy," she yelled. "Just head towards the sound of my voice."

"OK. But I'm not coming out until CALM have gone," I shouted back, rapidly regaining some control.

Poor Lisa hadn't fared much better. Having fallen asleep after an hour or so she was found by CALM, taken off site and cautioned. That night I stayed in Gardener Eight sleeping under the stars with Peter's daughter Debbie and partner John, a bearded photographer from the UK. We woke next morning beside the matriarch tree, had breakfast, then John drove us to Peter's bungalow for a well earned break.

It seemed as if half the crew were there and as evening drew in once again, it was 'frock on Friday!' The cult-cum-ritual had begun with guys showing solidarity for women's rights issues but continues today, 'cos secretly we all like to wear women's clothing. There was the added bonus that most women really like to see a man in a nice frock. It proves we don't always take ourselves too seriously, we can be sensitive and feminine and you can see who's got a nice arse!

The crew quaffed wine and beer, men in borrowed party dresses. I wore a miniskirt with my nut-sack bulging out in shocking pink briefs. Music played in the kitchen and outside on the veranda people were dancing and talking, making plans, telling stories and joking. This truly was the best. I was among real friends with an incredibly important common goal. I was where I belonged, but I was also very tired so I sprawled out on the living room floor with some others. There was a large Sony ghetto blaster with headphones by my side and on a pile of suitcases and household debris I found Peter's tiny collection of CD's. 'YES' gently lifted me up on a magic carpet and took me on a journey above silver clouds, looking down on snow-capped mountains and untroubled green river valleys.

DRAG-ON

It began as a fairly quiet day but late in the afternoon a group of action crew gathered together at Peter's, discussed strategy and formulated a plan. Then they were off, collecting various items of shopping: half a tonne of cement, eighty litres of water, heavy duty rope, digging tools, tarpaulins and torches. Hard man Dusty welded a chain at the bottom of an arm's length of steel tubing to be concreted into the ground for a lock-on. Finally, around 10pm everything was loaded into Canadian Scottie's ute and we set off to find the 'bongo van'.

The bongo van had originally been a tradesman's Toyota Townace before taking on its new role as a hippie runabout for driving into the backwoods and smoking a bong. Now it stood in a Northcliff protest sympathiser's back yard with grass growing through its wheels and floor. Whoever reconnoitred the bongo must have been spaced out at the time however, because when we rocked up it was quickly apparent she wasn't going anywhere on four flat, mouldy tyres. We piled back into Scottie's ute and tore off towards option two, twenty minutes drive from town.

Option two was a massive wrecked Holden saloon lying upside down on the grassy verge. Marcus and Paul slung a rope round the rear doorposts and back to the ute's tow hitch.

"Let me get this straight. You're going to drag this motor, upside down, all the way to Gardener Eight?"

The guys were busy checking rope security and making adjustments...

"Stand back," warned Paul. "If the rope goes it'll take your head off!"

...so Dusty explained.

"We drag the wreck on to the lock-on. That's why it's called a 'drag-on'. We've done it loads of times before, but using a bigger ute or a truck."

I tried to imagine how it would be, dragging the huge car thirty kilometres in the middle of the night, on gravel roads, on its roof. Only in Australia! The gutless 2.8 diesel skidded and strained until we could smell its clutch burning, but she couldn't budge the wreck. The Holden was just too heavy and with its wheels missing, we couldn't roll it.

Determination waning after our double failure, we arrived at Gardener logging road, but no one knew exactly where to dig the drag-on pit and no crew were there to show us. The plan was finally abandoned at around 1am and we kipped the night on Scottie's floor.

BRAVERY

I hadn't taken Lisa seriously when she said she wanted to use one of Stuart's hollow-butt lock-ons. CALM had found the first one and stuffed the opening with the root end of a pine tree to prevent its reuse. I assumed the same had happened to the other one and anyway, I was on another 'more important' mission when I reluctantly agreed to help her look for it. She was right though. The second lock-on was still there. Stuart had carefully protected the arm tube with plastic sheeting to prevent earth falling in and camouflaged the site with dirt and brush. There was no chain at the bottom to lock on to but the police wouldn't know that.

When the loggers came in that morning Lisa proved to be a real soldier, shoving her arm in the tube and rolling from side to side to prevent them gaining access. Vanessa was desperate to *buddy* for her but they broke their own rules and dragged her away. She could see them rough handling Lisa and using bully tactics. They threatened her with all kinds of shit adding resisting arrest to the list of charges, but Lisa held out and single-handedly prevented CALM from destroying more trees that day. They banned her from setting foot in the area again. Who gave them the right to do that?

Everyone played their part at the camps. People came and went as their lives, stress levels and health permitted. It's not easy to watch something you love destroyed, knowing you're fighting against a system with almost unlimited resources. Some members shone brilliantly, their beliefs and devotion pushing them way beyond the call of duty.

buddy - someone who stays with the lock-on to give morale support, supply them with water and food and make sure they are not injured while being cut free.

Debbie and Mat were due to lock-on to the skidder and loader respectively. On the big day, however, Mat buggered off unexpectedly, probably to save his sister from another of Darren's beatings. In the resulting emergency Bhakty, who'd intended to buddy for Debbie, took Mat's place and locked-on further down the road to the larger of the two loaders.

Bhakty was possibly the most mature and together eighteen year old I'd ever met. His confidence and positive attitude were an inspiration. Nothing fazed him and he showed no fear of any task, be it climbing to a branch thirty metres above ground and sitting there without a platform all day long, or being arrested and getting a criminal record for what he believed in.

I found Debbie in the monster skidder cab, already locked-on through an 'L'-shaped metal tube she'd placed behind the steering column. There was an unnatural quietness in the clear-fell area that morning. Even the parakeets were silent, as though they sensed the importance of the coming battle and at the edge of the dead zone, the last of the giant trees awaited their fate.

Despite her tough, logical exterior, Debbie was clearly distressed. I started to talk to her in her uncomfortable lock-on position and she began to sob. This was so wrong. The clear-fell desert, like a summer picture of the Somme. Endless piles of dead sticks and baked mud made from pristine ancient forest. Fucking madness! I trembled with rage as I tried to stay gentle and comforting for Debbie. Fuck CALM and Bunnings and all the politicians and liars. I started to cry too as my roots, that I had ignored and suppressed for twenty years, came right back around and smashed through my heart. The forest had always been my love, even before Debbie was born, but she and the others stayed pure and true to their beliefs.

"Tell me something to take my mind off this," she pleaded, so when I got a grip of myself I told her about the paragliding trip I made to Nepal, just before my big journey.

"It was a really emotional time for me," I began. "My dad had just died of cancer and literally one week later, I was on a Royal Nepal Airlines flight to Kathmandu."

Debbie didn't stir so I continued.

"We flew from Galam, a tiny village well away from the tourist trails, where we camped for three days. Our tents stood on a peninsula of rock perched on the edge of the world, with an awesome view of the neighbouring valley and mountains. They welcomed us as if we were kings and gave us food and endless top-ups of rakshi. That's the strong clear rice wine they brew up in the mountains."

"What's rakshi taste like?" Debbie asked, leaning on an elbow to let me rearrange her jumper under her for a pillow.

"Turpentine. And it has the same effect on your brain."

"Go on," she said, enthusiastically.

"News of 'the flying men' spread quickly and every evening the entire population of successively higher villages came down to dance and sing with us. There we were, staggering about in the freezing cold until the wee hours, pissed and stoned on local weed, while the locals tried to marry us off to their daughters.

"On the day we left Galam, the women made us garlands of flowers, or malas, which they placed round our necks, and the village elders sent us off with stirring speeches and rapturous applause. Then, we walked up to a plateau high above the village and when a gentle breeze came through, quickly inflated our paragliders above our heads, flying them like kites..."

"What? How'd you do that?"

I quickly described the principal of paragliding to Debbie: A row of fabric cells like giant socks joined together at the sides, form a crescent shape that supports a chair-like harness from a number of fine lines. By standing into wind and pulling up on the front lines, the cells inflate and the canopy, as it's called, tries to fly above you. It can then be steered and controlled by brake lines that pull down on the left and right of the trailing edge.

"Go on, go on!" urged Debbie, clearly getting into the story.

"My heart was racing fit to explode as I stepped off the mountainside into empty space. Soon I was soaring, working the cliff face back and forth and getting higher on every turn, buzzed occasionally by curious vultures as big as Labradors.

"Spiralling round and round in thermals I reached almost a kilometre above take off, arms aching from holding tight turns on the controls. The view changed as I turned, from towering mountains; Chirco Ri, also known as the Fish Tail because of its 'V' shaped peaks and behind it the snow-covered Himalayas. Then valleys and lowlands like a gigantic living relief map far below, bathed in shafts of sunlight shining through a roof of broken cloud. Hillsides ringed with rice paddy terraces trailed off into the haze. Lakes of mist trapped in valleys. Sunshine gleamed off a snaking river more than two kilometres below. And floating all the while high above the earth in all that space, dangling below a stretched out parachute, from sixty thin lines. The feeling was total euphoria. A stupefying feeling that nothing was wrong with me or the world, or could ever be wrong again. I flew for over two hours before steering out of the thermals and gliding down to the valley floor."

"Wow. It sounds awesome!" said Debbie, forgetting for a moment her fear and discomfort. "I'd like to go there some day. What are the people like?"

"Ah, the Nepalese people are very special. Incredibly hardy, quiet spoken and impeccably honest. High up in the mountains they have round Tibetan faces, wide eyes, sun-scorched skin and wear traditional brightly coloured clothes. Even their animals are so different from ours: the yak-ox cross with huge horns and shaggy black coat trailing down to the ground. Goats and chickens live in every yard or space around the villages."

"What happened next?" Debbie asked.

"After our warm up at Galam it was time for 'the big one', so we jumped on a Twin Otter plane and flew much higher into the mountains. It had snowed hard before our arrival and the snow killed off the thermals so we couldn't fly our paragliders, but it was worth going just to see it! Surrounded by a ring of blue-white mountains with Dowlageeri, almost as tall as Everest itself, towering above us.

"We took a walk one day, up to a temple called Muktinath. I guess I was searching for the spirit of my dead father and I remember feeling disappointed. There was no sudden revelation and I really thought he wasn't there, but now when I think of that beautiful memory I know that in fact, he was with me all the time."

Vanessa arrived and took over as Debbie's buddy. She was much more experienced and the cops would only allow one of us to stay, so I wandered off to 'do good' elsewhere. It took them four hours to cut first Bhakty, then Debbie free. By this time CALM and the tree-fallers had given up and gone elsewhere. Debbie and Bhakty were duly arrested and taken away for 'processing', the forest saved for another day because of their dedication.

Vanessa was a forest tigress and devoted mother to her young son and daughter. Her children and sick father were her first love, the forest certainly her second. She easily outran everyone else through the scrub-roll and her courage and stamina never failed. We stayed together that evening minding the giant matriarch tree - her tree - watching a spectacular display of glistening stars and a grey possum who scaled a crude wooden ladder set against the hollow butt.

* * *

Debbie and Bhakty's court hearing was a farcical media circus. Bunnings and Wesfarmers had strong connections with the local press and the cynically named Forest Protection Society thugs were called in to harass and jeer the two desperate criminals. Outside the court room they surrounded poor Debbie, all of five feet four, pushing and shouting vile abuse while a TV reporter barked the same question at her, over and over again,

"What's going to happen to the timber worker's jobs if you people are allowed to wreck the timber industry?"

MARCUS LOCKS ON

So few in numbers, protestors had to choose carefully when they were going to be arrested. When you were arrested you could get lucky - let off with a caution and charges dropped, or you could get a criminal record that followed you for the rest of your life.

Marcus was not arrestable. He had other convictions and knew the police would go hard on him, next time. There was Eli, his son, to consider. But this was the day Liz Davenport had promised media coverage and all kinds of publicity. Marcus had chosen this day to make a stand and would lock-on to the big loader. We assembled early and Jess Two-Fins convinced me I should buddy for Marcus.

It was a rush job and we had to finalise details as we went. The distance from the ground to Marcus's lock-on position in the steering swivel housing (these monsters steered by pivoting in the middle) was too great, so we packed mud underneath and laid mats of *marri* bark on top for him to lie on. Marcus was still struggling to close his thumb locks when a uniformed CALM official rocked up.

"I'm here to tell you that you're in breach of bla, bla, bla, bullshit section bla, bla, bla. What's your name?... Occupation?... Where are you from?"

Marcus never uttered a word but luckily Jess joined us, just as I was spilling my entire life story.

"Name, age and address. That's all you have to tell them. After that just say, 'No comment' to everything. They're only CALM," she said, in front of the guy's face. That was the last bit of cheap information they got from Gardener, and they left.

---

marri - Australian tree with coarse, fibrous bark and tapered trunk that can grow up to 40 metres tall.

"That's it!" said Marcus as he finally managed to snap shut the thumb locks in the awkward, confined position. (Who actually uses these?) But the left ratchet was a bit too tight and now impossible to adjust.

Completely run down and suffering badly from a chest infection, a result of the broken rib sustained in the fight with Darren, Marcus began to shiver. No matter how much I covered him with blankets and clothing he just got steadily worse. It had been so hot the last few weeks but today of all days it was overcast, there was a fine drizzle and it was cold. With my jacket and shirt tucked around his neck, Marcus continued to shake uncontrollably.

Jess stopped by again while doing the rounds and massaged Marcus's arms and legs to try and help his circulation. They didn't always see eye to eye. It must have been hard for him to admit that the slim intelligent woman less than half his age, commanded so much respect and was such a key figure in the movement. Jess in turn, often found Marcus's stubborn strong will and conflicting strategy hard to bear. For all that, a common cause made them part of the same family, and they knew it. The cops agreed to let me stay and I wrapped myself as close as I could to him.

"Your mate doesn't look so good," said the chubby cop.

"He's fine," I told him, knowing Marcus wouldn't release himself even if he could.

Just over three and a half hours after he had locked-on, the police finally managed to 'free' Marcus. He was taken to Edgerton police station and released pending a court hearing, then he returned to Wattle and found a quiet place to rest and sweat out the fever that had overtaken him. No trees were felled that day.

Further down the logging road Liz Davenport had wandered off with Gary Rabbit towards the cathedral tree and wasn't seen again for several hours. The press and police said she was lost, but she wasn't. She needed time to look around and affirm the significance of what was going on. She needed time to think, and to cry.

Gary, married with two young daughters, couldn't afford to be arrested, so after making sure Liz was safe he simply went bush to avoid the taped off 'temporary exclusion zone'. It was Gary who'd come to my rescue when I was presumed lost in the bush. Now Gary's wife was in floods of tears over her missing husband, and to my lasting shame I gave up after only a brief search telling her,

"Oh, he'll turn up OK. Gary was born in the bush."

Gary did turn up later that evening, dehydrated and completely exhausted. I suspect he took a similar route to me, pushing through the regen to Chessapeak road, but he never told anyone what really happened out there.

A film crew arrived from Channel Nine News closely followed by the notorious Forest Protection Society. It was quite a circus with dozens of pro-logging people, several CALM Hiluxes, three cop cars and two fire trucks. It seemed they were there to show on camera, how much tax-payers' money was being wasted dealing with worthless, troublemaking protestors.

Gareth bravely walked over to the FPS crew, introduced himself and began chatting with them. I joined him to lend moral support, followed by Jael and Bhakty. I was talking with a man in his late seventies. He didn't want to see the forest destroyed any more then we did, but he came from a time when the big trees were an abundant resource, when it seemed they would be there for ever.

The middle-aged muscular bloke with Gareth was willing to listen, although riddled with CALM and Bunnings propaganda. His wife however constantly swore, making obscene personal remarks about the protestors. She never listened long enough to understand what was being said and her own abusive ravings never made any sense.

Liz finally emerged from the forest late in the afternoon and was immediately arrested. A tall blond crew-cut cop dragged her away from the camera back up towards the cathedral tree and a short while later she was bundled, handcuffed, into a police van. Husband Tom blundered in on the situation quite unawares and was also promptly arrested.

"Arrested for what?" he pleaded vainly. "Don't you have to have a reason?"

Liz was in tears as they drove her away. I felt sorry for her at the time but the experience served only to strengthen her resolve and she gave more than thirty TV and radio interviews over the next few days, forcing the apathetic people of Western Australia to wake up and take notice.

* * *

Craig was a rebel. Young, slinky, with a bright red Mohawk and multiple piercings, he relished the thought of a brush with CALM and would make an excellent black-wallaby partner. Next morning we took the bow to fire a line over a tree he had chosen. It was a magnificent specimen with a splendid crown of three massive branches where a platform could fit securely, and the surrounding radius protected several other fine old karris.

Before long we'd lost the first arrow and the banana arrow became wedged. The line snapped as we tried to release it and Craig left in disgust. I wandered off to be alone for a while and when I returned half an hour later, the banana arrow had miraculously dropped to the ground. At the same time Craig returned re-energised, we fired the perfect shot, and hid the line and spool between buttress roots with twigs and leaves.

As night drew in Debbie and I collected supplies left by Vanessa at the log barricade. Darren had invited himself to the camp fire by the big tree, despite being asked repeatedly to stay away. We heard screams as we approached the cathedral tree and quickened our pace. Darren, now completely pissed, had attacked gentle Craig, punching him to the ground. Someone told me he actually held the back of Craig's head with one hand

and attempted to smash his nose upwards and into his skull with the palm of the other. Attempted murder, nothing less! Mercifully the blow missed, taking the skin off the top of Craig's nose. He somehow picked himself up and ran off into the bush to hide. I fumed with rage and searched furiously for something heavy to smash Darren's skull in, but there were no rocks close by and the sticks I found were too big, too small or eaten by termites. My adrenalin waned, fear replaced rage and before long I bottled out.

Darren had committed several other violent assaults on members of the group, he was an habitual wife-beater and Mat, his brother-in-law, feared for the safety of his sister and her unborn baby. The cops had told us that a successful arrest required all five previous assault victims to press charges and that wasn't about to happen. Some had left camp and were untraceable and the rest were just too scared. Opinions on how to deal with Darren varied from the extreme to the absurd. Andrew honestly believed that he could be 'cured' by a session in an Indian style sweat lodge. We followed mad dog Darren down to his car. He vomited several times and was finally driven away by Mat.

After collecting the last of the gear from beside the log barricade; rope, harness, karabiners, I searched for Craig's tree by failing torch-light. The mid-sized fir tree CALM had rammed into Stuart's hollow-butt lock-on was the only useful cover available nearby, so I climbed into its branches and began placing the gear under the trunk.

"You fucking cunt!" someone bellowed from the bottom of the coop. "You fucking wanker, stealing my gear. I've seen your light. I know where you are...I hope you got a big fucking knife!"

I froze in terror. It had to be Darren. He must have got out the car and made his own way back. A couple of weeks earlier Darren had stolen several hundred dollars worth of climbing ropes, harness and radios from the movement. Simon Two-Dogs and dope-head Jason had gone round to his place and simply taken them back when he wasn't there. Now I was hiding in the only bit of cover, on top of said gear. I crouched frozen with fear as the searcher crashed about in the dark yelling foul abuse and murderous threats.

The sound moved further away and I settled down to wait in a dreadfully uncomfortable squatting position, terrified that any movement or noise would lead him to me. Some time later he returned with help and a torch, and I wished I had escaped when I had the chance.

A light beam swept through thick bush at the edge of the coup as the hunter moved with alarming speed and apparent ease. The shouting had stopped, they were serious now and determined. Rumour had it Darren had spent time in the army. An enraged psychopath, skilled in army night search tactics and unarmed combat. As daylight approached, he was closing in.

Several hours had passed. My thighs and calves throbbed in burning agony, coursing with pins and needles. The sweeping torch beam grew closer and finally shone directly on my position. The blinding light appeared to define the silhouette of a man barely thirty paces away. I was made. If the mad dog carried a knife, he would probably kill me. "What a crazy way to end," I thought.

I knew I wouldn't be able to stand but something finally snapped inside me and I suddenly felt powerful with rage. I didn't want to die, but I had little control over that. The only thing that seemed to matter was that I put up a fight and now, for some reason, I was ready. I stretched out and when the pain subsided and the feeling began to return to my legs, stood and left my hiding place.

"The gear you want is over here. Come and get it," I yelled and made off towards the big tree, fully expecting to get whacked at any moment.

Debbie and Vanessa lay motionless inside the giant hollow-butt and as I approached I saw that others were with them,

Andrew and Jason. I gently rocked Debbie's shoulder and she woke with a gasp.

"Where have you been?"

I started to tell her about being hunted by Darren and the terrifying night I'd spent, cowering in a fir tree. Debbie leaned sleepily on an elbow and looked at me, bewildered.

"That wasn't Darren," she said. "It was Jason. It's his climbing gear."

"Jason?" I looked at the sleeping form a few metres away. "But why was he shouting and swearing at me? Why didn't he say who he was?"

"Shush!" said Vanessa and rolled back to sleep.

What could I do? There was no sense in waking everyone up just to tell them what a paranoid dick-head I'd been. Jason, that arsehole! I could have strangled him where he lay. Instead, I wandered back down the track until I was out of earshot.

"Aaaah!"

Craig fled to Bunbury next morning and wasn't seen again. At Pemberton police station Debbie and I gave statements about mad dog Darren's vicious assault. PC Adrian took our statements and showed genuine concern but with Craig gone there was nothing he could do. Once again, Darren got away with it.

On Sunday I felt completely run down with a sore throat and aching joints, so I rested back at Peter's. By early evening however, something was clearly up and I got myself together, determined to take part if there was action.

Marcus and some crew wanted to blockade Gardener Eight logging road and Dusty was already building the drag-on base; a very large steel post across which he welded three metal tubes, each an arm span in length. The others quickly gathered almost a tonne of cement and blue-metal (builder's gravel for extra tough concrete) and assembled the whole lot on Gary-the-builder's truck.

Work started and the diggers broke the back of the logging road with picks, shovels and a heavy crowbar. Feeling pretty rough I joined the women collecting firewood (there was plenty around) and rocks for the cement. Some Northbridge locals turned up and helped, which was great for morale.

It was back-breaking work in the warm night air but at least there was no sun and no March flies. I jumped into the pit to dig a couple of times and nearly passed out with the effort. The ground was rock hard compacted clay with thick, springy, tree roots running through it. You had to admire some of the diggers. Small but tough Shroom (mushroom), muscular Wayne and Bhakti were maniacs on the end of a shovel. On they went through the night and into the morning and then, around 2am, Marcus and big, bearded builder Gary returned in the truck towing the drag-on vehicle, a very large, very heavy Holden coupe.

The pit was finally finished, waist deep, as wide as the car and long as its wheelbase, and everyone helped to lift in Dusty's drag-on base. The concrete mixers began work and a couple of hours later, the two arm-lock tubes and the drag-on base were completely encased in concrete and rocks. Stuart and Shroom knocked holes in the car belly pan with a pickaxe for the tubes to come through. The pickaxe bounced taking a chunk out of Stuart's left shin, but his adrenalin was up and he kept working with his leg heavily bandaged.

Earth was packed around the concrete and the Holden was rolled into position alongside the pit. Its wheels were removed and all of us heaved it up onto its side like ants wrestling with a giant bug, underside facing the pit. A cable was attached from the front tow hitch of Gary's truck to the car's doorpost to prevent it slamming down as we pushed and levered her end for end, to the pit edge.

Marcus nearly had kittens as he eased the truck forwards, lowering the Holden into position. Everyone wanted to stick their heads underneath and have a really good look, like a little bonus, seeing the whole thing come together after all that hard work. The drag-on was finally finished at daybreak but the locals who'd promised to man it never showed up, so Stuart stood by.

Patrick Wier and Margaret Bannister, influential protestors from Perth, had organised two coach parties from various backgrounds on a three day 'forest awareness' tour, the climax of which was to be a visit to Wattle and Gardener. Many of the coach group were old and unable to walk very far and the problem now presented itself of how to get the coaches and accompanying vehicles past our drag-on and CALM's giant log barricade to the cathedral tree and clear fell area. Steve, a weekend visitor from Perth, came to the rescue.

"Maybe if we can get everyone behind pushing, we can tow the shorter of the three logs out far enough with my Discovery."

He drove Bhakty and myself down to recce the roadblock. There was a tree trunk as long as a bus with root stumps still attached. Neither it nor the much longer trunk in the middle were going to budge for anyone, but the third, almost as broad as I am tall, was perfectly round and lay on flatter ground. We set to work digging away any raised areas of mud and debris while Steve rigged up a flimsy tow cable. Bhakty and I found some logs we could barely carry to use as lever and fulcrum, and we were set.

The Land Rover strained and Bhakty and I saw stars as we heaved against our levers. The rope snapped, then the cable hooks bent, but finally, inch by inch we rolled the enormous trunk far enough to allow vehicle access. So the Discovery *did* have other uses than the school run. Whoops of joy! Steve could go home to his family knowing he'd made a difference and would be more inspired on his next visit.

An informer told us that the FPS were planning to disrupt the coach tour by blockading public roads to the forests. They'd already blockaded Northcliff town and occupied the environment centre run by Gary the builder, but we wondered what for. Northcliff was a one horse town and at that time of day the environment centre would have been deserted. The entourage of small vehicles accompanying the two coaches were sent ahead and gradually filtered through to us.

"What blockade? We didn't see any blockade," some of them said as they arrived. That was because the FPS silly sods, were in the wrong place. Even so tall white-haired Graham, our friendly freelance journalist, shot off in a major hurry to catch the illegal blockade on film. I jumped into the car with Debbie and Red to lend support, whether he needed it or not.

A few kilometres away round a sharp uphill bend we skidded to a halt in a cloud of dust. There they were, a mixture of huge bearded lumberjacks and FPS bully boys, angry and menacing, but Graham walked straight up and pushed a large, cumbersome video camera in their faces. They ordered him to stop but he carried on and the situation rapidly got out of hand. A short stocky bloke shouted out,

"Does anyone here want to be filmed?"

"NO!" yelled the blockaders in unison.

The short guy grabbed at the camera, pulling bits off and fiddling with knobs and buttons. Graham made a fatal mistake and pushed him back. He was instantly surrounded by huge honey monsters, shoving him around and shouting abuse in his face. At the same time, one of the ringleaders leaned into the car as if to talk and snatched away the keys. Now there was no escape. Just as the situation looked set to explode, demure Debbie leaned out of the front passenger window,

"Leave him alone," she screamed, "He's only doing his job!"

They backed off a little and Graham apologised to the short guy.

"Give us the film and we'll give you back your car keys," offered the ringleader.

Graham was an excellent journalist, if a bit hot-headed at times and there was no way they were getting his film. After a brief standoff he managed to turn the ignition switch with a blade from his trusty Swiss army knife and we were gone.

As the day wore on, visitors drifted back toward the crowd at the drag-on in varying states of shocked bewilderment, despair and anger. Some were in tears. We all felt a tinge of guilt that we hadn't prepared them a little better but it had to be that way. They would go home and spread the word. It was a tremendous relief to feel the tide turning and there was a positive feeling among the exhausted protesters that filtered through to the newcomers. Local cop Adrian rocked up and admired the Holden, dug into the logging road. He chatted freely with the crowd while children played in and around the old car, painted with sunflowers and proud in its new environmental role. It was a wonderful day.

The visitors asked questions and took group photographs. Occasionally there was a gasp as some revelation of horror was explained: 'The value of woodchip is as low as seven dollars per tonne! In many areas the logs are left to rot where they lay, Bunnings are in such a hurry to destroy everything before public opinion stops them!' but the overall feeling was positive and the atmosphere, fantastic. Ordinary people from all walks of life, brought together in a common cause. That's what the protesters had achieved.

Four-o-clock rolled by and the coaches never showed. Not because of interference by the FPS but simply because many of the people were old and frail and the itinerary was just so full. They'd seen timber mills eating whole forests of giant trees, clear-fell sites that resembled World War One battlefields, and the grotesque wood-chip mountain on the coast. The coach group had got all the information they needed from the crew at Wattle - and then some!

As things quietened down Jess and Jael showed up with some others to inspect the drag-on and drop off water and food. A moment later the small party left again, but as they walked back to the car Jael shouted,

"Andy still wants to live here. I can't marry him 'cos I don't have citizenship."

In a rare light moment Jess called back to me, "Ah fuck, Andy. I'll marry you!"

It was late afternoon. Stuart and Mike were leaving for Wattle in Peter's van so I hitched a ride with them. The coach groups were filing on board ready to head back to Perth and I joined Dusty and Lisa seeing them off. Even though I hadn't actually been in Wattle during their tour and despite my shaggy appearance, the visitors each came up and shook hands or hugged us before boarding. It was choking stuff, they all said such fine things about the protestors.

DRUNK DRIVER

A small group of us went in my van to a combined 21st birthday and engagement party at a farm somewhere in the sticks outside Northcliff. It was a cracking do with a live rock band, a whole spit-roast lamb and an endless supply of drink from a huge chiller bin. By the time we left I was pretty well pissed and stupidly got in the van to drive.

We were doing around 50mph on the dirt road when we hit a twisting downhill section and picked up speed. Suddenly the back end lost traction and slewed left. I tried to counter and lost control as she spun the opposite way, skidding sideways towards the bank. Bang!...and over she went. Dust, rice and all manor of cooking utensils and spare parts flew around inside. Hazard lights flashed, windscreen wipers and washer droned loudly. I couldn't turn them off, my left knee had smashed the wiper and hazard switches. I was comfortably nestled against the door while Bhakty hung down from his seatbelt above me.

Terrified the whole thing might go up in flames, we had to get everyone out in a hurry. Bhakty was soon out, holding the passenger door open for me while the others pushed back the sliding door and clambered over the side to safety. Our only casualty was when Mike burnt his bare feet stepping down off the exhaust. He hopped around flashing snapshots with his automatic camera, thanking me heartily for the best entertainment he'd had in weeks.

Luckily, Canadian Scott had been following a short distance behind and saw the whole thing. Against everyone's advice, I slung my tow rope around the sliding door bottom hanger and hitched up to Scott's ute. When he pulled away the door came straight off, so we hitched the rope to a chassis member, heaved her back upright and strapped the door on the roof.

At Peter's the following evening word went around that Darren was with some FPS in Northcliff Hotel drinking heavily and stirring up locals to attack the protestors guarding the cathedral tree, so it was decided a group should go to support the tree sitters.

Late that night John dropped Stuart, Paul, Ross and myself near the old camp. It should have been a short stroll to the big tree but after half an hour it was clear we were on the wrong trail. In the pale moonlight we tried to retrace our steps but became hopelessly lost. Fear of FPS thugs in gangs wielding baseball bats and chains rapidly spread through our little party.

Suddenly we heard a heavy vehicle approaching fast through the back of the coup without giving the agreed signal - two long blasts of the horn. We froze in terror as a dog barked in the distance.

"If it comes for you, gouge its fuckin' eyes out. That'll stop it!" gasped Paul.

Yeah, like huge vicious hunting dogs are going to sit there calmly and let you do that. Moments later, footsteps and the crunching of twigs nearby sparked a new level of hysteria. Our plan of solidarity went out the window as we dived for cover in the regen. Boing! Three times I hurled myself at the bush and each time bounced back onto the track. "What the fuck do I do now?" screamed my inner voice. Paul and Ross had more success and scuttled through to cover. When we heard Jason's voice calling us it took them some time to get back out again, slashed by brambles and thorns. "Jason, the prick! I might have known". Two hours wasted, everyone freaked out and exhausted, we found the cathedral tree and crashed down. The threatened attack never came.

* * *

Part of me wanted to stay with the protestors but the movement was definitely gathering momentum and the need to continue my journey was calling me away. In a relaxed moment Marcus told me,

"Don't go back to Britain bro'. Britain's fucked, it's sinking under the waves. Stay here where your friends are. We love you!"

He gave me a silver ring with the face of a hawk embossed. "This will remind you to come back here. Fly back to us soon bro'."

We hugged. I was totally choked and my eyes filled with tears. I felt that what Marcus said was true, but how could I suppress my own quest?

I left the following day heading back up the coast towards Perth. It was absolute torment and I already missed all my friends, but I knew that if I didn't go now I would never leave. Back in the city I immediately started to advertise on all the backpacker notice boards for two people to rideshare with me to Melbourne. My proposed route would take us across the middle of Australia via Monkey Mia, Uluru and Brisbane. I would need help with fuel costs, not to mention essential companionship.

Since her arrest, Liz Davenport had become a major radio and TV personality championing the cause of forest protection and now you couldn't switch on without seeing her face or hearing her voice. She was busy organising an evening of speeches, music and poetry to coincide with John's photographic exhibition about the forest. The event was to be broadcast live from upmarket Bay View shopping centre and about three hundred people were expected.

The evening was a resounding success. Some of the crew turned up and those who were invited to speak to the audience of middle class Claremont were passionate, sincere and made their point clearly. Mike, unfortunately but affectionately nicknamed 'Brad Pitt with brains' by Liz, brought his natural humour with an underlying deadly serious note and quickly won over the audience.

Sporting a Mohawk hairstyle and wrapped in a bright orange sarong, Gareth's stature and radical new image made him even more impressive. The audience was silent, waiting attentively for him to speak but Gareth, unable to come down from the amazing buzz of spending over a week up a thirty metre high tree platform, struggled to relate the incredible passion he was feeling. TV cameras rolled and newspaper cameras flashed. The audience wanted to follow him but couldn't quite make that leap. There was a light-year of difference between them but it didn't matter, they were taking the first steps.

Liz was surprisingly together and a tremendous ally to the cause. She called Vanessa and Debbie to the podium either side of her and introduced them. Vanessa recited one of her most heartfelt poems, then it was Debbie's turn. Many in the audience knew very little about the forest issue but her speech soon brought everyone up to speed. She got to the personal part about her own involvement and began to choke on her words, tears forming. Liz put her arms around them both and said in a loud voice,

"These are the dole bludgers, the layabouts, the ferals, that CALM, the government and the media keep telling us about. These young women standing beside me here!"
There were cheers and rapturous applause and she hugged them closer to her. It really was quite something! Finally, John rounded off proceedings with an inspiring speech. It was John's photographic exhibition after all and the whole thing had been his brain-child.

I hung with the 'ferals' for a couple more days. Everyone was buzzing, saying they were going to a douf that evening and would I like to come. I'd heard the word bandied about in camp before.

"What the heck's a douf?" I asked Stuart and young skinhead, Gavin. The two jerked their heads back and forth in unison like a pair of punk pigeons,

"Douf – douf – douf – douf – douf."

"Oh, I should have guessed."

Around fifty people gathered in the upper level of a disused warehouse in Fremantle. To begin with, members of Perth crew recited poetry, played guitar and sang. Then a number of Wattle protestors performed their superb version of 'The Lorax'. After that the disco continued into the early hours.

It was Perth forest protest day. More of our crew were joined by local activists and concerned citizens, completely blocking westerly traffic along Saint George's Terrace as they marched on the Parliament Buildings. The carnival noise of whistles and drums was infectious and everyone danced. Outside the government offices public address systems were hurriedly rigged and TV cameras set in place, while police and media helicopters buzzed noisily overhead. The main speaker introduced himself and thanked everyone for their support, then Jess Two-Fins addressed the crowd. Five thousand people fell silent as she said all that needed to be said, clearly, defiantly and from the heart. She made significant reference to the mishandling of the timber industry and described constructive measures proposed by the Western Australian Forest Alliance to save as many jobs as possible in a sustainable timber industry. I felt proud to know her and glad that the best people were on our side.

OUTBACK

Liesel, aged twenty-four from Cape Town and nineteen year old Anna from Essex saw my ride share advert and got in contact. We arranged to meet, discussed plans and it was sorted. Liesel was a good sport, good fun and game for anything but sadly after we'd passed the point of no return, Anna decided she thoroughly disliked me.

Every time I spoke or even moved she put on a face like a bulldog chewing a wasp and made a 'tut' noise of utter exasperation. She never took on her share of the chores, cooking, cleaning or helping with simple vehicle maintenance. Anna hated the outback and the concept of walking anywhere, which seemed to me the whole essence of being in Australia. She drove my aged van like it was her mother's Golf Gti and bitterly resented being asked to slow down. OK, so I did contradict myself and could be a bit of a schoolteacher at times.

"Don't go so fast on the sand! Go faster over the corrugations! Don't leave the lights on when the engine's off!"

For Anna it was always, "Too hot. Too dusty. Too many mosquitoes. Can't eat that muck. Sleep outside under the stars? You must be crazy! Why should I take a shovel with me when I go to the toilet?…It's only desert."

This wasn't how it was meant to be. Trip of a lifetime? How could I be wishing it was over already? I suppressed my natural instinct to ditch her somewhere in the bush, putting up with her bullshit until I could bear it no longer.

"Since you stepped on in Perth I've had nothing but bad attitude from you. I've no idea why you're being like this 'cos I've been as fair and straight with you both as I can!"

"It's just the li-'ul things I guess," she said. "You act like you know everythin' about cars, an' nature, and when your pushin' that environmental stuff on us…it drives me mad!"

We drove and drove, visiting all the tourist stuff: Geraldton with its fine old wooden fronted bars and balconies, Monkey Mia where a myriad pinnacles of sandstone stood like an army against invaders from the ocean. A film crew were there with trucks, arc-lights and big reflective silver screens making a car advert. Perhaps people could daydream about the stone slabs and swirling orange dust when they were stuck in traffic. Liesel had a go on the windsurfer and mastered the basics really quickly in the light breeze and shallow water of enormous Shark Bay. Anna of course, refused to join in. A manta ray over a metre across appeared from nowhere, its huge black form gliding alongside the board in the clear warm water.

On we went through Gascoin Junction and Meekatharra, names on the map consisting in reality of just a *roadhouse*, a shop and a petrol pump. In one such roadhouse - a small bar with walls covered in jaded photos of tattooed *road train* drivers and young women showing off their boobs - we met the roo-killer as he sat nursing a cold beer. A huge, solitary man in his mid forties with furrowed, sun scorched skin, short sleeved check shirt, tight shorts and working boots. Box section bars on the tray back of his ute carried the flyblown feet and heels of around twenty kangaroos.

"It's not so much that roos are a pest," he told us. "They don't overgraze like sheep or goats and when there's a drought the females have less young. But they compete with the sheep, and that's not allowed."

Normally, he explained, the carcasses were taken away for grinding up into pet food or animal feed but right now there was a glut and the animals he'd shot today were just left in the bush to rot.

---

roadhouse - inn or guesthouse on an isolated country road.
road train - large truck towing up to four trailers.

That evening I quizzed the silver-haired police sergeant as we collected a permit to travel through a large section of Aboriginal territory from the police station in the small, dusty, mining town of Laverton.

"We've been warned about gangs of kids breaking off petrol caps and siphoning petrol to get high on. What should we do if they attack our van?"

"Hit 'em over the head with a pick-axe handle," he said, without batting an eyelid. "You'll be passing through during the Men's Ceremony," he went on. "Boys from all over the territory will be coming to Warburton for the initiation to manhood. Some of them will be painted or wearing costume. Do not take photographs or stray from your vehicle in the restricted area, and don't stop to offer lifts. They're not after your property. If you get any hassle they probably want your petrol. Use *av-gas* and don't lock your petrol cap. You'll be fine!"

Women were a rarity in Laverton and it was fun watching the locals crack on to the girls in the bar that evening. A Fijian priest named Zak invited us to his house and we spent the night in comfortable beds before leaving behind the last human settlement for hundreds of kilometres.

The Australian bush is truly vast. I mean…it's enormous! At first it filled me with an overwhelming sense of my own insignificance and fallibility and I felt sure that if I'd been alone these thoughts would have driven me mad. As its name suggests, the land is covered in hardy bushes with little round leaves, just taller than a man and spaced a few metres apart. Giant earth movers, skeletons on wheels with a massive shovel mid-way along the spine, scrape away the crust of baked brown earth to reveal a deep layer of bright orange dust. These 'roads'

av-gas - alternative to petrol that doesn't give off such heavy fumes.

are often unnervingly straight and play tricks on the mind. Driving all day long, the terrain we looked out over in the evening was precisely the same as when we'd set off and it seemed like we hadn't moved at all. The heat was absolutely suffocating, only the movement of air evaporating sweat kept our body temperature below the red line and whenever we stopped for a break I found myself gasping for oxygen like a fish in a stagnant pond.

Corrugations are lateral ripples that form on unsealed roads and bake hard as concrete in the sun. Their effect on vehicles ranges from annoying vibration to violent suspension shattering and they can cover hundreds of kilometres at a stretch. In some particularly bad sections our road was covered in sharp, irregular, cannonball size rocks, heavily corrugated and slashed by vicious gullies all at once. There was no alternative but to drive fast and hope the L300 would hold together.

It was my turn at the wheel and we juddered along painfully at around 50mph. Liesel sat up front beside me, singing, while Anna lay in the back, slowly disappearing under a layer of fine orange dust that somehow always found a way in. All of a sudden there was a loud banging noise from under Liesel's seat and the steering became light and vague. Pulling over we found that the tread had completely lifted off the front nearside tyre and it was now perfectly round in profile like a doughnut. Worse still, with the wheel off I could see the shock absorber had smashed through the bottom suspension wishbone and was dangling uselessly.

At dusk we passed by Warburton township, an Aboriginal community in the middle of Aboriginal land and limped into the caravan park which was enclosed like a fortress by a high chain link fence. As it grew dark, the young campsite manager invited the three of us to his mobile home for beer and a chat. Backpacker types rarely came this way and he wanted to know all about our travels. He warned us about petrol sniffers, which was ironic because when we returned to the van later the petrol cap was lying on the ground beside an empty plastic Coke bottle and a length of garden hose.

The girls slept in our tent that night, leaving me in the van with the luxurious futon all to myself. It must have been around two in the morning when I was woken by a sound like scurrying mice. I hauled back the curtains and in the poor light, made out three or four young men huddled around the petrol filler.

"Get away!" I screamed, wrenching back the sliding door with a crash. The lads leapt at the high fence like kangaroos, clearing it with ease and had vanished into the night before I even stepped outside. Petrol sniffers, same thing as before - empty Coke bottle and a length of hose, but this time stuffed half way down the filler neck. I threw the stuff over the fence with an eerie feeling they were out there somewhere, watching us.

A tanned, muscular road maintenance engineer rocked up next morning in a shiny Toyota Hilux. He'd met the girls earlier in the roadhouse shop, and magnetised to Anna's tanned fullness between sarong and bikini top and Liesel's elegant lines, offered to show them the township. I continued working on the van removing two broken shock absorbers as Liesel and Anna bounded into the Hilux.

The girls returned an hour or so later, and they were full of it.

"It was unbelievable! They've got a new estate of modern bungalows where they've torn off all the roofs and doors for firewood. There's burned out cars and rubbish everywhere, drunks lying in the gutter and gangs of kids wearing rags, just hanging around with nothing to do."

I could just imagine the engineer explaining, "We build them roads, houses, schools and this is what they do with them," but I wondered if they'd ever asked for those things. Did they ever ask for anything more then access to their land or to be left alone?

While Liesel took a shower Anna came over to talk to me. That was pretty unusual in itself and I could see from her expression it wasn't going to be happy news.

"I'm stayin' here," she said, matter-of-factly.

My jaw dropped. She was a total pain in the arse, but I needed her petrol money and there was no way I could replace her now. I'd put up with her nonsense for so long and now she was ditching me! It turned out the road engineer was heading off towards Sydney at the weekend and had agreed to take her. Liesel already knew about the deal but mercifully decided to stay with me, perhaps thinking three was a crowd.

BOGGED

A cyclone had moved inland from the north-west and was catching up more each night. Finally it overtook us, drenching the road all the way to Docker River. Corrugations melted away and red dust turned to deep, soft, sludge. At floodways - shallow replenished riverbeds - the road was completely submerged. Most large trucks and four wheel drives would have ploughed through but my fifteen-year-old van was tired and only had a few millimetres of tread left on the tyres.

The sky swirled all around us, black and deeply menacing as far as the eye could see, filling us with a crushing sense of foreboding. Behind us and just to the north, dark curtains of rain stretched earthwards and jagged bolts of lightning rattled unpredictably. The road back to Warburton was awash and by now completely impassable, but it was at least three days to the nearest roadhouse ahead.

The mud got deeper and the submerged river crossings wider. Flooring the accelerator we crawled along in second gear with the engine screaming and choking smoke billowing from the engine compartment under the seat. Rear wheels spun madly and the back end slewed from lock to opposite lock as the front wheels sank deeper. If we stopped we'd never get started again until the cyclone passed and the road dried out, and that could take days, even weeks. Frightful visions of shivering on the roof, with flood water rising above the windows, filled my head. It was a titanic struggle to get through each floodway now, and emerging the other side after concentrating so hard on one tiny section, we looked out over endless miles of the same with a feeling of utter helplessness.

Then, the unthinkable happened. Half way across one particularly broad waterway the front wheels dropped into a gully and we slammed to a halt. We were stuck. I restarted the engine and tried rocking her in forward and reverse but the rear wheels spun vainly. Liesel took to the drivers seat and gunned the engine while I pushed and bounced the back end jumping up and down on the rear bumper, but she wouldn't budge. Wading through muddy, thigh-deep water, I checked out the rut with my feet. It was axle deep with steep sides and the wheels were wedged in tight. Taking a panoramic look at our surroundings I shivered as I realised, "We're not going anywhere."

The rain hammered hard and water slowly filled the L300's footwell above the foot pedals. Inside, Liesel had retreated to the back end and was cowering on the futon with a blanket wrapped around herself. Cold and wet through, I joined her.

"What are we going to do?" she asked in a wretched voice.

"I don't know."

Liesel looked away and stared dismally at a steamed up window.

"Don't worry Liesel. We'll be alright."

Secretly I wasn't so sure. There was no sign of the rain letting up and the water was steadily rising. Disconnecting the battery, I taped over the engine breather tube and tied plastic bags over the carburettor inlet, then we wrapped all our dry clothes in bin liners and moved them as high as we could. We weren't very hungry but we had a brew and cooked some food all the same. It gave us something to occupy our minds and boosted morale a little.

When I woke next morning the rain had stopped but to my horror, water lapped half way up the wooden floor compartments just below the mattress. That meant it was near the top of the engine and the fuse box, wiring harness, everything was immersed. Outside the water was up to my waist. I coaxed Liesel out of the van and we waded over to higher ground. All around us now was a vast lake with only the bush tops poking through. The sky was still grey and uncertain but it looked like the cyclone was moving south and the day passed with only an occasional shower.

On day three the water level had receded again to just above the footwell. We had enough food to last for several days: a large bag of rice, stacks of tinned fish and fruit, but the uncertainty and sheer boredom were getting to us. Liesel spent most of her time reading while I trudged through the slop around my van in ever increasing circles, to avoid confrontation.

Around mid-afternoon I heard an engine racing on the horizon and waded back to Liesel as she sat on the roof enjoying the first sunshine we'd seen for days.

Two men in their forties sat up front, the driver sporting a thick brush of beard and wild, wiry hair. In the tray, two sinewy young men stood against the roll bar while the ute bounced and ploughed through the brown water towards us. All had jet-black skin. The driver jerked on the handbrake as though trying to throw off his passengers and the lads splashed down, wading nearer. The young men gathered round, taking a keen interest in my van and its accessories. The roof rack with two spare wheels, spare water tanks and the curious windsurf board. The driver came straight over to me with his mate and spoke with an air of consternation.

"Mm. You well an' stuck boi."

The lads grinned broadly. One tugged at my scrap yard bicycle on its chair frame cycle rack.

"Y - yeah, we hit a rut," I told him, trying to conceal my fear.

Liesel went to climb down but I motioned for her to stay put on the roof rack. The driver turned to his mate and muttered.

"…'im fucked up pretty good…"

Matey approved with a smile and the lads chuckled. Suddenly the driver glared at me, taunting,

"What'cha gonna' do now, boi?"

The lads left off their exploring and glowered menacingly. There was a silent pause for unbearable seconds. I feared the pounding of my heart would be overheard and give the game away - that I was shit-scared and didn't know what the hell to do next. The driver turned again to his mate and the two babbled loudly in their native language.

All of a sudden the driver yelled something to the group, they piled back into the ute, and pulled away in a fountain of muddy spray. I felt giddy. Watching them leave I had forgotten to breathe. A large truck was coming our way, making light work of floodways and mud. I hadn't seen it while I was engaged with our first visitors but I guess they had. A few minutes later the truck driver slowed to avoid swamping us and pulled up ahead. Understandably he didn't want to step down from his cab so he called down to us,

"Take the chains off the back and hitch 'em up good."

Liesel rode up front with our rescuer and I held on for the white knuckle ride. The truck threw up a torrent of muddy spray like a water cannon directed at my windscreen. The windscreen wipers failed instantly when I tried them so I steered towards the centre of the spray jet.

As dusk loomed we pulled into the lay-by at Lassiter's Cave. Over a hundred years ago Lassiter walked there in fierce summer heat, after his camels ran off and left him stranded some one hundred kilometres due south. He continued north and was eventually found by a friendly tribe of Aborigines but despite this brave effort and the kindness of his Aborigine hosts, he died shortly after from exhaustion and malnutrition. Australia is full of similar tales of heartbreak and despair from the pioneer days before the Land Cruiser.

Kevin, the truck driver, was tall and gaunt with short cropped ginger hair and a stubbly growth of beard. He told us he worked in an Aboriginal community shop and was returning with supplies.

"They come in the shop high on fumes and try to steal stuff all day long. I have to whack 'em sometimes and sometimes their families threaten me. Usually it goes no further 'cos they all buy their food there and if they attack a member of staff, we close the shop. That pisses them off and the one that started it all gets payback, big time!"

When we woke next morning the cyclone had passed on and the sky was miraculously transformed, clear and blue. I checked the L300's engine and electrics drying what I could with rags and then, turning the ignition switch, she spluttered and farted into life. When he was sure we were OK, Kevin continued on his way.

Liesel and I needed some fresh air after being cooped up in the van for so long, so we explored the area surrounding Lassiter's cave. There was a natural pool, now little more than a moist wallow covered with reeds, brush and lilies. Picking our way through the small haven of vegetation we disturbed frilled lizards, parakeets and zebra finches while keeping a sharp eye out for poisonous spiders and snakes. The place teemed with life.

With Anna gone the atmosphere was much more relaxed. We weren't in a hurry any more and sometimes ventured up side roads to blistering white salt pans on the desert fringes, staying a couple of nights to really get a feel for the place. The outback came alive with the clearest skies I'd ever seen, the most beautiful sunset and sunrise anywhere in the world and a stark contrast of yellow, orange and purple shades that changed throughout the day. We became adept at reading trails. Roos, emus, dingoes, snakes and scorpions all left their distinctive mark in the dust, although we seldom saw them by day. The feeling of solitude left me breathless and sometimes just being there filled my heart with such extremes of sadness, wonder and joy, I thought it would burst.

LOST

Our walks became more adventurous. We'd set off before sunrise armed with a compass and day-sacks loaded with food and water, usually following a triangular route to minimise the number of course changes and errors, while always covering new ground.

By late morning the heat was ferocious, suppressing any will to move and we'd take shelter under a bush for a couple of hours before continuing. The flies were incredibly tenacious, getting into our noses, eyes, ears and mouths, so we made kepis by pinning strips of material to our baseball caps and fended off their worst attacks. When a breeze came, it blew hot dust around that clung to our clothes and sweat soaked bodies. Yet, there was something addictive about the outback, experiencing the hardship and struggle. A trial of strength and stamina that strangely, we came to relish. Our confidence grew and I convinced Liesel we should attempt a real challenge, a three day trek into the bush.

The first leg was hard work but unexceptional and by the time the sun dipped, painting the sky fiery red, we had covered around twenty-four sweltering kilometres. We made camp, cooked food and settled back to talk while counting shooting stars and lonely orbiting satellites.

By mid-afternoon on the second day we came across a partially dried up river lined with eucalyptus trees. Squawking parrots circled in flocks, almost deafening after the silence of open bush. I counted three different species. There were finches, egrets and water birds about the size of a moorhen that I didn't recognise. Animal tracks crisscrossed by the water's edge, so many, it was hard to tell who had made what.

As darkness fell we made camp, lulled by the faint rippling of water and a large flock of white crested parrots finally stopped squabbling, roosting high in a nearby tree. Now the air was filled with many different sounds. Dozens of frogs sang competing love songs to attract a mate, crickets chirped and there was an almost imperceptible shrill squeak from bats as they flitted above us, hunting for moths and mosquitoes. In the distance, kangaroos disturbed brush and dry leaves as they cautiously approached the water's edge and a group of guinea fowl wandered down to drink, silhouetted against the moon's shimmering reflection.

On our return leg we walked until dusk, compensating for the shorter stretch the previous day. Early explorers had travelled enormous distances across Australia with pinpoint accuracy and by comparison, our walk should have been dead easy. So why, after a full day's walk, were we still surrounded by featureless bush in all directions and why were my van and the road nowhere to be seen? I racked my brain, desperately trying to imagine what could have gone wrong. Weighing up the pros and cons we agreed to stay put rather than hunt around in the dark and fuddle our position.

The sunset and stars were beautiful that evening but I was filled with a deep sense of dread and it was impossible to sleep. We had just under one litre of water each and precious little food. By midday tomorrow the temperature would soar to forty degrees and there was very little shelter. Our vehicle was on an abandoned trail, leading off a dirt road that almost nobody used. We were somewhere in the middle of Australia's vast outback...and we were lost. If we couldn't find the van tomorrow we'd be in serious trouble.

I felt a crushing sense of guilt for putting us both in danger and showing lack of reverence to Australia's bush-land and Aborigine spirits. You just don't go there unprepared without proper training and equipment, the land was far too harsh and unforgiving for that. I could almost hear them saying,

"You knew not to mess with us, to come here and think you could live like our people. You have angered us!"

Leaving Liesel huddled by the campfire, I walked off a short distance to be alone and said a prayer to the ancestors.

A little while later, overcome with emotion, I rejoined her sharing the fire's dwindling warmth.

"I'm sorry for all of this," I told her in a shaky voice, but she was drawing in the dust with a stick, so engrossed in her own thoughts my words barely registered.

"If we carry on tomorrow on the same heading for a couple of hours," she said, "we'll either cross the road or know that we're going in the wrong direction. Then, if we still haven't found it, we'll have to take the same heading all the way back to the river to load up on water."

In the darkness she couldn't have seen my jaw drop with surprise and I suddenly felt a powerful wave of encouragement.

"You're bloody marvellous," I told her and leaned over to kiss her forehead.

Setting off before sunrise we continued walking in the same direction as Liesel had suggested, but after two hours the terrain looked exactly the same, red dust baked hard under foot, bushes all the same height, maddeningly just tall enough to obscure our vision of the horizon and any landmark that might have helped. There was nothing to climb, no higher ground for a vantage point and no distinguishing features whatsoever, so we began our depressing march back towards the river.

We reached the familiar line of eucalypts by nightfall exhausted and dehydrated, threw off our clothes and collapsed in the cool, shallow water. Then we filled our water bottles and discussed our plight. We couldn't expect to be rescued. Nobody was waiting for us at Uluru and our van was too far off the main road to be spotted. We could follow the river downstream because it should get broader and maybe lead to a sheep station or settlement. The downside of that was it would take us in the opposite direction from the van and if we didn't find a settlement we would slowly starve.

Under bright moonlight we checked our remaining food. One and a half packets of digestive biscuits, a small packet of dry roasted peanuts and a tin of peaches wouldn't go far, but it was better than nothing. I emptied out the contents of my trusty survival tin - never imagined I'd actually have to use it. Candle, whistle, pencil stub, a condom? "Give me something I need." Snare wire, fishing line and hooks. A three barbed spinner. "Excellent!"

I wanted to make a start trying to catch something the next day but Liesel's logical side was shining through.

"How confident actually are you, that you can catch us something to eat with this stuff?"

"Well, er…"

"I think we'd better go back to the search area tomorrow and try for the van. Without food we'll get weaker every day, and if your fishing expedition is unsuccessful we may not have the energy to search later."

This wasn't the frightened young woman who had cowered in the back of my van during the flood and what she said made perfect sense. I knew how to make a deadfall trap or set a snare in theory but I'd never actually done it in earnest and we could wait all day for a fish to bite - if there even were good size fish in the shallow river - so we agreed to go back out and search.

Starting early the following day we set off again for the general search area. It seemed madness to be walking away from the river and I fought hard against all my instincts, screaming at me to go back. By mid morning the heat was ferocious and a suffocating wind blew through the bush, rustling tiny parched leaves and thorns, sucking precious moisture from our bodies. Not even India could have prepared us for this. My van, our passport to safety, was hidden somewhere in all that bush. I wrestled constantly with a sickening feeling of panic, knowing it could be just a stone's throw away and we'd never see it and only Liesel's tough, cool example kept me sane.

We searched in a large diamond shape allowing two hours at a steady pace per side, but saw nothing. Not a damn thing. The only logical conclusion was that we weren't where we thought we were and by mid afternoon, stomachs raging with hunger, heads throbbing and giddy from dehydration, we trudged back towards the river in dismal silence. There would be no more searches for the van and to me, the feeling of despair was as real and painful as when I watched my mother's coffin being lowered into a deep, dark grave ten years earlier.

Back again at the river, bright moonlight sparkled on the gently rippling water but the tranquil scene only made us feel worse. Desperate for something to occupy my mind I took out my Swiss army penknife and began shaping pieces of stick to make the trigger components of a deadfall trap - another trick I had learned from Ray Meers. When I explained the principle, Liesel began taking an interest and helped me scour the riverbank for a suitable flat rock.

We set two traps on clear areas of sand bank, one on each side of the river. I used our last two biscuits, one for crumbs to attract a victim and the other in halves, secured with fishing line to the trigger arms. Birds would fly down to drink at first light checking the area for seeds and insects and I tried to think like them, to see if their habits might bring them within striking distance of our traps. Frogs taunted us cruelly. We could creep to within hopping distance of a noisy individual, then it suddenly went silent and its neighbours started up to torment the hunter.

We must have been exhausted because the thud of the nearest trap failed to wake us. When I woke and saw it laying down I bounded over to check the result, a sad little finch pressed flat against the sand. All that biscuit for such a small bird. I plucked and gutted it, which didn't leave a whole lot, then Liesel cooked it over a fire.

Time for fishing, but without a rod and reel it was difficult to make the spinner wriggle like an injured fish and it tended to dredge along the bottom forming a lifeless clump of weeds and silt. We found worms and all manner of creepy-crawlies for the plain hooks and Liesel fashioned a simple float from a dry piece of stick, then we shared and ate the tiny bird, bones and all, and wandered downstream until we came to a natural dam.

The river was much broader here and just above our knees, a likely spot to find fish. I trawled the spinner without success while Liesel stood on the dam using the plain hook and bait. Before long she had six glistening minnows in a neat pile beside her and we devoured them ravenously. Then, with hearts heavy as lead, we turned our backs on the last remnants of certainty and began walking downstream in deadly earnest.

Over the next four days we made slow progress along the meandering river. We didn't catch any more fish, but we had spectacular success flattening a good size parrot with a deadfall trap. Needs must, but our situation was becoming desperate. My stomach felt like an empty chasm burning with constant cramps, while my lips and fingertips tingled worryingly with pins and needles. We hadn't had a proper meal for over a week, we were weak and emaciated, and the geckos and insects we ate weren't much benefit because we rarely managed to keep them down.

My initial optimism had been replaced with blind persistence. Whenever I'd thought about it in the past, I had imagined the end would be feverish and fretful as the mind fails to come to terms with reality - 'Hey, it's over!' - and fights itself to the point of breakdown. Now it was actually happening, I found that far from caring too much, I didn't actually care much at all. No fear of ceasing to exist. No worries about the life that might have been, and no concern that our bodies might never be found in all this vastness. My only thought was to keep going like a machine, until my body refused to do what I told it. And what kept me going, what made me force one foot in front of the other, was not the thought of friends and loved ones back home. Nor, I'm ashamed to say, even a desire to save Liesel and bring her safely through this, but simply the knowledge that I really had nothing better to do with my life.

And so, late in the afternoon of the ninth day, we rounded a bend and saw the river widen. Staggering on, we found that the cause was a man made dam and I could have sworn I heard the faint sound of country and western music in the distance.

It wasn't my imagination, I wasn't dreaming, we'd found people. My head spun, I sank to my knees and prayed. Liesel splashed on frantically but her legs failed her and she collapsed in the shallow water. Drained from hunger and days of walking in searing heat, we didn't have the strength any more and lay there for a while.

When I'd recovered enough energy I picked myself up and, taking Liesel by the arm we stepped up onto the crude stone ford and headed towards the sound of Shania Twain. The music blared from a ghetto blaster in a large, metal frame barn. There was nobody about so we split up to check out the other farm buildings.

"Jesus!" yelled a huge bloke in shorts and check shirt, swinging open the door and almost bowling me over. "Where the heck did you come from?"

But before I could explain my vision blurred and the lights went out.

It was late evening when I came to under a naked electric light in a small, whitewashed room. It felt odd to be on a bed with springs after so long. I made to sit up and my head immediately started to throb and swim. Then, like an old man of ninety, I carefully stood and shuffled to the hallway. Liesel was lying in the room next door. She woke when I sat on the bed beside her, but made no attempt to rise.

"We made it," I whispered.

Liesel just smiled through cracked, sore lips and squeezed my hand.

Some time later, an Aborigine in his early thirties wearing dirty blue overalls came into the room.

"How ya feelin'?"

"I've felt better," I told him. "Where are we?"

"Dungalara sheep station, about three hundred kilometres from Uluru. Me an' Jim, that's the fella' that brought you's in here, was wonderin' how ya' got here? We couldn't find any vehicles on the access road, an' nobody'd be crazy enough to walk in along the river!"

It turned out that Benjamin, or Tope as our Aborigine host was nicknamed and Jim ran the sheep station with currently around two thousand sheep. Jim called the police and doctor in Uluru on the radio, but there was little point in sending anyone out as all we needed was food and plenty of rest. The police thought we had been incredibly stupid but we hadn't broken any laws, so they gave us a stern warning and left it at that. Tope said he had an idea where the van was when we explained how long we'd been walking and the general direction, and offered to take us to look for it when we felt better.

We only stayed for two days. There was little to do and Tope and Jim were out most of the time working with the sheep. You might think we'd had enough of the bush to last a lifetime but we found ourselves going for gentle strolls finishing down by the river, just lazing back on a rock and watching different birds coming down to drink. I felt at peace. The simplest of things gave me pleasure. The sun on my face, watching courting doves drink from the water's edge, the sound of Liesel's voice.

It was a hot, dusty ride along Dungalara access road in Tope's ute and I told him about the first group of guys who found us when we were bogged by the flood.

"Aw, they was just havin' a bit of fun with ya mate," he said. "They wouldn' a' done you's no 'arm. We got warriors an' that, but Aborigine isn't a fightin' people. Most of the trouble nowadays is on the settlements, with grog an' that, an' 'cos white people taken our land away from us. Everybody knows that!"

Tope had been touched by Western influence and decided long ago, to play white society at its own game. He shared ownership of the sheep station with Jim and by all accounts was doing pretty well for himself.

We hit the Uluru road and started back to look for the turn-off Liesel and I had taken. After about twenty minutes we turned down a familiar-looking track heading north and sure enough, a few kilometres later, there she was, just as we'd left her. The battery was flat so we hooked my jump leads up to the ute. She spluttered a bit and then burst into life with a puff of exhaust smoke. Tope loaded us up with water and tinned food then we bade him farewell and were back on our way, still weak as kittens but in high spirits.

We travelled on to Uluru, swarming with tourists. The mighty rock shone reddish brown in blinding sunlight and looked as if it had grown straight out of the flat surrounding land. More than twice the height of the Eiffel tower, it covered roughly the same area as Disneyland. On the east side of the rock was a modern tourist information centre, a supermarket and kiosks selling model Ulurus that looked like glowing dingo turds and T-shirts that read, 'I *was* going to climb Ayers Rock…but fuck it!'. Nowadays large numbers of visitors climb the mountain every day even though its Aborigine guardians ask them not to. In the past however, only the young men of certain tribes were permitted to climb it to fix wooden poles, indicating which tribes were requested to attend local ceremonies. Liesel and I made the two hour Mala walk around the base where a narrow band of vegetation supports a variety of birds, reptiles and fist-sized spiders. We watched with satisfaction as a number of climbers' hats blew off in the breeze and tumbled all the way down to the bottom.

In the evening we pulled into a large deserted parking lot a few kilometres away and climbed a small hill to watch the sun set. At the top we were surprised to find a coach party of elderly sightseers with folding tables and chairs set out, drinking champagne and eating petits fours from silver platters. We blagged our way into the group and were offered crackers topped with kangaroo, crocodile and emu meat, but somehow it all tasted like chicken. As the sun dipped behind us the rock glowed brilliant orange against a clear purple sky to the rapturous sound of "Oohs" and gasps, then it was gone, replaced by the first stars as the rock became a dark silhouette.

King's Canyon a few hours' drive further east, echoed with the sound of sightseeing helicopters, but was still a wonderful green oasis in the endless expanse of hot, dry, bush country. The plateau of multi-layered brown and yellow silt stone stood out like a great wall and has been eroded over millions of years to create a rock pool and waterfall, nestled between overhanging rock faces.

From here on the roads were mostly tarmacked and smooth with no more suspension-busting corrugations or tyre-shredding rocks. No more red dust on the bed, our food, or in our hair. I checked the damage to the van. Two failed tyres, a ruptured water tank, various loose bolts and electrical connections and two broken shock absorber fixings. We'd been lucky.

Our journey eventually took us over a line of forested hills that separates flat, arid plains from the north-eastern coastline. A broad river stretched out below us, shining in the morning sunlight as it meandered through marshland towards the Coral Sea.

Lost

Cairns was like a massive drive-through shopping mall with numerous fast food outlets, giant supermarkets, furniture warehouses and multiplex cinemas. The rain forest just to the north was lush and green, supporting countless endangered species found nowhere else in the world. It generates its own micro-climate on which the surrounding mango and sugar cane plantations depend, but this magnificent jewel was being ransacked as developments sprung up all over the place with names like 'Rainforest Motel, Rainforest Caravan Park and Rainforest Restaurant'. Dozens of 'for sale' signs were nailed to trees alongside a new road that slashed through the heart of the forest and everywhere stood fresh plots of land where the trees had been bulldozed and burned. Ironically, when the rainforest has gone, the rain will stop and the whole area will dry out and die, but nobody seemed too bothered about that right now. In a sheltered cove away from the worst destruction, giant ferns and trees draped with creeping vines extended right down to the sandy beach and heavy mist rolled out from the forest like breath in a cool afternoon shower.

We pulled over for the night near long rows of sugar-cane like tall billowing reeds, but the network of irrigation ditches attracted swarms of mosquitoes. Unable to shut the van windows in the hot saturated night air, we were slowly being eaten alive. Liesel finally cracked and cursing wildly, drove us to a lay-by where we slept on a sandy beach looking out over moonlit surf, well away from the "evil little fuckers."

When we arrived in Brisbane, Liesel chose to stay with some friends she hadn't seen for years. Parting was very difficult after all we'd been through together, even though it obviously had to happen sooner or later. The authorities discouraged street camping and most of the city's attractions were now beyond my budget so I carried on down the coast.

Surfers' Paradise is famous for its long white sandy beach, high rise apartments and joggers, but the breakers aren't particularly big and there are nasty sandbanks to contend with as I found out when I tried to use my windsurfer. Swimming was confined to an area not much bigger than a tennis court within a floating barrier and nets; protection from large numbers of deadly box jellyfish that visit these waters in spring and summer.

Further south the classic wooden buildings of Byron Bay nestled in a leafy green cove looking out over the Pacific Ocean and the town buzzed with a constant throughput of backpackers from around the world. Sometime during the night an over officious parking warden stuck tickets on dozens of camper vans as their owners slept in a seafront car park. Nobody was ever going to pay and it seemed a bit of a pointless exercise.

Next morning the sky was overcast and the air cool and muggy. Walking around a rocky peninsula past canoeists and a group of youths taking surfing lessons, I spotted a pod of eight or nine dolphins hunting fish half a kilometre or so offshore. They bobbed out of the waves herding their sparkling prey into a tight formation before lunging into the middle for the kill. Below a lighthouse built on a prominent point of rock, a pair of white headed fish eagles soared on the sea breeze, occasionally turning with astonishing agility to make mock attacks on an outcrop of vegetation.

The coastal track bent steeply upwards to a thickly wooded plateau, where a small group of flying students assembled 'V'-shaped hang-gliders in a tiny clearing. The look on their faces ranged from apprehensive to shit-scared as they approached the short wooden take-off ramp, and with good reason. The breeze was barely strong enough to keep them airborne and immediately ahead was a sheer drop to the forest and beach, with no clear landing space in sight. An instructor was already

The cyclone – just before we got stuck

Liesel is overjoyed after our ordeal, Kings Canyon

Uluru

A working replica of HMS Bounty - used in Mel Gibson's 'Mutiny on the Bounty' -
taking sightseers around Sydney Harbour.

The Twelve Apostles, south east coast of Australia

The Vauxhall Chevette was a bloody good motor! Hannah
(left) and Emma

Pahia Bay

Rotorua where many of the buildings are heated by underground steam vents

Lake Taupo

Kaikoura Bay

Mount
Tongariro

Milford
Sound, most
photographed
site in New
Zealand

First day
on
Routeburn
track

Ray and
Mike take a
break on the
Routeburn
track

Ray at the foot of
Franz Joseph Glacier

Dramatic skyscapes over Monte Alban

Huge breakers, Mazunte Beach

Tulum – view from the 'City of Dawn'

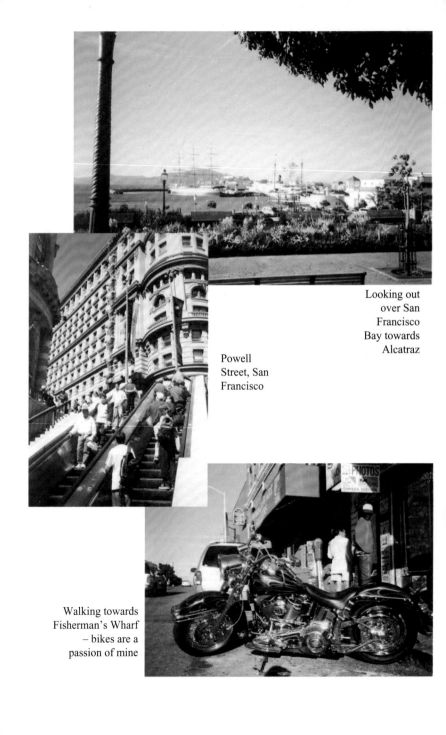

Looking out over San Francisco Bay towards Alcatraz

Powell Street, San Francisco

Walking towards Fisherman's Wharf – bikes are a passion of mine

in the air with a passenger soaring back and forth in front of the cliff, proving that for the brave and foolhardy, it was possible.

Taking a detour from the coast I followed winding dirt roads up into the Blue Mountain range, hazy in the morning drizzle. Leaving the van I went on foot to climb a small peak and get more of a feel for the area. The forest of young, narrow leaved gum trees was eerily silent as I followed a trail to the top, when suddenly an emu bolted from between the bushes up ahead and ran right past me. I nearly jumped out of my skin. The ungainly creature stood taller than myself, like an ostrich in drag with a bare blue head and shaggy brown feather duster plumage. It blundered drunkenly as though its head and body wanted to go in opposite directions and was gone in a flash.

On reaching the top the weather turned evil, driving rain from a blackened sky and blinding bolts of lightning with instantaneous, ear splitting claps of thunder almost directly overhead. The few surviving trees were scorched ominously from previous lightning strikes so I scrambled back down the track, occasionally disturbing grey, deer faced kangaroos that bounded off into the bush.

Sydney is one of the highlights of any Australian trip, with endless partying, friendly people and heaps to see and do. Everything takes on a different look however, when you've got no money and your visa has almost expired. In Charing Cross - the gay capital - I went into a run down pub for a quiet drink and was immediately propositioned by a smelly old bloke in a raincoat. I felt like a vagrant, scuttling off at night to find a quiet side street to sleep in the van because the backpackers were too expensive. I was terrified of being rousted by the cops during the night and my van yellow stickered - registered as un-roadworthy - rendering it impossible to sell.

Just being there, however, was a buzz in itself. I stood beneath the colossal iron archway of Sydney Harbour Bridge beside a restored paddle steamer that doubled as a floating restaurant and function room and across the water, a working replica of HMS Bounty ferried sightseers gracefully around the great harbour. Approaching Sydney Opera House, I was stopped by a photographer taking pictures for a tourist information leaflet. He got me to cycle past, but unfortunately only wanted my legs and $5 bike in the shot with the famously artistic building as a backdrop.

THE CARNEY

Be afraid. Be very afraid!

Back in the early eighties I met Mervin Carney during my apprenticeship as a fitter/turner and we gelled, a pair of misfit Beavis and Butthead punks. Mervin emigrated to Melbourne with his parents when he was twenty-two.

During their tour of Eastern Australia, close mutual friends Simon and Sarah took a short break to visit Mervin and were deeply disturbed by what they found. Mervin had no friends and rarely went out. He watched telly continuously and from this severely restricted input, had formed some extreme views about society and the outside world. Unemployed for more than six years, he had sold a piece of land for a profit and bought a bungalow on a new development in the suburb of Dandenong. In an e-mail while I was apricot picking in Edgerton, Simon mentioned his concern.

"I'm afraid our old mate is madder than a sack full of squirrels. He sleeps on the bare concrete floor surrounded by empty beer cans and gun catalogues…Please, if you go and see him, drill a hole in his head to let the evil out!"

It was almost an hour's drive to Dandenong from the centre of Melbourne and I finally tracked down the new estate. The bungalows had been completed but there was still a lot of building debris strewn about the place and some of the streets and gardens were unfinished. Mervin's living room curtains were drawn and it looked as if no one was home but I parked in the driveway and rapped loudly on the front door. No reply. Around the back the kitchen door was slightly ajar so I leaned against it, pushing back a pile of rubbish bags, and squeezed through.

Inside the kitchen was gloomy with a single narrow window at eye level. There were more bulging bin bags and some were open or torn, spewing their contents of empty beer cans, pizza crust and chicken bones onto the floor. The sickly sweet smell of rotting food and garbage was vile.

"Mervin," I called out. "Anyone home?"

There was a groan from further inside and I walked through the hallway, stepping over the mess. Lying on a mattress on the living room floor was my old friend Mervin. He looked up at me from his drunken stupor.

"Bloody 'ell, Jock!" he exclaimed. Jock was my nickname back home.

I went to switch on the light but it didn't work. Angry that nothing had changed since Simon and Sarah's visit, I stormed over to the living room curtains wrenching them apart and we winced in the sudden brightness.

"Hell's teeth, Merv, look at the state of this place…at you!"

Mervin ignored my harsh tone.

"Jock. Jocky-boy," he slurred. "When d'you get here? If I'd known you were coming I'd have got something in for breakfast."

"Merv," I told him gravely. "It's three o-clock in the afternoon."

I helped my old friend to the bathroom and ran him a bath. Then I found a roll of plastic bin liners and set to work bagging up the worst of the rubbish.

Mervin emerged an hour later, still the worse for wear but a lot cleaner. There was no furniture so we sat on beer crates drinking black tea. An army of tiny black ants formed a living stream stretching all the way from the kitchen to the front door and I watched them impassively as we talked.

I stayed for a couple of days, sleeping in my sleeping bag on a manky mattress in the spare room, but I was already finding it pretty depressing. Poor Mervin was firmly entrenched in his lonely rut.

"I wish I could do what you're doing, Jock," he told me over lunch.

"It's nothing special, but you've got to make a start. You can't do anything without money, so you'd have to find a job. Anything. Just to save a bit of cash."

Mervin thought for a moment.

"Nah!"

And so we went, round in a circle. I looked at my crazy old friend. He grinned, displaying a large gap in his front teeth won in battle as a teenager, high greasy forehead glistening in the bright afternoon sunshine.

"I can't believe you're happy like this Merv. And if you are, it's only because you don't really know what else is out there."

It must have been about three in the morning. I was dreaming nicely, when somehow I became aware of another presence. My eyelids cracked open and there, standing at the foot of the bed in the light from the hallway, was Mervin.

"Jesus. What the... How long have you been standing there?"

Mervin completely ignored the question.

"You're a good bloke, Jock."

"Oh, thanks Merv."

"You're one of the best blokes I know," he continued inanely.

"I'm not, Merv, I'm average. I've done bad things in my life."

"No Jock, you shouldn't say that. You're a really good blo..."

"Merv!" I cut him off. "What the fuck's this about? It's Christ knows what time in the morning. You come creeping into my room..."

"I've got a gun, Jock."

Oh boy. Why wasn't I surprised?

"Are you afraid?"

Secretly I was trembling. He'd been crazy when he left England but I couldn't know how far round the bend he'd gone out here since. It would take nothing for him to put something in my food or drink. I could be chopped in pieces and embedded in the patio concrete before you knew it, and if he really had a gun...

"No Merv," I told him sternly. "I'm bigger than you and if it comes to that, I'll stick your gun up your arse!"

The bizarre conversation dwindled on for what seemed like ages. I tried ignoring him. That had little effect. Mervin seemed quite happy to carry on a monologue, but eventually he left. I was shaken but desperately tired, so I dragged a heavy wardrobe in front of the door. He wasn't getting in the room again without waking me.

Later that morning I quizzed Mervin about his spooky appearance in my room but he refused to discuss it. Instead he started banging on about how difficult it was to find his ideal partner and showed me some dog-eared photos of a Phillipino woman he'd met through a dating agency specialising in Asian women. I found the whole thing a bit sordid. Most of the girls came from abject poverty and there had to be a hint of financial motivation behind their desire to come to OZ and marry.

To lighten the mood that evening we drove to a bar near the centre of Melbourne before visiting 'The Casino', a hideous Mecca of gambling and gaming pursuits. There was a hyperactive buzz about the giant, glitzy, modern complex and you could actually see a look of greed and desire on people's faces as they drooled into their emptying wallets.

The following evening we bought pizza and were sitting munching in a children's play area. All of a sudden Mervin dropped his food to the ground and spoke without looking at me.

"I think you oughta leave, Jock."

I was shocked. I had decided to go soon anyway, but not like this. From a practical point of view it was a disaster. Time was running out to sell my van. I'd already placed an advert in the local paper giving Mervin's phone number. Now I was going to have to move to a hostel in the city and start again from scratch.

I passed a restless night and was woken by the dawn chorus. By 7am I was dressed and went to look for Mervin. There was no sign of him but he'd left a note pinned to the kitchen door.

Jock
I've gone for a walk. I'll be out for a couple of hours.
I don't want you to be here when I get back.
Mervin

Considering myself lucky to get away with my life and sanity, I dumped my few belongings in the van and left.

* * *

Melbourne is Australia's second largest city with a cluster of modern tower blocks set out on a very sensible grid pattern, a large affluent marina and a busy commercial port. There's a lot going on but it's pleasantly more subdued than Sydney, attracting less of the rowdy drinking element and the prices are more sensible. Moving into Packer's Palace on Hoddle street forced me once again to rely on my social skills. The age group was very young, drawn by the cheapest rates in town and easy access to the city centre, but they were a good bunch and I soon lowered my guard and started to make friends. I shared a dorm with an Asian and two Dutch girls all in their early twenties and none of us gave it a second thought.

Selling my van was number one priority and the rest of my trip depended on getting a good price. I made a blitz on all the city backpacker notice boards with a photocopied advert. She had such a lot going for her - a rugged, tough camper van with heaps of useful and unusual accessories. If I'd had plenty of time she would sell easily but there were now just five days before my flight. Each day I toured the central Melbourne backpackers knocking 250 bucks off the asking price.

For a treat one afternoon after doing the rounds, I cycled towards my favourite café. The road was busy, cars and vans parked all along the cycle lane, so I rode carefully on the pavement.

"Arsehole!"

In the corner of my eye I saw a young bloke shout out and knew it was directed at me. Throwing my bike down I stormed back towards him, I was just in the mood. Other pedestrians looked on alarmed but in the toffee-nosed part of town no one stopped to help him.

"What did you say?"

He stepped back, putting his hands up in defence.

"I - I don't want any trouble."

"Don't bloody start it then!"

I was furious. It seemed like all my troubles manifested themselves in this twit and he wouldn't give a stuff if I got run over. I walked back and remounted my bike, dropping onto a clear stretch of road.

"That's better," I heard him call after me, clearly not knowing when to quit.

With just three days to go I got the price I needed for my trusty van and hoped she'd be as good for her new owners as she had been for me. Then, flushed with success I caught up with a couple of ladies, Kim and Julie whom I'd met way back in Bombay and Kim took me to an Aussie-rules football match - Melbourne Tigers verses Adelaide Bulldogs.

It was an awesome spectacle. Late in the evening the giant, floodlit oval stadium thrummed with a capacity crowd of fifty thousand. We walked out onto the first terrace in dazzling arc-light and I gazed across the field at a sea of faces. Sadly most of the supporters, including Kim and myself, left in disgust as the Tigers virtually threw in the towel two-thirds into the match.

* * *

It was time to for me to leave Australia. Hard to believe the continent had swallowed up seven months of my life in the blink of an eye, but maybe that was a small measure of the country's greatness. Kim and Julie took me to the airport. We hugged and I said goodbye to amazing Australia.

AUTEAROA

NEW ZEALAND

TANGETA WHENUA
(Island of clouds)

An airport bus dropped me on Queen Street, central Auckland, on a drizzly overcast afternoon. The broad straight road lined with a tasteful mixture of five storey buildings from Victorian to the present, sloped down towards busy Auckland harbour and the Tasman Sea. Auckland's suburbs spilled out over several valleys and bays but the central skyline was tall and highly developed and there was even a telecommunications tower with its head in the clouds, looking like some gigantic football trophy.

In Kiwi Backpackers I found myself once again looking at car ads on the notice board. A Vaxhall Chevette for one hundred and fifty quid? "Blimey, that's Cheap."

"Are you interested in zis car?" asked the young German who had materialised beside me.

A couple of hours later he handed me the keys and registration document and I became the proud new owner of thirteen hundred cc's of roaring British iron.

I wrote a brief reply to a ride share ad on the notice board and was just about to walk away.

"Ooh look!" exclaimed the blond girl to her friend as she studied my note. "Someone replied to our ad. We have to find Andy in room five."

"That's me," I told her.

Sorted.

The Vauxhall Chevette GL Estate was a bloody good motor! No, really. It seemed dreadfully unfair that wherever we went in mine people giggled and smirked. Undeterred, we carried on around the northern coast of North Island, students Emma, Hanna and myself.

Late in the afternoon we stopped near the town of Waipu to ask a farmer if he knew of a campsite in the area and without a thought, he let us camp on his land for free at a thoroughly beautiful location by an estuary. The place was a bird watcher's paradise. Black swans, red billed oystercatchers, herons and sandpipers settled down for the evening beside the still water as the sun retreated behind a grassy spit of land. We cooked pasta mixed with tomatoes, herbs and fish over a small petrol stove that came with the car and enjoyed a beautiful sunset and cold, clear night.

Waipu was a picturesque little tourist town overlooking broad, sheltered, Bay of Islands. The Maori Land Rights Treaty, drawn up to return areas of confiscated land to the Maori, was signed there in 1840 but never adhered to.

The Maoris arrived in New Zealand almost one thousand years ago. Many tribes were cannibals, fearsome and warlike, and they soon made an end to the spectacular, flightless giant moa and all its close relatives. The moa, slow to breed, had no defence against such skilled hunters.

The issue of Maori land rights was only re-opened in 1995 and it still caused uneasiness between white landowners and Maoris. Visitors stood in the middle ground wondering what the outcome would be but whatever settlement was reached, it wouldn't please everyone.

From the Whare Runanga - Maori Meeting Hall (Wh is pronounced Ph), we walked along the raised wooden boards of Waitangi Trail through pristine mangrove to magnificent Haruru falls, a crescent of thundering water wide as a six lane motorway. I sat gazing into the endlessly tumbling mass, completely absorbed. The water seemed to represent time, hundreds of tons of it disappearing over the edge every minute. I thought of my life in relation to the falls. What were they doing when this happened in my life, or that? Always different in subtle changes of season. Forceful and silt laden after heavy rains, weaker and clearer in the heat of summer. Emma's voice calling my name jolted me back into our world.

We moved into cosy Mousetrap Backpackers further up the coast in Pahia. The small town consisted of a hundred or so tasteful wooden two storey houses overlooked by forested hills. A handful of fishermen tried their luck from the white sandy beach and sailing boats rested on the still water like swans. The girls quickly made friends that evening, guitar playing and shouts of laughter from the balcony in the cold night air.

Next morning it was, "Goodbye Andy."
Luckily, while the girls had been plotting to abandon me, I'd been chatting in the living room with a stocky young Texan called Frank. Frank and I agreed to meet up on our return to Auckland and travel together in his more spacious, red Datsun Bluebird estate.

To clear my head I followed a trail through regenerated forest to a viewpoint overlooking the beautiful, tranquil bay. Several hours later, tired and thirsty, I paid a visit to the Roadrunner Tavern in Orapahasi village in time for happy hour, where local characters made a pleasant change from fellow backpackers. A bearded man in Wellington boots and lumberjack shirt joined me, complaining bitterly that a chunk of his farm had recently been sectioned off and declared a National Park, apparently without his consent.

"How would you feel if it was your land?" he demanded.

The following day I went with a fellow Mousetrap resident, a late middle-aged American from Hawaii, to Kerikeri in his hired car and for once I didn't feel like the oldest traveller in New Zealand.

A river zigzagged through the quiet little town of trinket shops and shingled wooden cottages, slowly turning the water wheel of a restored flour mill. Just a short walk away the tranquil river disappeared over the edge of Rainbow Falls in a great curtain and crashing onto the rocks far below, formed a billowing cloud of spray that haloed the scene.

Continuing alone next day I followed the road north between rolling green hills and sandy coast, occasionally cutting inland to skirt bays or estuaries. That night I camped in a field overlooking pretty Taipa Bay with its small fishing fleet moored in the placid waters.

While cooking breakfast the following morning I chatted with my neighbour, a seventy-five year old lady from Hamilton. She warned me that crime was escalating on North Island and told me the story of how she and her husband saw off a burglar at their home a few months earlier, bashing him repeatedly with a walking stick.

Driving on up narrow Aupouri Peninsula I was passed by fifteen logging trucks before lunch time. The early settlers had cleared the entire area of native forest, replanting with fast growing pine in neat rows for timber and paper production. A sign in a drive-through village boasted a 'Tree Museum', so with nothing better to do I pulled in to take a look. Part of a giant, prehistoric tree trunk had been pulled out of a local quarry preserved in clay, and the museum constructed around it. Cleaned up and varnished with a doorway and staircase now built inside, the massive section was believed to be over 1,500 years old when it fell and had lain buried since the stone age. On the museum walls were photographs showing white settlers at work at the turn of the century, chopping down the ancient forest. Bearded men in shaggy tweed clothes, up to their knees in mud struggled like ants with oversize felled trunks, or sat proudly on top of their labours smoking clay pipes. The logs were loaded onto great carts pulled by oxen and brought to a narrow gauge railway, specially built for the purpose. One photograph showed a long chain of carriages piled high with the last of the mighty trees, disappearing between denuded hills that stretched off to the horizon. They hadn't left a single tree standing and if it wasn't for the photograph, no one could ever have guessed the place was once covered in forest.

Windswept grassy hills tumbled down towards stark and desolate Cape Reinga, New Zealand's most northerly point, where a lighthouse stood watch over the empty ocean. The next speck of land, New Caledonia, was more than 1,600 kilometres away. Shards of evening sunlight burst through the grey sky and danced off gleaming wave tops towards the horizon. I felt as if I was the only human being on the planet, grateful to be there but also sad, sensing it was a milestone in my life and I would never pass this way again.

Stopping for the night a little further along the coast at deserted Tapotupotu Bay campsite, I walked back along the shingle beach to a rocky outcrop just as the sun was setting. The tide was half way out and I clambered right round to a place where crystal clear blue water surged with tremendous force through tunnels deep in ancient volcanic rock. With the sea's ebb, tons of water cascaded into an opening. Then, as the surrounding water rose again it boiled up, blasting out into the foaming sea. Water channelled through a great archway, the entrance to a dark tunnel in the rock face leading deep into the hillside, but without a boat I could go no further. As I made my way back to my tent the sun's last beams lit up the cliffs at the opposite end of the bay with a brilliant golden sheen.

From Rotorua road I made my way down to Great Exhibition Bay and sat alone on the white sand beach for a while. A Maori warrior parked his car in the sand dunes next to mine and pulled a long wooden pole from the rear door. He walked down the beach occasionally twirling the pole like a bandsman's baton. Then, wading knee deep into the ice cold breakers, he held it firmly in front of him at waist height, legs a stride apart and slightly bent at the knee, and uttered a prayer to the ancestors. The pole was a ceremonial spear and the beach a sacred site.

Evening drew in as I continued south and the tranquil landscape of green hills dotted with grazing sheep ended abruptly in the dark gloom of Waipoua *kauri* forest. It had been raining, and now ghostly wisps of mist hung in the cold, still air. I arrived at the Department Of Conservation campsite where I met a young woman called Irene, about to start her kiwi count for the evening. Part Maori and in her mid-thirties, she managed the site and lived in a bungalow by the entrance. As she showed me to my pitch, Irene told me she'd been working with a group of researchers currently staying in one of the dorms, assessing numbers of New Zealand's endangered national emblem. In her assigned area she could usually expect to hear the calls of up to eight individuals from 5.30 to 6.30 pm, the bird's most vocal time.

"Those are non-native trees," she said, nodding to the pine forest in front of the camp, "and they're scheduled for harvesting. Normally I wouldn't mind if they dropped the lot, but they're right next door to the National Park and the undergrowth that's grown up between them is habitat for kiwis." I remembered the huge areas of clear-felled pine forest I had seen on Aupouri Peninsula.

"It's nesting time. They'll be slaughtered if tree felling goes ahead now."

kauri - massive coarse-barked tree like a gigantic oak but with small, rounded leaves. Can grow up to 35 metres tall and live over a thousand years.

Irene explained that before the Maori came to the islands, New Zealand had only three species of mammal - all bats, and that two of those were now extinct. The only other native inhabitants were insects and a bewildering variety of birds, many of which were flightless, because there had been no predators and the forest undergrowth was so dense. The Maoris brought with them dogs and inadvertently, a small species of rat, but the European settlers introduced a further fifty-five animal species, thirty of which survived today with devastating consequences for native birds.

While fixing supper in the kitchen hut I chatted with Bruce, a part time tutor of horticulture at Auckland Technical College and member of the kiwi project. He told me that the more sporting settlers had introduced the Australian possum some time ago, in order to give themselves something different to shoot at. Possums had no natural predators here and were breeding out of control, currently estimated at a staggering seventy million. They ate literally all the young leaves from the trees, easily defoliating and killing a thousand year old kauri in a matter of days. They also stripped the trees of berries, competing with native birds and taking their eggs and young.

"They should have brought in the mongoose," said Bill, a lecturer of environmental studies and member of the kiwi team. "We nearly got those too, you know."

"Yep," agreed Bruce with a wry grin. "That would take care of the possums alright. Have you seen the way they deal with a cobra?"

Possums and just about every remaining species of ground dwelling bird in New Zealand. I learned that a top government official had actually proposed doing just that. Thank goodness he was stopped.

It hadn't taken long to realise that the introduction of rabbits was a dreadful mistake, and the subsequent introduction of stoats and weasels to kill the rabbits hugely compounded the error. Flightless birds were completely defenceless against the new killers and the effect was catastrophic. Myxomatosis virus was deliberately introduced to deal with the rabbit infestation but had little effect. Then, in 1997 Calisivirus was illegally introduced, possibly by despairing farmers, and later sanctioned by the government because it seemed to have the desired result.

Bruce invited me to join the group the following morning collecting *manuka* seeds as part of a non-government re-forestation program. Bruce's other main job was issuing certification of organically grown produce to farms and food producers and he told me about his visit to Japan a few months earlier.

"Organic food is becoming big business around the world and it's essential to sort out genuine from fraudulent producers.

Giant Mitsubishi invited our certification team over to Japan. Three of us sat at an enormous mahogany table faced by thirty top executives from the department of toxic waste disposal, petrochemicals and pesticides, weapons and car manufacture. It made no difference to Mitsubishi, their only interest in 'organic' was as another money spinning investment."

Ten of us assembled outside the kitchen bright and early next morning and drove a short distance to the home of Stephen King, better known in New Zealand as 'the barefoot ecologist'. Stephen, a renowned botanist and scientist, was a dynamic character with a great vision: to re-forest areas of New Zealand cleared years ago by the settlers, with native trees and plants.

Stephen had a rugged, weathered appearance with long matted hair and a thick growth of beard. He always wore a traditional, heavy woollen Swan Dry smock and as his nickname

manuka - hardy, invasive bush that grows up to 3 metres tall. Called teatree by early settlers because its leaves were used to make tea.

suggested, he never wore shoes, not even in the city. He didn't criticize or ridicule our modern, materialistic way of life. He just pointed out that it is unsustainable, there is no need for it and that there are better alternatives.

Stephen showed us the view from the back of his house, an area of outstanding natural beauty he called 'his office'. In the distant hills the edge of Waipoua forest contrasted starkly with adjacent velvet smooth pastureland. He and a small group of fellow ecologists bought up strategic blocks of land across the country whenever they became available. We, his disciples, were fascinated and eagerly fired questions at him.

"Where do you get the money to buy so much land?"

"We don't really have all that much yet," Stephen told us. "Our original aim was simply to create a gentler, more natural boundary between national park forest and farmland, but nowadays there's such a need for native habitat we acquire land wherever we can. A small amount is bequeathed by converted landowners. Mostly the money comes from donations or is collected by the group members. A lot of the land is marginal, so little use for farming anyway."

"So how does what we're doing help re-forestation?"

"Well, you can't just go out there and plant baby kauri trees," said Stephen. "The soil is in a poor condition after years under crops or pine forest. First we need a good covering of bush. Manuka is ideal because it grows vigorously and it's invasive. It's one of the few plants that'll take over grassland unaided. Its roots fix nitrogen and begin improving soil quality immediately. Today you'll be collecting seed branches so we can sprinkle the tiny seeds directly into furrows. We leave the rest to nature."

We went back inside and were shown photo display cards that helped explain the work being done. There was a picture of a giant kauri tree Stephen called the phantom kauri, because only a handful of people knew of its whereabouts. The aerial photo showed numerous parasitic plants living on the massive tree including a two hundred year old *totora* tree growing in its crown.

"There's more variety in that one tree than in all the redwood forest of North America!" he proclaimed proudly.

We drove out to a site where the manuka was abundant and walked down to a steep ridge overlooking the national forest. Stephen pointed out how different shrubs and trees exploited different conditions of soil, water level and sunlight. Clusters of palms marked the banks of a hidden stream while bush prevailed where the soil was poor. Birds spread berry seeds in their droppings and tiny seeds from their feet and feathers, so around the base of large roost trees grew the greatest diversity of new plants. Everything had a reason for being in its own particular spot.

"Kauri saplings don't start to photosynthesise until they reach almost three metres, so they grow right through the manuka. When they develop foliage, they shade out the manuka and it dies back."

Stephen pointed out an area of land that had been under manuka for nine years and was showing healthy signs of forest plants pushing through: giant silver tree fern, rimu and native red pine. Then he showed us another area where new techniques were giving similar results in under five years.

We set to work stripping off branches from thickly growing manuka bushes and piling them on glass fibre sheet. As the branches dried the seedpods would open releasing the tiny seeds. At around 1pm we knocked off and walked back to the vehicles. On the way I chatted with Sonny, a Maori with long jet-black hair and a big muscular body covered in tattoos. He looked younger than his fifty-two years and told me he had seven grandchildren.

"Were your ancestors ever...er...cannibals?" I asked.

totora - parasitic fern like tree.

"Oh yes. Most of the Maori tribes were cannibals at some stage."

It was a terrifying thought. The war chants that tattoo-faced groups of Maori men performed in ceremonies were conducted in deadly earnest. Few other dancers had so much at stake or were so expressive.

As I left Waipoua that afternoon it was greatly encouraging to know that a small number of dedicated people were giving their all to preserve native wildlife and habitat for future generations.

Back in Auckland I sold my Chevette and teamed up with Frank, then, after loading up with supplies we headed south in Frank's Datsun. Wash Beach Caravan Park was home to a population of Kiwi pensioners and Chinese immigrants. The smell of Chinese cooking was wonderful but they weren't used to western style ovens and laid their fish straight on the oven grill above the element, where it baked on hard.

The weather was turning colder and in the morning a sharp layer of frost had settled on our tents. While Frank and I ate breakfast an old chap poked his head inside the cooker to find where the burning smell was coming from.

"Jesus bloody Christ," he exclaimed, "What a bloody mess! I'll have to tell Maggie about this."

And off he went to fetch Maggie. The two duly returned and Maggie took a look inside the oven.

"Bastards!"

She slammed the oven door shut and stepped back in disgust. Opening it again a moment later to confirm the horror she'd found inside, she took a closer inspection.

"Those dirty bastards. Pam 'll have to see this!"

And so it went until a small crowd had gathered inside the kitchen. A heated argument followed as to the appropriate course of action and a lot of very un-Christian things were said.

Frank and I missed the campsite lynching, instead making the all day return walk to Mount Tarawea. It was a glorious trek up through deciduous forest to the summit where we were rewarded with spectacular views of the surrounding hills and wide, still lakes. An eruption in 1886 ripped the mountain in half, leaving giant craters connected by a steep gorge. The scene of vivid red and yellow sulphur trails and volcanic ash resembled some desolate planet from another galaxy as we bounded down the steep scree slope to rejoin the trail.

A collection of hissing steam vents, bubbling chocolate coloured mud ponds and yellow sulphur pools known as Hell's Gate just east of Rotorua town, reminded the visitor that the violent past which created our world was still very much alive and simmering under a thin crust, right there in New Zealand. Rotorua was built over an active volcanic seam and the rotten egg reek of sulphur was picked up several kilometres away on the prevailing wind. Many of the town's buildings were heated by pipes sunk into the molten chaos below and steam clouds rose like silent ghosts from gardens and parks all around town, forming a spooky shroud of mist in the evening chill.

The local campsite had tent pitches that were heated naturally from underground and stayed warm all year round. There was a two stage jacuzzi - too bloody hot and just right, and for cooking, a steam heated hangi or underground oven. We bought a large shoulder of lamb and left it cooking all afternoon while we went sight-seeing at the nearby blue and green lakes. Algae flourished, fed by warm undercurrents of minerals, giving the water its distinctive colour.

Frank and I ate in the TV room above the kitchen that evening and the lamb, cooked to perfection, literally dropped off the bone. It was delicious. Unfortunately our neighbours, a young British couple cycling their way around New Zealand, enjoyed watching back to back soaps and game shows and after two nights of the same routine I'd had enough. The Simpsons were on the other side so when the commercial break came I switched over.

"Excuse me. We're watching the other channel," said the young woman in a commanding, school teacher voice.

"But the other channel's shite and you've been watching it all evening," I remonstrated.

"You can't just come in and switch channels when people are watching something else." exclaimed the television Nazi.

"No one ever gets a chance to watch anything else because you're always in here hogging the TV!"

"Turn it over!" she demanded.

"Oh for fuck's sake."

"Don't you swear at us," ordered the boyfriend, keen to get in on the act.

"Don't tell me what to do!"

As the situation degenerated into a playground slanging match they got up and walked out.

"We don't have to put up with his sort," muttered the boyfriend slamming the door.

Oh dear, that could have gone better. Poor Frank, alarmed by my brutish behaviour, kept pretty quiet for the rest of the evening.

Without warning, next morning Frank announced he was going back to the USA to join the Peace Corps. He told me he'd been trying to join for some time and had just received an e-mail saying there was a vacancy. The nights were becoming bitterly cold with a likelihood of miserable weather ahead and Frank, used to the warm Texas climate, wasn't at all happy about the prospect. He made me an offer I couldn't refuse on the Datsun and included our ferry tickets to South Island. I figured if the car shat itself I'd just have to hitchhike back to Auckland or catch the bus. Driving on past beautiful, still lake Taupo I spent the night at a picnic spot where the mighty Waikato River thundered deafeningly through a narrow gorge in a surging, foaming green mass.

The following afternoon I walked along the riverbank to a place where it broadened out and gave up much of its ferocious pace. Here the trout leapt from the gently swirling water, kingfishers screeched up and down the banks and herons stalked their prey amongst swathes of reeds.

There was something very special about New Zealand with its fierce Maori history, the staggering beauty of the landscape and the unconditional friendliness of its people. Even the young manager of the burger bar in Taurangi, when I was on my own and feeling low, treated me to a coffee. New Zealand was a tough place to make a living with its harsh winters and hot summers, and in the days of the early settlers it was essential to have a strong community spirit - it could be you next who fell on hard times. Abandoned by the Commonwealth, ignored by Europe and spitefully dealt with by the US over its refusal to allow an American nuclear base, that spirit was as important today as ever.

TONGARIRO CROSSING

I bought a ticket for an early bus ride to the base of Mount Tongariro and late afternoon pick-up from the other side of the mountain. Olwyn, manageress of Alpine Scenic Tours, was also our driver and a most friendly and knowledgeable courier. She took delight in sharing her considerable local knowledge with an Australian traveller in her early thirties and myself, as she steered the aged bus past open moorlands of imported Scottish heather.

"The haka," Olwyn explained, "is the ritual Maori war dance you see the All-Blacks perform before a match. It was first performed near here by a Wharitoa Chief on the island of Moti-O-Pai in lake Rotoairo, when he realised he'd escaped his enemies and wasn't going to be eaten."

More disturbingly, she told us, "There was a great battle here several hundred years ago when the Hautu tribe from the south-west invaded the Tu-Wharitoa tribal lands east of Mount Tongariro. The Tu-Wharitoa killed all the Hautu, cooked their bodies in an enormous hangi and ate them! They knew the bodies were properly cooked when mucus ran out of the nose and ears."

Olwyn told us she could trace her own family history back to when her great, great grandmother, Margaret S. Peace, sailed from Newfoundland to Auckland in 1864 with her family aboard their tiny vessel, Clara. Margaret Peace kept a detailed journal of the voyage of which Olwyn and her two sisters each had a copy.

The Peace family originally emigrated to Newfoundland from Scotland to take advantage of a promised 'bountiful fishing industry'. After several years of poor catches and mounting debts however, they decided it was time to leave the harsh Newfoundland climate for a fresh start in New Zealand

and together with two other large families, thirty-seven souls in all, they purchased the Clara with the last of their savings and prepared to set sail with a crew of seven.

The Clara was a small cargo ship, just thirty metres long and weighing approximately one hundred and twenty tons. Sailing was delayed by a day when tragically a little girl, one of fifteen children on board, died during the night and had to be buried. There were numerous encounters with dolphins and whales and the crew caught sea birds and turtles when food supplies ran low. From her account the captain was a bit of a drunkard and it was a miracle they made it to New Zealand at all: there were numerous accounts of conflict between the passengers and captain as they fended off his amorous advances toward the womenfolk.

Olwyn dropped us off at the start of the crossing, making sure we knew the pick up time and place. It would be bad news getting stranded on the mountain for the night in freezing conditions without proper kit. We began the seven hour mountain walk and the young Australian woman told me she worked as a community nurse on an Aboriginal settlement back in the Kimberly district of Australia. I was struck by the stark contrast between the seemingly downtrodden and dejected Aborigines and the spirited defiant Maoris.

"The Aborigines were a gentler, more spiritual people," she explained. "They were thrown off their land and their culture was brutally suppressed. The Maori on the other hand, were warlike and were never fully dominated. If an uneasy alliance hadn't been reached, they would probably all have died fighting the militia."

While I rested at a plateau above a huge secondary crater, my fitter companion stormed up towards the peak of Tongariro itself. I watched her steady progress up the steep scree and black lava face until she was lost against the massive cone-shaped volcano that towered into a perfect clear blue sky. A tiny ant toiling in shimmering midday heat. Other walkers arrived catching their breath, stared up at the majesty of the sacred volcano with its white sulphur collar and narrow plume of steam, and thought better of it.

Having recovered from the first stage I turned my back on the mountain and continued the walk, joining an Irishman called Ray and a guy called John Smith from Australia. Our awesome surroundings seemed to demand reverence and utter silence like some gigantic mausoleum but instead we chatted and joked as we slipped and stumbled in the caking grey clay of the great crater, wide as three football pitches end to end.

"What were your parents thinking of?" Ray asked John.

"It's really not such a big deal in Australia," he replied.

"I knew a girl in America once, called Sandra Gash!" exclaimed Ray. "Can you believe that? You'd think she'd have changed her name to Geysh or something."

Ray had worked on the Ariane space program for three years in Spain, designing experimentation equipment carried on satellites. An Irish rocket scientist.

"The women in Spain are beautiful," he told us with a longing sigh.

"But very religious and quite unapproachable," I added.

"Myt, myt. In Spain I fock like a prince!"

Ray continued to blow apart my stereotype of Catholic peasant farm-girl with moustache and hairy legs, watched jealously by an overbearing father.

"Spain is a very modern, advanced country. The climate is excellent and the people are lovely."

Ray was tall and slim with short cropped hair and scholarly glasses. He was quick-thinking, easy-going and had a terrific sense of humour, qualities that would make him an excellent travel partner. We scaled the crater's rim to a knife edge ridge before clambering down the other side to a pair of emerald green lakes far below. Then, after another break, it was a long gentle descent across the grass-covered mantle to our pick up point.

Ray didn't have any transport and we both wanted to explore South Island, so we set off in the red Bluebird the following morning. Wellington, on the southern tip of North Island, was built partly on a hillside with steeply sloping streets like San Francisco. The city was very exposed to the elements and while Ray spent the night in a dorm at Rowena's City Lodge, I slept outside in the car lashed by howling winds and torrential rain.

When I woke next morning I cooked porridge for breakfast over a little gas stove, not the easiest task inside a steamed up estate car loaded with gear, and afterwards sneaked in to use the showers. We spent some time exploring Wellington's impressive museum and sampled the city's pubs and clubs in the evening.

It was still dark when we arrived at Wellington docks early the following morning. Our ferry weaved its way through narrow Tory Channel and Queen Charlotte Sound avoiding pinnacles of rock like giant shark's teeth, to Picton port on the northern tip of South Island.

After some helpful suggestions from Picton tourist office we drove to the fishing village of Marahau, starting point for the three day Abel Tasman walk, and stayed overnight at The Barn backpackers. Inside The Barn was a very cosy living room warmed by a glass fronted wood stove and there was a relaxed, friendly atmosphere. Dagmar, the owner's German girlfriend, looked after the place while he was away. Her head was shaved perfectly smooth and to begin with it was hard not to stare at the lumps and bumps and her accentuated ears, slightly at odds with one another. There was no television so we relearned the art of conservation, talking well into the night with the only other guests, two Austrian students.

After breakfast Ray and I set off at a gentle pace on the long coastal trail, winding up and down through deciduous woodlands with Tasman Bay to our right, cutting across sheltered beaches and babbling streams. By late afternoon we arrived at Bark Bay, so called because tree bark from the area was once used nearby in the leather tanning process. With daylight fading we settled into the Department Of Conservation hut by the side of a broad tidal estuary, lit the woodstove and cooked supper. The spacious wooden huts were dotted along popular trails, making the experience more comfortable and enjoyable for the numerous visitors while limiting our impact on the environment.

We were joined by more walkers including a frail looking Japanese lad named Hiro and a young German student called Franziska. Hiro and I huddled round the stove by the light of a candle and when we'd got to know one another a little I asked him about his views on whale hunting.

"It is Japan culture to hunt whale," Hiro proclaimed. "Japan hunt whale many year."

"That's not what I've heard."

"Yes," said Hiro, quite animated. "For many year we hunt whale in Japan. It is our right!"

"But Japan is making many species of whale extinct. It's our right that we, and future generations should be able to see living whales swimming in the ocean."

Hiro pondered for a moment. His English was sketchy and it must have been difficult to make an argument which deep down he probably knew was indefensible.

"Do you love whale?" Hiro asked. It seemed that if I loved whales then my judgement must be clouded and irrational and therefore irrelevant. After all, everyone knows that whales are simply gigantic lumps of unthinking, unfeeling, blubber to be harvested like a shoal of mackerel.

"Yes, I love whales…and I respect their right to live."

Hiro hurriedly looked up the word in his dictionary.

"R – E – S – P?…"

"Yes…E-C-T. Like the song."

Hiro looked quizzical, then the light switched on behind his eyes and his face beamed.

"Ahh! In Japan we respect also. But we still want to eat whale. It is our culture."

I tried a different tack.

"Have you ever eaten whale?"

"No," Hiro laughed, mockingly. "Too expensive!"

"Only the very rich can afford to eat whale meat, yet you still defend whale hunting?"

Out came the dictionary again.

"D E – F – E?…"

"DEF-E-N-D"

"Ahh!"

The conversation went on like this for a while. Poor Hiro. Now he had a bit of a complex and went around the dimly lit hut asking the other occupants in turn,

"Excuse please. What you think of hunting whale?"

It was a good job I didn't discuss war crimes with Hiro...

ELEVENTH HOUR

In the morning I lent Franziska some waterproof clothing and together with Ray and Hiro we set off in light rain for Awaroa Bay, twelve kilometres further up the coast. The trail meandered round shingle bays and rushing river outlets through dripping woodland and ferns. Despite miserable weather the walk was exhilarating and thoroughly head clearing. When our small party arrived at the DOC hut in the early afternoon, we began drying our sodden clothes and warmed up in front of the stove.

One of the first requirements when living in the huts was light. Torch batteries didn't last very long and people sucked up to anyone who had the foresight to bring candles with them. The poor, shadowy light created a very different atmosphere that made people more reliant on one another for conversation and warmth.

At the large communal table there was heated discussion about environmental issues and I moved closer to listen.

"OK, our world's becoming a little overcrowded, but that's inevitable," said a heavily built American traveller. "...and global warming isn't so much a man made problem, it's simply part of a natural cycle."

"Bollocks!" said a Kiwi backpacker sitting opposite. "The biggest problem facing the world today is us humans. We're like a virus, killing the host we rely on and ultimately ourselves. No other species has so grossly overpopulated beyond the Earth's capacity to sustain it. No other species is so effective at destroying its environment and exterminating its fellow creatures. We are heading for environmental disaster and social collapse, my friend. We are quite simply, in our eleventh hour!"

There was uproar inside the hut. Questions were shouted from all directions and I thought he would be lynched but the

Kiwi pleaded for quiet and when order was restored he continued.

"There are far too many of us and we consume and pollute far too much. We've lost contact with nature, our roots. As a result we no longer respect or care about our planet or our own long-term future. We urgently need to break the cycle of greed and ignorance and start living within our means."

"Well that all sounds pretty gloomy," said a guy with a north London accent. "Shall I cut my wrists now? You're so critical of humanity and the way we live. Do you have a better plan for mankind?"

I was as anxious as anyone to hear the reply but was increasingly aware of a pungent smell like burning hair, permeating the hut. Just then Hiro returned from the outside toilet.

"Fire!" he yelled.

There was pandemonium. A sock had fallen onto the wood stove and the hut was rapidly filling with thick acrid smoke. The offending item was quickly removed and thrown outside. It was late and when the air had cleared we filed back inside and everyone went to bed. I guessed the world's problems wouldn't be solved that evening.

Fumbling about in darkness Ray, Franziska, Hiro and myself assembled our gear ready to leave the hut. We had to cross the wide estuary and needed to leave by 5.30 to avoid being swept away by the incoming tide. Boots and socks were removed and we set off for the opposite bank under misty moonlight. Wading through icy streams in the silt we crunched over millions of tiny sharp shells that cut our feet.

There was no way of knowing where the track continued on the other side because it was much too dark to see, but we eventually reached the bank. Ray pushed a large stick into the sand for a marker and we split into two groups to search. The pressure was on. Soon the tide would be racing in, everything would be under water and there wasn't time to make it back to the hut. Just as frigid seawater lapped at our feet Hiro spotted an opening through thick forest and undergrowth and we called Ray and Franziska to join us.

For the final stretch of our walk we were bathed in glorious sunshine. New Zealanders we had talked to told us that in summer, swarms of tiny biting sand flies were a nightmare and the trail was overrun with hordes of walkers. Right now though, the chill of autumn kept the sand flies at bay and we had the track entirely to ourselves.

By mid-afternoon we approached Tataranui bay from a long stretch of golden sandy beach at the edge of the forest and the end of our walk. We celebrated with a bottle of wine Ray had held back and cooked lunch while waiting for the daily taxi-boat pick up, then we said goodbye to Hiro as he was travelling on by bus. The aluminium boat fairly flew along, hugging the coastline in the flat calm sea and we passed by lazy seal colonies basking on small rocky islands, shags and cormorants.

After breakfast next morning we drove south and dropped Franziska at a petrol station on the outskirts of Blenheim. We had seen her wet through, shivering with cold and exhausted from hours of walking but never once heard her complain. She had grown on us and we were uneasy about leaving her to thumb a lift, but that was how she travelled. She'd already hitch-hiked her way right around North Island and a number of other countries.

"I keep getting picked up by old couples," she'd told us. "They always say they wouldn't normally give a ride to a hitch-hiker, but they don't want me being picked up by the 'wrong people'."

We watched from the edge of the forecourt as she stood by her rucksack, thumb in the air, long blonde hair billowing on the wind. Moments later a car drew up alongside her, there was a brief discussion, she tossed her Bergen in the back and was gone.

Ray and I arrived at the small town of Kaikoura on the north-east coast just as the sun was setting. I dropped my companion off at a backpackers and went to look for a quiet spot to park up and spend the night.

One of the main reasons visitors come to Kaikoura is to see whales close up from a boat. Sadly, along with sleeping in a comfortable bed, this activity was beyond my budget now, so while Ray went whale watching I enjoyed a pleasant beachcombing walk around Kaikoura peninsula.

A couple of hundred metres offshore a layered wall of lime and siltstone formed a safe platform for fur seals to rest and sun themselves. Sunlight gleamed off the bay and behind me in the distance, snow-capped mountains rose up into the sky, piercing their own halo of cloud. The weather was unseasonably warm. Few people were complaining but this time of year it should have been cold and wet. In a sheltered cove below the chalk cliff face I came across an adult seal in a really bad way, rocking its head back and forth with every breath. Pneumonia? Poison? Killer whale attack? I wondered what had killed the other three seals I found on my walk. I passed a school teacher with a party of thirteen year olds collecting small marine animals for study and she told me she would inform DOC about the seal.

"The sick ones often come here to die," she said. "The DOC will help if they can, but often all they can do is put them out of their misery."

The trail took me to a vantage point high on the grassy cliff top where I could see for many kilometres in all directions. The ocean was immense and flat calm, thought-provoking and beautiful. Wind and sea currents formed contrasting shades of deep blue and I watched tiny boats on the horizon with my binoculars, wondering if Ray was on one of them.

Arriving in Christchurch next day the city centre seemed grey and impersonal. Some of the pubs and bars had old photographs on their walls showing how the place had looked in the days of sailing ships and horse-drawn carriages. It was a great pity they had demolished much of the classic architecture to make way for unattractive, functional office blocks.

We visited the museum in an area townsfolk proudly named Canterbury because of its ornate red brick colleges, spires and archways. There was a fascinating exhibition on Antarctic exploration, Scott of the Antarctic, fragile early motorised snowmobiles and vehicles, but the highlight was an exhibition by German and French photographers in black and white. The variety of subjects, dates and places was astonishing: Jews being herded out of the ghettos, construction of skyscrapers on New York's 100th Street in the 50s, bridge building in China, all manual labour. Starving and desperate Tibetan refugees fleeing Chinese occupation, escaping over the Himalayas into Nepal. Destruction of videotapes at a checkpoint in Taliban-held Afghanistan. Stone throwing Palestinian youths facing Israeli tanks and heavily armed troops. Moslem women grieving over a mass grave in Yugoslavia. A young man in overcoat and tie dragging his baby daughters past a disabled Tiger tank in a shattered Dutch town. The pictures stirred all kinds of emotions. Life or death scenes, as real today as they were then.

One particularly striking image was taken in Japan, 1993. Research workers in a test laboratory, covered from head to foot in protective suits were separating a mother macaque monkey from her baby. There was an intense expression of suffering, loss and despair in the animal's eyes. Next to the photograph was this inscription:

'Since we have had weapons, animals have been our victims.

Since we have eaten, animals have been our food.

Since we have built societies, animals have been our companions and helpers.
Ultimately we too are only a certain kind of animal. We have to learn that our fellow creatures have some worth. We dominate them. We can use them. We can destroy them.

Every animal species that dies makes it less probable that we will live. Only when we consider their forms and voices can we remain human. Animals must become powerful in our thinking again, as in the time before their subjugation.'

Heading west out of Christchurch the road snaked up over Arthur's Pass, lying between snow-covered mountains. We hit the coast expecting to camp and cook food in darkness and bitter cold but a little north of Camerons village the manager of Tramways pub told us,

"Ah what the heck, my caravan's empty, you can sleep there tonight."

Visiting awesome Franz Josef Glacier further south along the coast the following morning, we walked beyond a rope barrier to get a better picture. I have seen glaciers before from a distance but standing just a few metres away directly in the path of the gigantic ice snake was an awesome experience. The whole mass creeps forwards about eight centimetres every week and everything in the way is either pushed to the side or squashed into the valley floor. A crystal clear river ran through a great cavern at the head of the glacier and blocks of blue-green ice as big as a truck broke off now and then, smashing to the ground with a resounding crash.

That evening Ray and I both squeezed into the back of the Datsun and we slept in a lay-by on the edge of misty lake Mapourika. That was, until something started to eat the car. Rats, mice, or maybe even possums were up around the engine compartment and from the sound of it, up to some serious mischief. I was terrified they might chew through the wiring or cooling hoses and leave us stranded.

"Ray," I hissed, jogging him through a thick layer of sleeping bag.

"Whah?" he moaned. He'd pulled the sleeping bag right up over his head against the cold and yanked the draw chord tight, leaving only a small breathing hole. In the moonlight he looked like an enormous maggot.

"Ray, wake up. Something's chewing through the wiring. We've got to stop it!"

The maggot sat upright, head still obscured as it realized the seriousness of the situation, and we listened in complete silence.

B L A R T!

For a moment there was silence again, then the maggot began convulsing in hysterics.

"Whatever it was," I said, "I think you killed it."

On the way to Wanaka town the Bluebird began to cough and splutter and finally conked out altogether on a long gentle incline. It was a cold gloomy evening spitting with rain as I got to work under the bonnet removing spark plug leads one by one, trying to isolate the fault. We'd been there just a few minutes when a silver-grey Lite Ace van pulled up ahead and the driver walked towards me. My mind was playing crazy tricks. I could have sworn I recognised him.

"Do you need any help?" asked the young man, golden dreadlocks peeping out from under a woollen beanie in South African colours.

"Don't I know you from somewhere?" I blurted out, immediately feeling stupid because he looked very puzzled. Of course I didn't know him and anyway, that thought was completely tangential to the problem at hand – my broken car. But as I looked at him...

"No, I do know you. Didn't I help you start your car when you broke down in Australia?"

He thought for a moment.

"Yeah. That's right...Hey that's incredible!"

It bloody was too. Mike was his name, from Germany. Liesel and I had pulled into a petrol station in the middle of nowhere and I went over to help him as he struggled under the bonnet of his Ford Falcon. The positive battery lead was loose so I asked him for a spanner to tighten it.

"I don't have any," said Mike, innocently.

"What, no tools?" I shrieked. "Your driving across the outback and you haven't got any tools?"

"I haven't got any tools because there isn't any point. I wouldn't know how to use them."

I secured the lead and the Falcon burst into life.

Back in the van I did my Victor Meldrew impersonation.

"I don't believe it. He's driving right across Australia and he hasn't got so much as a flamin' spanner!"

"Leave him alone," Liesel scowled. "He's cute!"

"Cute won't get him out of the shit when his car breaks down in the middle of the bloody bush!"

Mike laughed when he remembered how over the top I'd been.

"Sorry about that," I told him and we agreed to meet up later in Wanaka for a beer. By now the Datsun had cooled down and once again ran well enough to continue.

Matterhorn backpackers was fairly quiet this time of year and the young Irish manager very kindly let me use the facilities.

"Told ya," said Ray, beaming with pride. "Irish...salt of de earth!"

We were joined in the pub by fellow Matterhorn resident Ken from Derby, a sturdy chap with a round face and glowing red cheeks.

"I'm here for the hunting," he told us unashamedly. "All the animals here are introduced and they're tearing the shit out of the native forest and wildlife. But that doesn't justify what I do. I hunt because I love it!"

Much as I disagreed with his views on hunting I couldn't dislike Ken. He was rugged, good humoured and straight as a die and anyway, nothing I said could ever influence his opinion. In New Zealand, Ken liked to shoot deer. There were no natural predators and without some form of control the animals would overpopulate and steadily convert New Zealand's forest to heathland.

As we supped our beer Ken told us about an experimental DOC-sponsored possum cull he had been on. Unlike deer, it would be almost impossible to eradicate the possum because they simply climbed from tree to tree to escape hunters and were becoming more resistant to poison.

"The DOC marked out an area for the hunters to go through an' we went in a line blastin' anythin' that moved. I didn't enjoy it. It were a bloody slaughter. As we swept through it started a sort of momentum goin' and all the possums seemed to bunch up just ahead of us. It were a bit cruel an' all 'cos there were a lot of injured animals. Normal bullets pass straight through and if you don't hit 'em cleanly the animals just bleed to death."

Mike joined Ray and myself the following day in his little van and we drove to the ski centre of Queenstown, passing between spectacular snow-capped mountains that towered above us. Ray and I were preparing to tackle the famous Route Burn Track, a three day walk over the mountains with overnight stops at DOC huts. Our plan was to leave my car at the end of the trail near a village called Paradise, then Mike would drive us all the way round the foot of the mountain range to The Divide, our starting point.

Mike decided not to walk the whole way with us so we paid for his petrol and hoped he wouldn't change his mind. It might just work if our tired old vehicles didn't break down and the weather stayed fine. It had been snowing up in the mountains but the TV weather reports and staff at the DOC office in Queenstown told us there should be a three day 'clear window'. It didn't seem possible in the freezing drizzle of early winter with thick grey cloud overhead.

That evening Mike and I went to see Ray in Bumbles Backpackers, but for some reason the old woman who ran the place wasn't happy about our visit.

"So you've come to collect your friend and now you're leaving."

"Uh-hu."

She had a strangely abrasive nature but it was OK. We'd go in a minute.

"You've come to collect your friend and now you're leaving, with your friend. Yes?"

"For goodness sake, leave us alone", I thought, "We'll go in a minute. It's not a big deal".

"Yeah, that's right," and we turned back to talk with Ray.

"Alright. So you've come to..."

"Do you mind?" Ray exploded, "You're being extremely rude to my friends here!"

"The rules are..."

"I've read your rules and they're not breaking any. What's your problem?"

Nice one Ray! She really was an arsehole, but I kept my mouth shut. No sense in getting Ray kicked out as well.

Around lunch time the following day we drove up over a narrow mountain pass and down across broad marshy floodplains to Paradise, leaving my car as planned. Then we all piled in to Mike's van and drove almost 240 kilometres round the mountain to spend the night in the little town of Te Anau. As Ray moved his bags into the local backpackers the manageress and her Maori assistant kindly let Mike and I stay a while in their TV room.

"Thanks," I told them. "You're so different from the manageress from hell we met yesterday in Queenstown."

"Bumbles!" they exclaimed in unison. "That'll be Pam. She's got quite a reputation."

"Obviously the product of an unhappy childhood," Ray mused.

"And a failed marriage," speculated Mike.

"And a failed moustache waxing," Ray added.

Mike drove us to Milford Sound early the following morning along a breathtaking route of mountains, deep gorges and broad river valleys. The sea was absolutely still giving a perfect mirror image of snowy peaks across the bay and a clear blue sky, at one of New Zealand's most photographed sites. After a breakfast of porridge it was back up the steeply winding road through a crumbling tunnel in the mountainside, to The Divide. Mike joined us for the first day's walk.

In summer the mountains thronged with tourists making it almost impossible to get a place in the huts but now, out of season, we had the whole area to ourselves. The weather was usually dreadful in June with annual rainfall almost nine times higher than London. The day before we set off it had snowed hard on Harris Saddle, a pass 1,400 metres above sea level and roughly mid point of the walk, but now the forecast was spot on and we were bathed in glorious sunshine.

Climbing up through temperate forest, we occasionally paused near gullies or clearings to rest and look out across a great valley at the neighbouring ridge of mountains. A narrow waterfall cascaded down a sheer rock face from far above our heads, spray saturating our clothes as we passed. We reached a plateau where the track wound through an eerie, fairytale forest of gnarled, stunted silver birch, boughs and trunks draped in thick green moss dripping with moisture. The track was marshy under foot, cut here and there by rippling brooks of icy water. In a small clearing sheltered in the lee of the great mountain, we spent our first night in a basic but comfortable wooden cabin known as Mackenzie hut.

Mike left us early next morning and the trail snaked steeply up towards Harris Saddle. Leaving behind the distinct tree line we continued up through a wide band of tussock and low shrubs, before entering the final layer of snow-covered peaks streaked with landslides and rocky outcrops. The sky was a perfect blue, not a cloud in sight, giving a tremendous feeling of space and clarity.

There was a sharp dry chill in the air approaching the Saddle and as we carefully picked our way to the top of the pass over a layer of crunchy frozen snow, we knew we had been extraordinarily lucky with the weather. Looking along our ridge and down the valley the sky was so clear we could see all the way to the ocean, nearly thirty kilometres away. Ray and I stopped for lunch on a hillock overlooking an icy crater lake at the highest point of our walk. On the other side of the lake was a steep scree and rock slope leading to the summit: the eerie silence was broken occasionally by the call of choughs and the echoing clatter of rock slides.

Perched on the mountainside in the next valley, Falls hut was a sturdy, modern timber building resembling a Val D'Isere ski chalet, with balconies and huge viewing windows. There were comfortable dorms with inviting wooden bunks but we rolled out our sleeping bags close to the woodstove in the spacious living room in order to gaze out at the awesome panoramic view. Stars sparkled in the clear moonlit sky and the mountain towering above us stretched all the way down to the valley below, where a glistening river meandered back towards Milford Sound.

Our shins and knees ached as we clambered steeply down into the valley the following morning. As we reached the tree line the sky clouded over, it began to drizzle and the trail's end came all too soon.

We drove on to the city of Dunedin paying a visit to Otago museum, and in the natural history department found a section devoted to New Zealand's recently introduced species. The settlers played God when they arrived at the islands, thickly covered in forest and inhabited only by birds and cannibals. They chopped down most of the forest to make way for agriculture and introduced animals that reminded them of home. Some of the exhibits were starting to look a bit moth-eaten: a stuffed family of white tailed deer with patches of fur missing, goats, dogs, rabbits, cats, rats, stoats and weasels in awkward poses standing unnaturally close to one another.

Another display showed how the tectonic plates moved millions of years ago: Australia with its smooth barked, high crowned karri trees and marsupial mammals, breaking away from Indonesia, and New Zealand inhabited only by birds, with coarse barked kauris like gigantic oaks, from Polynesia. That's why the two islands originally had no flora or fauna in common. The theory is that New Zealand became cut off from the mainland before mammals and reptiles had a chance to populate the land. Birds that arrived earlier eventually lost the power of flight because there were no predators to escape from and food was abundant and easy to get to.

Entering the section on native birds it seemed so sad that the first albatross I encountered were dead and stuffed. Tragically, the albatross is now critically endangered because of long line tuna fishing. In a disturbingly long, neat row of glass display cases were a number of stuffed birds, ranging from a tiny flightless wren to large wading birds, representatives of entire species made extinct by the settlers and the creatures they brought with them. Many others like the kakapo, a near flightless parrot weighing up to 2½ kilos and the kiwi, New Zealand's national emblem, are now critically endangered.

We left the museum and drove to a beach a few kilometres out of town on Otago Peninsula where a small colony of yellow eyed penguins regularly emerged from the sea. The birds swim around fifteen kilometres out to an area off the continental shelf rich in fish and squid and when gorged, they swim back home again. The species is endangered with only three thousand breeding adults left in the world. They are very shy and easily scared off, so we were horrified to see dog walkers strolling nonchalantly along the beach at the critical moment. We waited for things to quiet down in a specially constructed hide and at dusk our patience was finally rewarded when the first of the unusual birds hopped out of the sea, landing neatly on some rocks at the far end of the beach. Out of the frigid sea, their ideal element and now heavy and clumsy on land, it was just possible to see their feet change colour from pale orange to bright red as they became engorged with blood. This helped prevent them overheating as they slowly made their way up a steep grassy hill a few hops at a time, to their nesting grounds.

Sadly, it was time for Ray to leave New Zealand. His contract in Spain was over and now he was going home to "rainy Derry", so I dropped him off at Dunedin airport, shook his hand and wished him luck.

The Datsun was playing up badly and I had to keep stopping to let her cool down. Pulling over to give the engine a break in an area resembling the sweeping treeless hills of the Scottish highlands, I watched a family of hawks attacking a lapwing in a neighbouring paddock. The adults wouldn't kill it outright because they were training their young. The young birds didn't know how and kept flying away, but their interest was triggered every time the lapwing tried to escape. Nature can be very cruel and their attacks were relentless.

With the help of the registrar of births, deaths and marriages in Christchurch, I finally tracked down my aunt and cousin. To my dismay, they had moved from Christchurch several years ago and were living in Dunedin, about 500 kilometres back south where I'd just come from.

My Uncle John emigrated to New Zealand when he was twenty-four, desperate to escape escalating unemployment and poverty in Glasgow, and he became a Jehovah's Witness some years later with his wife, Heather. Whenever I asked my dad about them he always told me,

"You don't want to go there son, their religious views are extreme. Very strange people, son."

Now I was here in New Zealand my curiosity was thoroughly aroused. I couldn't ignore the strong feeling of family bonds and I set off early, back to Dunedin. Luckily I found an auto wrecker in a small town along the way and set about replacing most of the ignition system. (For the spanner and sprocket minded, it turned out to be the carbon impregnated fibre lead from the contact breaker to the breaker body, an essential but piffling little component that the workshop owner let me have for free). That finally cured it and I quickly phoned my rather surprised aunt to tell her I was on my way.

Far from religious fanatics, my long lost relatives turned out to be very warm and welcoming and I was so glad I had made the effort to find them. I stayed for two days in my aunt's bungalow and the subject of religion would never have come up at all if I hadn't mentioned it myself, out of curiosity. They were not so unlike other Christians, with just a couple of quirky differences. I met the whole family over supper and a few glasses of surprisingly good home brewed beer, and was touched by their generosity and kindness.

In a quiet moment my cousin told me, "In his later life, my father suffered from bouts of depression. Towards the end he couldn't cope and spent his last years in a nursing home. Maybe that's what your father found so difficult to deal with. He remembered dad in happier times as a strong and dependable brother, a character, bit of a joker even, so he invented an excuse not to keep closer contact with the rest of us."

I was heartbroken. Poor Uncle John. I wished I could have met him. It must have been so hard for my own father too.

Back again on North Island, remote White Bay was racked by a cold east wind. A narrow horseshoe-shaped wall of rock had been drilled through by the action of waves and sand to form a massive archway. Clambering down to get the best possible photograph I stood precariously just above violently surging surf. Back on the mainland a dogfish and a huge conger eel lay amongst debris washed up on the sandy shore. As I left, a lone surfer came down to the deserted bay and paddled out into the icy foaming water. Tough as nails, these New Zealanders.

In Napier on the edge of Hawke Bay, I admired the Art Deco architecture for which the town is famous. Paintings of the Art Deco / Bauhaus era were stark and heavily stylised. People were depicted caricatured and angular, having depth and form but lacking human detail, while buildings were cold and grotesque.

In 1931 a devastating earthquake completely levelled Napier. Architects began with a clean slate and rebuilt the town entirely in the style of the period - Art Deco. Not since the ancient Egyptians had a people expressed their character so boldly and vividly in their buildings, their clothing and their art. Most of the central facades still had tremendous character and were extremely colourful with bright pinks, blues and yellows. Much of the residential area was built on a hillside where the houses had walls of overlapping timber slats, ornate balconies, shuttered windows and window boxes overflowing with flowers. I left Napier as the sun was setting and followed the coast road for a while. On my right the clouds formed a gigantic ceiling of fiery red, leaning over at an angle of forty-five degrees above the sea and trailing off to the horizon. I reached an area of forested hills, parked up and slept in the car near lake Waikaremeana.

When the sun rose next morning it started to burn through cold mist that clung like a ghost to the lakeshore. The place truly looked as if it must be the home of the Maori spirits. An assault course of limestone caves had been eroded into the lakeside ridge, and following a trail that led all the way through

I emerged at magnificent tranquil Aniwaniwa falls. The falls were in two tiers roughly the height and width of a two storey house, surrounded by thick deciduous forest. At the nearby visitors' centre I learned about local history.

Te Kootie Rikirana was born in Gisbone in 1830. In 1865 he was wrongly accused of being involved in the Hau Hau rebellion against the colonial government and deported without trial to the lonely Chatham Islands, far out in the Pacific. In 1869 he escaped, commandeering a ship and sailing it back to Poverty Bay from where he was originally banished.

Enraged at the injustices committed against him and his people, Te Kootie murdered thirty-three Europeans and thirty-seven Maori collaborators. Fleeing to Urewera forest, a £1,000 reward was placed on his head but he always managed to stay just ahead of the militia. On one occasion he relaxed enough to take part in a horse race with the local tribe, but on hearing the militia were close by he escaped by swimming the horses across lake Waikaremeana. He left the following letter in a conspicuous place for his pursuers.

> 'Sirs,
> A word from me to you. This murderous purpose of yours is like a rat rooting dung. Send a man to tell me to come into the open where we can fight. That would be fair.
> I sent two messengers to you in peace but you attacked them treacherously. It seems to me there is more to be gained by men from cultivation of crops then by making war. I have no interest in this lust you have for battle but beware I should choose to fight.
> That is all I have to say. If you dislike these words what does it matter. All the worse for you.
> From your enemy.'

Te Kootie was never caught and in a bid to tie up loose ends and prevent him becoming a martyr, the authorities finally pardoned him. On hearing this, enraged militiamen burned crops and villages where they suspected Te Kootie had hidden and that winter many starved to death as a result.

In museums and art galleries around New Zealand there were many paintings of the lost Maori tribes. Thankfully there had been some excellent artists in the early days of the settlers and the likenesses of fearsome tattooed warriors and women tattooed only on the chin and lips were beautifully detailed and lifelike.

I followed the winding gravel track over the last wooded hills surrounding the mystical lake until suddenly the road ran straight and tarmac smooth, dropping down to flat arable plains.

The following morning the road to Hamilton was completely deserted and if I hadn't stopped to pick up the lone hitchhiker there was no telling how long he'd have to wait in the biting cold. Mick was in his mid-fifties but his weathered features, huge white beard and shaggy, matted white hair made him look a decade older. Despite his filthy clothes, (and I hope he'll forgive me for saying he smelled pretty ripe) he looked for all the world like Father Christmas, the genuine article.

Of all the people I'd met on my trip, Mick was the most serious traveller. Hitching, stowing away on ships and jumping trains around the world, he had been travelling for over thirty years and knew no other way of life. He slept in woods or by the roadside in a sleeping bag and the clothes he wore, but he would always accept an offer of food, shelter and occasionally clothing.

"That's how I get to meet people," he told me. "They give me things I need and in return I tell them about my travels. It's hardly a fair trade but they always seem quite happy with it."

Mick was making his way north to beat the worst of the cold, wet season before heading back down to Queenstown for work as guess what?...a department store Father Christmas. Dropping Mick off at a small village to visit some friends, it wasn't long before I picked up my last hitch-hiker, a heavily built Maori in his early twenties.

I wasn't sure what to make of my new passenger and no matter how I tried, I couldn't seem to strike up a conversation even though I had so many questions about the Maori way of life past and present and his views on land reforms. We spent most of the journey in uneasy silence and I was glad when we finally reached Hamilton and he got out.

In the city of Hamilton I felt cold, tired and self-conscious about not having showered for several days. Biddie Mulligan's was named during the current Irish pub epidemic, probably before the new owners realised that Biddie Mulligan had been a traitor to the Irish cause, siding with the English. The Gabriel Hounds were playing live with flutes, accordions and violins, and it wasn't long before some of the regular customers were up dancing. As the pace picked up and the pub filled it was great to watch them. Celtic fever was sweeping the planet with a resurgence of traditional Irish music and dancing spurred on by the recent Riverdance phenomenon. The dancers spun in circles, in pairs and groups of four. Finally, a young Japanese tourist was dragged protesting onto the floor and whirled around like a rag doll by buxom ladies, until he had made a sufficient fool of himself.

Back in Auckland I found the address of a young couple Julie from Melbourne had given me before I left Australia. Originally from the UK, they were incredibly warm and welcoming and let me stay at their flat for my last few days in New Zealand. I sold the Bluebird to a group of girls for around £150 confident that if they were gentle she'd get them around OK.

MEXICO and the USA

MEXICO

There were no direct flights from Auckland to Mexico so I boarded an eleven hour flight to LA. There was a five hour wait in the airport followed by another three and a half hour flight down to Mexico City. Arriving late at night jet lagged and knackered, I spent my first night in a cheap seedy hotel in Revolucion district not far from the city centre, with cockroaches scampering over my bed sheets and face. I didn't mind their little feet so much as the ooze of squashed bodies against my skin when I rolled over.

Rising early I moved into nearby 'roach free Casa de los Amigos, a clean, safe, Quaker owned guesthouse with a surprisingly warm and friendly atmosphere that became my home for the next couple of days.

Mexico City was hectic with visible poverty, decline and a constant danger from pickpockets and muggers prowling among bands of unemployed young men. It felt safe enough in the city centre though, and walking back to the hostel that evening I stopped off at a municipal garden where a large crowd had gathered to listen to competing bands of musicians playing popular Mexican music. Each group of up to a dozen wore matching costumes, tight waistcoats with rows of polished silver buttons, enormous shoulder pads and masses of swirling braid, large matching sombreros and painfully tight toreador pants. They strutted about like bullfighters, carrying acoustic guitars, trumpets, violins and accordions and it seemed the posing and posturing were even more important than the music itself. I mingled with the audience for quite some time waiting for them to start up but all they gave us was little tantalising bursts so I figured I'd already missed the main event and left.

I was keen to learn about the early civilisations, what their cities looked like in their heyday and what happened to them, so the following day I visited the excellent Museo de Antropologia.

A wandering tribe of Aztecs founded the city of Tenochtitlan in 1325 AD. They settled there by a lake when, as the legend goes, an eagle was spotted standing on a cactus, eating a snake - a sign that the people would be safe there.

Hernan Cortes, after devastating the Aztec people with muskets and cannon, levelled their great temples and in 1521, began building the city of Mexico on top of the ruins. The ground was marshy and had to be drained and filled in. Since then it has proved to be completely unsuitable for such a large city and now the grandiose churches, cathedrals, hotels and state buildings, lean terribly from subsidence.

It was sad to see the roof and pillars of the great Catedral Metropolitana held together inside by thousands of scaffold braces in a vain attempt to postpone the inevitable. The effort and workmanship that had gone into its construction was incredible and I sat in awe gazing up at the apse. Gilded statues of the saints surrounded by paintings depicting their deeds formed a great archway, and in the centre a dazzling golden sunburst was bordered by skilfully carved marble pillars.

One church near the museum of Templo Mayor actually made me feel dizzy because its geometry was so chaotic. My eyes told me that a gigantic steel frame standing in the centre was perpendicular, but the stone walls and pillars leaned heavily away from it. While my mind was dealing with that, the floor sloped steeply downwards from the door, so I found myself staggering about inside like a drunk.

The Mayans were astonishingly advanced architects producing breathtaking, geometrically perfect structures with only hard stone tools. They were great farmers too, growing a variety of crops on built-up blocks of land. Fertile soil was layered on the raised plots and conifers planted around the edges to prevent it from washing into surrounding irrigation channels. The trees provided a windbreak for more fragile crops and irrigation was controlled by a complex system of sluices.

...But the Pre-Columbians were also incredibly bloodthirsty, none more so than the Aztecs who believed it was essential to appease the rain and sun gods with daily human sacrifice. So many victims were taken from neighbouring conquered tribes that when Cortez arrived with only a small number of soldiers, he easily mustered an army of over forty thousand natives to fight the hated Aztecs.

Fifty minutes' bus ride from Mexico City, The great city of Teotehuacan was one of the largest and most well-preserved ruins of the Mayan period. Built on a flat plain surrounded by arable land, pyramids were arranged either side of a broad highway more than three kilometres long, with the massive sun temple at its head. On top of each pyramid once stood a parallel sided sacrificial temple, painted inside with murals and adorned with complex carvings of birds of prey, animals and gods. Eagles with tearing beaks and talons, panthers and dragons with deadly jagged fangs.

To consecrate the sun temple on its completion, it is believed that a staggering sixty thousand human sacrifices were made. That's equivalent to the entire population of the city itself at that time. During sacrifice, the heart was often torn out of the victim and placed, still beating, on a ceremonial urn. I shivered with revulsion when I climbed to the top and saw an urn in the shape of a jaguar lying on its back, face turned towards the victim, and tried to imagine what it must have been like when the Mayans lived there.

The entire city centre was dedicated to worship, sacrifice and matters of state. The suburban area would have been enormous with stone and timber dwellings, public buildings and farms stretching for many kilometres in all directions. Walking over steep steps between two large pyramid temples, suddenly facing me was a row of demonic dragon's head gargoyles each as big as a fridge. The frightful beasts with piercing black eyes and vicious teeth seemed to jump out from their pyramid base. In a time when superstition and mysticism dominated people's lives, such figures struck terror into the hearts of the Mayans and their captured enemies.

On the bus back to Mexico city I sat beside Mo, a primary school teacher from Ireland.

Mo and I travelled together to Puebla city next day and moved into budget priced Hotel Avenida in the city centre. The outskirts of Puebla were very ugly, with large open refuse tips between clusters of crumbling whitewashed houses where the poorest of the poor foraged for anything salvageable. Lines of shanty dwellings made from bits of corrugated iron and polythene sheet stood on the banks of drainage ditches, threatening to tumble in when the rains came.

By stark contrast the city centre was boastfully ornate, clean and bright, unchanged from the turn of the century during Mexico's prosperous era. Unfortunately a number of buildings were off limits with large cracks in walls and fallen masonry, the result of an earthquake just two weeks earlier. There were no tower blocks, factories or superstores and broad streets were arranged in an easily negotiable grid pattern. Most town houses had lavish courtyards accessed from the main street. Some had plain, high walls painted yellow, red, or blue, with wrought iron balconies and shuttered windows on the upper floors. Others were tiled with bright patterns, sporting detailed masonry work and carved stone window arches that might have been more at home in a church or cathedral.

Strolling the city centre that evening we heard loud dance music coming from a club, so we approached gingerly and the manager ushered us upstairs to have a look inside. It was oldies' night and there was no one under fifty except for the band. Chairs were quickly rearranged and places cleared for the new guests as we nodded and smiled politely to our new friends. Mo had already picked up a little Spanish and was busy making small talk with her neighbour while a constant procession of suitors invited her to dance. I had my own self-appointed dance instructress, a smallish lady in her mid fifties, who clearly wanted to dance but didn't have a regular partner. After a couple of beers I felt relaxed enough to give it a try and before long they couldn't keep us off the dance floor.

Next morning, Mo and I made a day trip to the small town of Cholula, around thirty kilometres west of Puebla. During the Mayan era there had always been a shortage of water in the region and it was recently discovered that large numbers of children aged six and seven had been sacrificed to appease the rain God, Tlalac. Here, the Spanish invaders committed the ultimate act of destruction. First they decimated the native population and ransacked their ancient pyramid temple. Then, they built a church on top of the ruins and tortured the remaining natives, forcing them to take up Catholicism. In actual fact before the Spaniards arrived the original temple had already been built over, three times in succession.

Late in the afternoon we caught a bus for Oaxaca city, arriving after dark. We took a wrong turning and got lost because of my hopeless navigation and by the time we found the *zocalo* most of the cheaper guesthouses were already full. Mo was determined to find a particular hostel she'd read about in her guide book and was getting more wound up by the minute. Trouble was, she had a very strong personality and always liked to make the decisions. I had long since lapsed into passenger mode, following her up and down familiar looking streets like a puppy. I suggested we split up and settle for anything we could find and she boiled over.

"That's bloody great," she yelled, a small crowd of bystanders turning to listen. "All you've done is get us lost, and now you let me down and go swanning off by yourself!"

zocalo - central square.

After she'd vented her fury she relented a bit. I felt pretty hurt and inadequate for a while. Then I thought, "Hang on a minute. I'm almost at the end of my trip, I've been travelling for fourteen months and I've seen and done some pretty amazing things. I may not always get there in style but I must have been doing something bloody right!"

Eventually, we found the Danish Youth Hostel and moved in for the night. It was a grubby place full of noisy teenagers experiencing sex, drugs and alcohol for the first time. Mo chose it for the social scene but neither of us really had much in common with the regular clientele.

Early in the morning a group of lads came in pissed and kept everyone awake singing Bob Marley songs, very loudly and very badly. Another lot arrived some time after, laughing and shouting until daylight. I left later that morning and moved into the hostel Isabella Rosa a few blocks away, quieter, cheaper and with laid-back, friendly residents.

Tom from the States was a very sociable young hippie and we wandered around town that evening in the warm, still air. In the back of a little pet shop on Independencia, Los Simpsons were showing on TV. I hadn't seen the show for weeks and it seemed even funnier in incomprehensible Spanish. We ambled into the large church of Santo Domingo with gilt pillars and woodwork, but stopped just inside the entrance - a wedding was going on inside. How would we like it if an uninvited hippy and scruffy backpacker wandered in on our big day?

These fantastically ornate Mexican churches demonstrated a powerful devotion to faith. No expense was too great, no detail too complex. It was as if the architects wanted to mesmerise the congregation into a state of beguiled acceptance. As we gazed in awe it was easy to forget that mere humans created them. Tourists wined and dined in the open restaurants around the zocalo while locals took a gentle evening stroll in their extended family groups. On the pavement in front of a row of civic buildings squatted around twenty Indian women with brown skin, round faces and long, jet black hair, dressed in traditional brightly coloured shawls. Evicted from their farms by the ruling Mexican landowners they had been begging during the day with their small children and now rolled out sleeping mats and blankets for the night.

Next morning I went with Mo to Monte Alban, spectacular Zapotec ruins dating from 300 BC to 1200 AD. The temple complex was built on a hill overlooking Oaxaca town and cultivated land that trailed off to a ring of surrounding mountains. By late lunch time the grey-blue haze shrouding the mountains was burned away by a blazing sun and now, towering clouds formed rapidly over the distant ranges, sharply contrasting with the deep blue sky and stark angular Zapotecan pyramids at either end of the plateau. On the western side of the holy city stood two parallel walls, remnants of the ritual ball game once played by teams of warriors to decide matters of state. On the east side was a large tomb fronted by stone tablets bearing caricatured carvings of gods and rulers standing on the skulls of sacrificial victims.

In this spectacular setting I tried to imagine warriors dressed in elaborate bird or jaguar costumes, and high priests wearing long flowing robes and headdresses of brightly coloured feathers. All pumped up into a state of frenzy on a cocktail of drugs made from local plants, they prepared their victims for the terrifying ritual of sacrifice, illuminated by flaming torches under a blood-red sky.

Next day in the huge, bustling, covered market by the second class bus station, every imaginable item of fruit, spice, vegetable, clothing and hardware was on sale. Butcher's stalls strung with skinned rabbits, goats, massive bulls heads with bulging eyes and naked poultry dangling from hooks in the sweltering afternoon heat, somehow reminded me I was hungry.

As I passed a food stall a girl of around eighteen blocked my way ushering me to sit at her table, and minutes later she brought me a spicy chicken enchilada followed by a large glass of lemonade to cool my searing taste buds. Neither of us spoke the other's language but she managed to tell me her name was Laura and this was her mother's eatery. We tried several lines of conversation that only ended in confusion so I finished my meal and asked for the bill. She seemed to be saying it was on the house, then she asked where I was going next on my journey.

"San Francisco and then home," I sighed.

Laura gestured to herself, "Take me."

Slightly embarrassed I left a handful of coins on the table, excused myself and left.

That afternoon I explored art galleries and a museum dedicated to the ancient civilisations of the region. It had been fashionable locally for people, especially those destined for life in the priesthood, to have a high, sloping forehead. Carvings depicted children lying down with heavy stone callipers placed on their heads to deform the skull into the required shape. Who knows how long they must have spent each day subjected to this unbearable torture.

Back at Isabella Rosa I went for a quick wash in the shower room before bed and met a young Californian woman called Linda brushing her teeth, mouth full of foam. She was exhausted having just endured a nineteen hour bus ride.

I overslept next morning and missed my bus for Mazunte village and the turtle sanctuary I wanted to visit on the west coast. Linda was up and about and asked me if I'd like to join her for breakfast. In the small local market she demonstrated how you could eat a healthy nutritious meal in Mexico for less than the price of a newspaper, if you knew what to look for and how to ask for it. On our return Linda broke into easy conversation with Enrice, one of the young hostel managers. Enrice pointed to a framed picture of a beautiful ruined church and neighbouring convent on the office wall, telling her in Spanish,

"This is really worth a visit and it's quite easy to get to. Tourists seldom go there and it's not mentioned in the guide books."

He told Linda the legend of how the place fell into disrepair and she translated for me.

In around 1700 the Spanish settlers began constructing a church at the trading outpost of Cuilapan, but the town ran out of money due to its remoteness and the building lay unfinished. In desperation, so the legend goes, the local priest and congregation made a pact with the Devil, who promised to help finish the roof. He told them, "If you can complete the roof before the cock crows tomorrow morning, I will help you finish the church free of charge. But if you fail to keep this deadline you must forfeit your souls." The priest agreed, work continued through the night and it looked as if they would easily meet the deadline. Seeing this, the Devil plucked a feather from the cockerel's tail to make it crow early, then he snatched up the souls of the priest and settlers and with that, the unfinished roof collapsed.

Linda and I caught a *collectivo* taxi to the site. Enrice was right, it was a wonderful place, even more dramatic in ruins then perhaps if it had been finished. The long roofless nave was fronted by two stone towers with spiral staircases leading into empty space. At the end of the low brickwork shell stood a modest, more recent, domed church and adjacent this was a large courtyard surrounded by the two storey convent made up of small adjoining cells. Complex murals depicting local scenes were just still visible in the stairwells but the plaster walls were mildewed and crumbling and they could not last much longer. One of the upper corridors opened out onto a large flat roof and we stood there in the sunlight gazing at the beautiful green hills,

collectivo - taxi shared by several people.

orchards and cloudscapes around us.

Linda was tough and independent, having hitch-hiked right across Alaska on her own and more recently from New York to LA. Four years of committed forest protesting, arrested three times for the cause before the age of nineteen, nowadays her idea of entertainment was to go camping and hiking for a long weekend. She had never owned a car and cycled everywhere back home in Santa Cruz.

I was crazy about her and desperately wanted to say what I was feeling, how I'd felt since I first met her in the shower room but didn't dare, terrified it would only drive her away. I made up my mind that regardless of what happened, I would try to be grateful for whatever time we spent together.

Leaving the church we wandered through town until a man in his early thirties, slightly the worse for drink, invited us into the front yard of his unfinished house for refreshments. Andreas and Linda talked for ages and occasionally Linda paused to translate a little for me. Andreas declared his admiration for her saying if she and I weren't together, he'd ask her to marry him. His wife looked on with disdain as she and two of their young children pottered about the yard among the chickens. The two beers Andreas quickly drank rekindled last night's hangover and he swayed on his bench as he tried to focus on Linda, eyelids drooping heavily.

"Beware of drunks on the streets when you walk around town!" he warned us with a sternly waved finger. We were more concerned about the drunk facing us and decided, amid great protests from Andreas, it was time to move on.

TURTLE SANCTUARY

In the morning I packed early ready to leave. I needed to get underway, occupy my mind and not mope around thinking about Linda but I was anxious to say goodbye. She was milling about too and told me,

"I can't decide whether or not to go to Mazunte with you."
I had no idea she was even thinking about it but to my astonishment she agreed and we set off together.

Everyone felt sick on the bus. It was raining too hard to open the windows and the stifling humidity and stale breath combined with endless pitching and rolling around hairpin curves up and down mountains, took its toll. Linda really had it bad. In between stomach cramps she'd been giving me my first serious Spanish lesson, but it's not a good idea to peer over a book when your bus is lurching about all over the place and I struggled to hold onto my breakfast. Despite the discomfort, I saw through steamed up windows that the whole countryside was completely coved with a lush greenness, always ready to move back into any scarred or exposed area the moment people left off. All the big trees were gone but there was a sort of low jungle of broad waxy-leafed shrubs, giant ferns and vines that flourished in intense all year round heat and frequent heavy rain.

After seven hours we finally got off at Pochutla town and caught a canvas backed collectivo truck for the last few kilometres to Mazunte. We were dropped outside a tiny cluster of huts, in the middle of a deluge so heavy it was hard not to breath in water. There was no looking round for pretty beach huts or checking out the cheapest prices. A few enquiries led us to the home of a young couple and their three kids. Linda refused to haggle with the owners, Hernan and Maria, over the price.

"They're poor enough already," she said.

We were shown to our room and I felt a little guilty as the children's things were hurriedly turfed out to make space. The rain eased a little and after a short stroll to see mammoth waves pounding up the steep, white sand beach we sat on the front porch, while our hosts relaxed in hammocks under a thatched roof in the courtyard kitchen. Terriblé, the family's gorgeous brown and white terrier puppy, lay belly up asleep on my lap while I struggled to read a Sesame Street book in Spanish to Hudit aged eleven and her younger brother José. Rain dropped heavily from the roof's edge and Linda leaned over me from behind with her hands on my shoulders, to translate. I was truly in heaven.

Early next morning we made the short walk to the Centro Mexicano de la Tortuga and were introduced to Rodrigues, one of the permanent workforce. He showed us around and set us to work cleaning a large concrete holding pen of turtle pooh and algae. It wasn't pleasant but as Linda said,

"We can't just cherry-pick the best jobs."

We had missed the egg-laying season for green and rarer ridleys turtles: all night watches over nest sites, egg collection for incubators and the glorious mass return of turtle babies to the ocean - a frantic, deeply rewarding time from Rodrigue's account. The sanctuary was on tick-over with a skeleton staff but there was still plenty of work to be done. When we finished cleaning, our tank was filled ready to accommodate a Kemp's ridley turtle who had just lost most of her left rear flipper in a shrimp net.

Kemp's ridleys are critically endangered with fewer than 1,500 surviving today. Rodrigues told us that they breed on only one beach further up the west coast of Mexico and are susceptible like other turtle species to drowning in fishing nets and ingesting plastic bags, debris and long line fish hooks. He reminded us that picturesque Mazunte beach had once been a slaughtering ground for the gentle turtle.

Four of us struggled up the beach with the 40kg turtle laid on a tarpaulin. Before she was lowered into the tank her wound had to be cleaned, sprayed with disinfectant and covered in a water resistant dressing. It was most disturbing to see this beautiful, gentle creature so clearly in distress. Rodrigues gave her a shot of antibiotics to fight infection and a painkiller to reduce the effect of shock. Then Linda got to swim with her in the pool for a while.

Rodrigues said, "To keep her company and let her know that all humans aren't so bad."

The following day's task was to release a green turtle to the ocean. He had been in rehab after a collision with a motor launch had smashed and lacerated part of his back. Heavily scarred but now fully recovered, it took six of us to drag the 140kg leviathan down the beach and onto the rescue dinghy. We were taking him several kilometres out to sea. Rodrigues explained this made the returnees less likely to come back to the heavily fished shores around Mazunte.

At the drop site the great beast was heaved unceremoniously, flippers flailing wildly, over the dinghy's side into the clear blue ocean. Linda, myself and one of the regular team quickly donned facemask, snorkel and fins to follow. The big male headed for the open ocean making powerful sweeps with his front flippers, clumsy and awkward on land but sleek and graceful underwater and it was a wonderful moment as the three of us swam with him. Although Linda and I hadn't been there at his rescue, we were filled with a great sense of pride and purpose. I had never seen a turtle in the wild until a couple of days before and now there I was, swimming alongside one of the largest and most impressive species. A piece of living history, he had changed very little from his ancestors millions of years ago. Saved from certain, painful death, there was now a real chance that this individual would father generations of turtles to come.

The sanctuary was quiet again so we took the next day off and made our way to the line of bamboo tourist huts bravely standing on stilts at the top of the beech. While I played in the enormous Mazunte waves under a searing sun, Linda went for a swim out to a spit of land at the edge of the cove. When she finally re-emerged from the foaming surf she complained of stomach cramps and within half an hour she had chills, fever and barely enough energy to walk.

Back at the house I sat on the porch chair feeling nauseous and listless, nursing a pounding headache. I was suffering from heat exhaustion and so badly burned that my blistered forehead and nose began to ooze.

Feeling a little better the following morning Linda was determined to keep to her schedule, so I went with her to Pochutla to see her on her bus. Perhaps it was for the best that our last day together had been so messed up, otherwise I might not have been able to say goodbye at all.

I spent three more days helping out at the turtle sanctuary, trying to keep my mind occupied. I stripped and rebuilt a small outboard motor that had seized, so now both the sanctuary's dinghies were up and running. When I left, the green turtle with the missing flipper was recovering well. She would soon be ready for release, but it was time for me to leave.

* * *

The first class bus left Pochutla around mid-morning on its thirteen hour journey east to San Cristobal De Las Casas. My neighbour, a Danish medical student called Ulrich, was amiable enough but his toxic garlic beer breath made me heave. We passed through low mountain ranges and broad sweeping plains on the thirteen hour journey. The hot, humid climate and fertile soil made everything grow and the landscape was surprisingly lush and green.

One of the disadvantages of first class was the appalling B-movies foisted on the captive audience and we were treated to the worst two films I have ever seen: The Halfback of Notre Dame and Jungle Boy. It was raining when we arrived so we made our way quickly to the Albergue Juvenil, one of the cheapest hostels in town. Ulrich immediately set off to find some friends of his in a hostel across town and I settled down to sleep in my top bunk, while two Mexicans in their mid thirties lay on the lower bunks.

At some ungodly hour of the morning, Ulrich rattled the door lock open and 'sneaked' in with a girlfriend. Loud whispering ensued making it impossible to sleep and I could hear every sound, even the condom wrapper tearing open. Then, for goodness sake, they started shagging directly above the older of the two Mexicans. The giggling, gasping and rhythmic humping went on for ages but the Mexicans didn't seem to mind and eventually I nodded off, only to be woken a few hours later when friends of the couple rapped loudly on our door, shouting to them in Danish. Ulrich and partner dragged themselves out of bed and wandered down the corridor to chat with them, leaving the door wide open. They talked loudly and the hallway amplified the noise. That was it. I leapt out of bed and padded down the hall towards them.

"D'you mind. It's four o-clock in the morning and the rest of us are trying to get some sleep!"

They looked at me dumbstruck for a moment. How could I be so intolerant? As I walked back to the room they started up again. I stormed back down the corridor and stood inches from Ulrich's face.

"What's going on, are you taking the piss?" I took their silence as a small victory.

Later that morning I was shunted upstairs because of a shortage of beds and Ulrich, of course, was sleeping like a baby.

The group of young Spanish travellers in my new dorm were impeccably polite and when it was time for bed, wonderfully silent. Unfortunately the night manager wasn't so considerate and invited some mates round for a tomcat howling and vomit party that evening. They made such an appalling racket that once again I was forced out of bed while my incredibly tolerant room mates slept on or pretended to sleep.

The hallway floor was awash with water, used to slosh away the sick that was spattered everywhere. A door opened in the room directly below mine and the noise was ear-splitting. A young man staggered out half carrying, half dragging his mate towards the washroom. Bypassing sinks that were already blocked and overflowing with chutney soup, they never quite made it to the toilet. Whoosh - splatter, all over the floor and toilet pan. Then they wheeled around and quite oblivious of me, rejoined their comrades.

Nobody noticed as I eased open the door and studied the scene for a few moments in disbelief. Popular Mexican fiesta music blared at maximum volume from a ghetto-blaster with an enormous single speaker in a wooden box. The guys who were still conscious howled along as they sat huddled together. At the end of each phrase there was an,

"A i e e e e !
Aai ! Aai ! Aai !
Ha - Haaa !"

"Guys - guys - guys," I shouted, attracting their attention. "Turn the music down please, We're all tryin' to get some sleep!"
It seemed to work and a short while later all was quiet.

After breakfast the following morning I set off for Canyon Sumidero, half an hour away by bus. Narrow open boats laden with passengers sped up and down the brown, fast flowing Sumidero river from the embarkation point to a hydro electric dam some 40 kilometres downstream.

In places, the canyon walls towered high above us like Manhattan skyscrapers, with a scorching sun almost directly overhead. Lush vegetation clung to every remotely hospitable surface, thriving on humidity and the promise of daily rain. In the rock face were clearly defined orange and yellow strata that plunged earthwards at crazy angles. The gorge walls lowered to a steep bushy bank where opportunist Indian families grew small crops of maize and tended goats, oblivious that this was a designated National Park.

Vultures scoured the riverbanks for carrion, soaring in thermals and swooping into overhanging trees, while egrets floated downriver on logs, bobbing in our wake. Grey pelicans patrolled less than a wing span above the surface, looking like cumbersome flying boats. Now and again one would climb sharply, flip over on its back and dive for fish. Cormorants perched in trees or on rocks drying their wings and a large crocodile lay on a mud bank, putting up with the endless stream of loud, annoying tourists who came much too close to take photographs. This was the safest place to be until they all went home.

We passed slowly under a waterfall that sprang miraculously from high up in the vertical cliff face. Dozens of large rock formations, shaped like half umbrellas, grew out from the wall at right angles and deflected the tumbling water, turning it to gentle rainbow-streaked rain.

Speeding on we swayed wide around bends to avoid driftwood or the huge flotillas of plastic bottles, general litter and human waste that choked the great river. Suddenly there was a resounding crack! and all heads snapped round to see that two boats had collided. If either sank it could be a real disaster, spilling children, adults and pensioners into the swirling, crocodile-infested water. The boat that took a broadside righted itself and mercifully stayed afloat. Its stunned passengers ordered their pilot to put them ashore on a narrow sandbank while they regained their composure but there were no injuries, so we raced on.

On a minibus tour of two nearby Indian villages the following morning our guide Javier, a small wiry *Mestizo* told us what to expect.

"These-a peoples, they sit down in the street to shit and pees. They have-a free schools but they no like to use them. They always drinking posh."

Posh, he explained, was the fierce local brew distilled from corn and tasting like turpentine. In San Juan Chamula many of the men were seriously under its influence staggering and swaying along, while others were out of it all together lying comatose in the gutter. The place was filthy with plastic litter and garbage strewn everywhere and small kids surrounded us constantly begging. Most of the buildings were ramshackle with corrugated iron roofs and polythene sheet doors, but luckily a few traditional adobe thatched roof houses survived representing the traditional way of life.

We were treating the inhabitants like exhibits in a zoo and there were hostile glances as we walked across a large open square to the church. It seemed the government of entirely Spanish descendants, wanted to make the Indians conform to the modern Mexican way of life by taking away their land, their religion and their language and when it failed to control them, it simply ignored them.

The people of Chamula may have looked dejected, but it was there in 1994 that around two thousand Tzotzil Indians rose up against the minority ruling class at the start of the Zapatista rebellion. Government buildings were destroyed in San Cristobal and many large farms were taken over throughout the state of Chiapas. The rebellion was quickly suppressed and the

Mestizo - of mixed Spanish and Indian decent.

rebels retreated to the jungle, but the incident brought the plight of the Chiapas Indians to the world's attention.

Inside the central church photography was strictly prohibited, the law being enforced by local police dressed in sheepskin waistcoats, carrying long wooden clubs. The hall was filled with a thick haze of burning incense and two large veil curtains hung from the ceiling, gathered in at the walls. The floor was covered in a layer of dry grass and pine needles and villagers knelt or squatted facing hundreds of candles while they chanted or prayed. Javier told us the original church on the edge of town was destroyed by fire when the candles burned low, igniting the dry grass on the wooden floor.

On the left was a line of large glass cases with ornate wooden frames containing carvings of various saints, which were carried around the village on wooden platforms during special ceremonies and festivals. Further inside, small groups of people crouched on the floor holding chickens ready for ritual sacrifice. During sacrifice illness and disease were transferred from human host to chicken and the infected birds buried soon afterwards, to avoid re-infection. The Tzotzil belief that Jesus, upon resurrection, literally became the sun, was hard to grasp although it was a beautiful thought.

We left Chamula and drove on to another Tzotzil village about twenty kilometres away. Zanacantan was much cleaner and there were no beggars or drunks lying in the gutter, but the Indian language was not taught at all in school and the only traditional house was kept solely as a tourist attraction. This was Javier's 'model village' and he eagerly pointed out all the advantages the people had there.

Inside the village hall land issues were being hotly debated between men in bright red and white ponchos and sombreros of woven palm. Apparently a group of farmers had claimed a plot for themselves which was already designated as communal land.

Next, Javier took us to the tourist show house with its clay and straw walls and thatched roof, standing uncomfortably

355

among neat rows of small concrete and brick dwellings. A tiny master bed stood in the only private space surrounded by untraditional polythene sheet on a wooden frame. The women inside paused from weaving and cooking over a clay stove, while we checked out beautifully carved wooden tools and utensils. Before we left, two French girls from our little group handed out boiled sweets to the women and children, which surprised me because all the modern guide books discouraged this as condescending and encouraging begging, not to mention rotten teeth.

Early next morning I bought a bus ticket for Palenque, almost on the border with Guatemala. The bus was an ancient, ramshackle affair with numerous body patches randomly riveted in place. It belched filthy grey smoke, ran on slick tyres and had falling-apart seats and broken windows. The conductor assured me we had enough time while I bought some food but to my horror, I returned a few minutes later with a small bag of *tamales con pollo*, to see the bus pull away without me. I chased it down the road and luckily the conductor made the driver stop.

The only other tourists onboard were a very smartly dressed French couple in their late fifties sharing a front seat with extra leg room, who looked completely out of place among working class Mexicans and peasant farmers.

Hours rolled by. A group of Indians climbed aboard, the men wearing bright red zigzag patterned ponchos, women carrying babies wrapped tightly in shawls on their backs. The journey was only around one hundred and fifty kilometres but we trundled along winding country roads at barely a jogging pace, picking up and dropping off passengers all the time and stopping at every village. To be fair, you got much more of a

tamales - little food parcels made from mashed maize filled with rice or meat.
con pollo - with chicken.

feel for the country this way and if you spoke a little Spanish it could be a very rewarding experience.

We stopped to pick up an old chap with his tiny granddaughter and our driver revved the engine impatiently while the old man stood in the doorway complaining about the hiked up fare. The driver slowly let out the clutch and the bus edged forwards. Suddenly, there were piercing screams and shouts.

"Go back! Back-back-back!"

"You bastard," I thought, "You've driven over that little girl's legs!" The old man snatched up the girl, still screaming blue murder and dragged her onboard. He seemed determined just to get going and made his way down the aisle as the bus moved off. The other passengers looked on blankly with wide staring eyes. I caught up with them, ignoring the conductor who wanted me back in my seat and knowing a little first aid, gave her a quick once over to check for injuries. There was a little blood around the toes of her right foot. The edge of the tyre must have squashed it into the mud but nothing was broken, thank God. We were several hours drive away from anywhere, let alone a hospital. What would we have done if she'd been badly hurt?

By the time I reached Mayabell campsite near Palenque ruins, a dose of food poisoning from the morning's chicken tamales was taking dreadful effect with constant runs and total lack of energy. I just managed to put up my tent before collapsing on my sleeping bag.

By lunch time next day I felt a little recharged and made the twenty minute walk to the ancient Mayan city. All around lush jungle was closing in on the temple complex, a reminder that when we have gone nature reclaims everything. To the right of the entrance was an elongated pyramid the size of a four storey office block, with a parallel-sided temple of huge limestone slabs on top. The structure was remarkably intact giving an eerie feeling that its owners could return at any moment.

Several carvings of Mayan leaders and warriors survived in the grand palace and their proportions and features were much less stylised so it was possible to get a good idea what the people actually looked like. Lord Pacal, whose hieroglyph was engraved on the walls as the sun and shield, ruled Palenque until 690 AD. His son, Chan-Bahlum the second (hieroglyph - jaguar-serpent), succeeded him during Palenque's most prosperous period and ordered the construction of the central palace, a beautifully preserved labyrinth of rooms and corridors in the foreground, and the impressive sun temple pyramid behind. In the palace there was a small section of painted wall but elsewhere damp and erosion had destroyed all the murals. The walls were also slowly changing shape as water seeped through the massive limestone blocks creating stalagmites and petrified, glassy water trails.

In thick jungle surrounding a crumbling well I was buzzed by a humming bird, a tiny darting glistening emerald. No other bird can fly at full speed to a given spot and then hold that position with such pinpoint accuracy, again and again in rapid succession. I was lucky. The male bird was defending its territory and kept returning to the same branch where it called in a surprisingly loud, shrill voice.

Palenque had been abandoned by the year 790. One theory is that the city had reached the end of its predicted lifespan and it would have gone against the Mayan belief system to stay longer, but no one really knows what happened to the mysterious inhabitants.

A dark figure popped out from behind tall reeds by the roadside as I walked back to camp.

"Mushrooms? Mushrooms señor?" he hissed.

The mushroom man could hear your footsteps from way down the road and was always hiding, ready to supply. Maybe he lived there. I caught up with a couple of tough looking

New Zealanders I recognised from Isabella Rosa, Oaxaca and they told me they had tried some.

"Seventy pesos gets you a large bag full," said one. "They're quite difficult to get down but we ate the lot. It takes about twenty minutes for them to kick in but when they do it's a really good feelin'."

"I couldn't stop laughin'," said his mate. "Everythin' you say seems to come out funny and the effect lasts for hours. If you stare long enough after takin' 'em, the jungle starts changing shape. It comes alive!"

The original inhabitants of Mexico knew the powers of these natural hallucinatory drugs and used them in everyday life. Their amazing beliefs and frightful rituals must have become even more charged when they got high and stepped over into the spirit world.

The guys assured me the incredibly loud bellowing noise that woke me early in the morning was made by howler monkeys. That was a relief, I thought I was going crazy. Mayabell campsite backed onto a wonderful patch of jungle where ripe avocados dropped from the trees. At night the air was filled with the sound of frogs, crickets and owls, while glow-worms dazzled like tiny stars in the undergrowth.

Dining at Mayabell involved service with a scowl from a surly chef and a plump, intolerant waitress but travellers still flocked to the restaurant to be frowned at and abused. Strangely, it added to the character of the place. Meals cost a little more than in Palenque town but were usually pretty good if you didn't mind the incredibly long wait. The trick was to order long before you were hungry. There was a pool to relax in when the day became unbearably hot and accommodation ranged from well appointed chalets to the most popular thatched roof open shelters for slinging hammocks. I slept in my tent because the mosquitoes in Mexico could bleed you dry.

Late the following morning I found a gap in the fence at the back of the campsite and went for a jungle walk. I slipped over several times in soft mud, rivulets of sweat ran down stinging my eyes and causing my clothes to stick to my body, while biting insects and savage spiny plants punctured my skin. For all that, the place was utterly fascinating with unusual colourful birds, butterflies, giant droning hornets and horned stag beetles. Magnificent orchids and lilies peeped through undergrowth into dappled light. Bats chirped and flapped underneath the giant calcified mushroom formations of a waterfall that waited patiently for rain.

In the afternoon a tall Germanic-looking guy rode into camp on a big BMW motorbike. Otto had travelled extensively in Central and South America living with small Indian communities. Mexican-born with German grandparents, he helped out with daily tasks: planting and harvesting crops, repairing a leaking roof or tending livestock, in return for somewhere to stay and a little food. He supplemented his Spartan lifestyle by sales of thirteen short novels with titles including: 'The Feathered Dragon', '20.13' and 'The Enchanted Mountain', a blend of stories told by village elders about the creation of life, the universe, plants, birds and mountains and tales from his own imagination.

Otto took me on his bike around the national park surrounding Palenque ruins. We rode up a rough dirt track, arriving at a village where he had stayed for four months, a few years ago. Some of the villagers still remembered the wild haired, fair skinned young man, who always wore a smile and had a good word for everyone. We stopped to chat with some old friends before being invited to the home of the family he had lived with. A revolting potion of curdled butter milk was ladled into plastic mugs and handed round so I sipped slowly to avoid getting a top-up. Pullets, cats and children played on the dry mud floor while Otto and our hosts caught up on each other's news. On the way back Otto proudly showed me a winding gravel road he had helped to build and a nearby coffee plantation where he'd worked for fifteen pesos, around £1 per day.

Heading for Campeche on the west coast of Yucatan peninsula the following day, the bus made a brief lunch pause at the seaside town of Champoton. The sun directly overhead reflected in a blinding glare from white sand and the calm, sparkling ocean. My eyes slowly adjusted after so long on the darkened coach and there were flashes of silver as small fish leapt from the water, fleeing predators. Frigate birds, pirates of the air, swooped on smaller gulls forcing them to disgorge their catch and brown pelicans cruised close to the water's surface like lumbering sea planes.

In the dilapidated hostel dorms of Campeche university buckets and pans lay under the leaking roof, but it was cheap and the open air swimming pool was a Godsend after the long bus journey. Most of the other residents were young students but Jorg, my German room mate, was only a year younger than myself so I didn't feel so much like a father figure. Jorg was tall and painfully slim, with a goatee beard and single long plait growing from the left side of his short cropped hair. At first he seemed to take himself a little too seriously, but I soon warmed to my well-travelled companion and as we walked around the coastal fortress town we made plans to travel together.

In town there were a number of Mennonites from surrounding farms, whose ancestors came to Mexico two centuries ago escaping persecution in Europe. The Mennonites had no churches, refused military service and rejected the state's authority. They all wore very similar clothes like a uniform, the women with wide brimmed black felt hats, shawls and flower print ankle length dresses and the men in straw cowboy hats and dungarees.

That night an awesome electrical storm boomed across the ink black sky. Great fingers of lightning flashed weirdly upwards, spreading across the horizon like the roots of some enormous upturned neon bush. We heard next morning that the power station 100 kilometres north in Celetun had been knocked out by the storm.

Jorg and I continued eastwards next day and pitched tent on the grounds of Ranchero guesthouse, a couple of kilometres from the ruined city of Uxmal. The mosquitoes were the largest and most vicious I'd ever seen attacking in the full afternoon heat, so we jumped into the guesthouse pool to escape.

Strolling through a nearby hamlet late that afternoon, a gang of local kids shouted after us. At first I thought they were a bunch of yobbos calling names, but it turned out they were just being friendly and wanted to show us their menagerie of pets. The eldest boy of around ten, jumped into a small concrete pig pen to point out his favourite piglets while turtles and terrapins were thrown into a water trough to demonstrate their swimming skills. Next, armfuls of squirming black kittens were brought for our inspection, but they didn't do very much and were soon abandoned as our entourage approached the family's cattle. The cow was fawn coloured, tall and skinny with wide doughy eyes, long down turned ears and a huge hump over the base of its neck. She looked on indifferently as dozens of small hands petted and stroked her big soppy calf. Tourists came and went on their way to the ruins but no one ever got the grand tour of the village and we left feeling quite privileged.

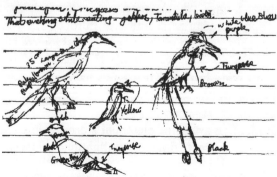

The evening was wonderfully peaceful and as we walked back to Ranchero crickets and birds serenaded on the warm, pollen scented air. During supper on the restaurant veranda, geckos called loudly to one another and bats flitted hunting moths around a single dim light overhead. A tarantula skulked across the dining room floor towards the shadows in search of crickets. Back home that would have put me right off my food, but out here it all seemed perfectly natural.

Setting off early next day to avoid the fierce afternoon sun, Jorg and I walked the four or so kilometres to Uxmal, coming under fierce attack from Kamikaze mosquitos. White stone temples looked out from the midst of lush jungle that threatened to envelop them. On top of a great wall built in a 'U' shape, stood a row of stone cells that opened inwards to a football-pitch sized courtyard. The air was thick with thousands of screeching finches that roosted in the cool dark spaces. Inside each room their droppings had formed a springy pungent mattress over the centuries, almost knee deep in places.

Unique in the Puuk style of architecture, the magician's temple south of the courtyard was a conical tower the height of a small block of flats. Cornices had protruding turtle god figures with great stone tongues. The legend goes that turtles prayed for rain on behalf of the Puuk Mayans because there was no natural water source at Uxmal. To the west was the tallest structure of the complex, an oblong sacrificial temple standing on top of a giant pyramid base. From one of the supporting pillars a menacing gargoyle surveyed the courtyard and encroaching jungle.

Hitching a lift that afternoon to bustling Merida, Jorg and I picked our way through the crowded bus station, where small ramshackle buses with bumpers hanging off and smashed indicator lights pumped smoke into the hot air. Shop front displays overflowed with leather handbags, sandals and wallets while others sold icons, brass candelabras and figurines of the saints. The town was so busy we were often forced off the pavement by milling pedestrians before hopping back up again to avoid hooting motorists.

Moving into the Casa de Huespedes in the town centre, an elaborate marble staircase, high ceilings and ornate stained glass windows over each door were evidence that this was once a very lavish residence. The upper floor overlooked a cool dark courtyard and its walls were covered with faded paintings of lovers and well fed, partially clothed women in over-emphasised romantic poses. In contrast to the huge guestrooms with twin double beds, the manager and his entire family lived in a dingy ground floor closet strewn with makeshift washing lines, having a bed sheet for a door.

I walked through a large dimly lit kitchen with red tiled floor and white tiled walls thickly covered in grime. Now silent apart from a prowling cat, the place had once buzzed with cooks and maids. There was a massive stove over which heavy iron pots hung from 'S'-shaped meat hooks. The kitchen led on to a rudimentary toilet and shower room and beyond that, the floor sloped precariously under the weight of a great brick oven before opening out into the laundry area patio and brilliant sunshine.

An hour's bus ride away, the ruins of Chichen Itza were some of the most intriguing and well preserved in all Mexico. The great ball court was the largest ever built with carvings on its two parallel sloping walls depicting ritual decapitation of the losing team. That upped the ante a bit, knowing that if you lost you got your head chopped off. The game involved keeping a hard latex ball in the air using only elbows knees and hips, through incredible twists and physical jerks. To score points the ball was knocked through one of two stone rings, carved with the feathered serpent figure and set high in the centre of each wall. Nearby, the small square temple of skulls was faced with gruesome carvings of eagles and jaguars devouring hearts torn from human victims, possibly supporters of the losing team.

The giant pyramid-shaped main temple housed an inner temple accessed by a steep staircase, barely wider or taller than a man's shoulders. The humidity inside was suffocating and moisture streamed off dimly lit walls covered with green and orange algae and glassy mineral deposits. Letting my imagination run wild I tried to picture life back with the Mayans, my fellow tourists as high priests in head dresses or bird costumes, but now my head swam from claustrophobia, heat and exhaustion. My ears filled with a murmur from the tortured souls of sacrificial victims, getting louder and louder like tinnitus. The staircase opened out into a narrow chamber and through poor light I could just make out a gutter trench and drain built into the floor. Suddenly I had to grip the wall to stop myself collapsing and I shuddered with revulsion as I realised what they were for.

Jorg and I were resting in the shade of some trees when he noticed an expensive-looking camera unattended on a fallen log. As he watched, a large Mexican woman placed a T-shirt over the camera and sat down beside it. Then, checking sheepishly around she opened her bag and slipped the camera wrapped up in the T-shirt inside.

Only a week earlier Jorg's day sack had been stolen while he slept on an overnight bus. He lost money and an expensive Ricoh camera, but most important of all they took a number of used film rolls and his irreplaceable journal and address book.

Jorg elbowed me awake and we walked over to the big woman. She was with a female companion and two guys; all of them in their mid-thirties, but Jorg was unperturbed and waded straight in.

"The camera you just put in your bag. Is it yours?"

"No," she replied indignantly, "Is it yours?"

Her friends gathered close to intimidate Jorg, but he stood his ground and I pushed my way in to lend support. Just then a park security guard walked by, Jorg explained the situation and the would-be camera thieves reluctantly accompanied us to the supervisor's office.

The supervisor removed the camera from the woman's bag and Jorg, peering over her shoulder, spotted another two inside. Convinced they were all stolen, he held on to the bag like a Jack Russell while the woman shouted and cursed, trying to yank it free. Finally the supervisor grabbed the bag away from both of them and calmed the situation. The bag was handed back, minus the SLR and telephoto lens and the thieves left. We never did find out who the camera belonged to or whether they got it back.

Leaving Chichen Itza, Jorg and I headed for Tulum on the east coast of Yucatan peninsula. It was a long, uncomfortable walk from the inland bus stop to the beach carrying full packs in sweltering afternoon heat, but we finally arrived at busy Santa Fe campground. Warm, clear blue water lapped gently at the broad white sandy beach strewn with tanned young bodies. Clusters of broad, squat, palm trees provided shelter from the fierce sun and a windbreak for tents. At the top of the beach a dozen or so comfortable looking huts with thatched reed roofs stood on stilts. Behind these were shower rooms with proper toilets - not the dreaded squat down ankle splatter type - and close to the quiet road was a large restaurant serving food and cold beer all day long.

Sadly, the idyllic atmosphere had been marred by a spate of thefts. A couple staying in one of the huts told us they'd been robbed while they slept and a camera and some cash taken and some of their neighbours had lost a lot more. Nobody knew how long it had been going on and the police and campsite owners seemed to do nothing.

Early next morning we visited Tulum, 'city of dawn', in its fabulously beautiful setting perched on coastal cliffs just a short walk further up the coast. Abandoned by the Mayans only four hundred and fifty years ago, Iguanas now prowled the derelict stone temples basking in the sun, while pelicans and terns soared the low cliff and people played in the azure waves below.

It seemed crazy to leave such a fantastic place but I was almost broke and getting dangerously close to my plane ride home. Jorg was heading for Guatemala and it was time to go our separate ways. Tearing myself away from the peaceful, refreshing ocean and easy lifestyle, I hopped on an overnight bus for Mexico City, arriving the following evening. Unable to face the fifty hour bus ride to Tijuana, the border crossing in the north west corner of Mexico, I headed for the town of Durango, about a third of the way up.

The bus arrived a day later and I hitched a lift to the local hostel, Villa Deportiva Juvenil. Having showered and settled in, I walked into town and sat on a bench in the shady zocalo. People joined me to chat and pass the time of day: a middle aged woman who asked me to send her a postcard of Big Ben when I got home, a young dentist who told me a little about the town's history and finally an old man carrying a metre tall gilded wooden crucifix with a beautiful carving of Christ as a present for his niece in Texas.

Back at the coach station the following day I thought I recognised the same two drivers who had brought me from Mexico City.

"You and me, we old amigos," one of them smiled.

As darkness fell a young girl on the neighbouring seat curled up by her baby sister to rest. It wasn't quite comfortable enough to sleep properly, we had to put up with noisy kids endlessly running up and down the aisle during the day and freezing cold air conditioning through the night - turning it down was apparently out of the question. Aside from that, our greatest inconvenience were the frequent army and police checkpoints. On one stretch of road we were stopped three times in an hour and barely covered thirty kilometres. It was the same routine each time: wait for ages in a traffic queue, then made to pull over and stop. Eventually, someone with a gun would come on board and order everyone off. Outside they'd be throwing off luggage and going through bags. One scruffy looking road block crew all wore bright yellow T-shirts with their logo emblazoned in bold letters like some street gang and the whole thing seemed like a huge job creation scheme. From my neighbour I gathered they were looking for guns, drugs and bandits posing as regular passengers.

In the orange glow of sunrise we drove through the low rise outskirts of Chihuahua and on into the desert. Eroded yellow sandstone ridges cast giant shadows across broad red dusty plains of tumbleweed and cactus. So different from the sprawling, overpopulated towns with open rubbish tips and broad boulevards packed with gaudy American pickup trucks.

After 36 hours on the coach we finally arrived, completely shattered, on the outskirts of Tijuana and I looked for a local bus to take me to the border crossing and San Ysidro in the US.

"San Ysidro?" I asked a driver as he sat in the cab.

"No se."

I asked some other drivers standing about talking to one another.

"Yes, he goes there," pointing to the guy I'd just spoken to. "Try again."

I asked him again. "No se," and he went back to reloading the ticket machine. I tried the office.

"Yes him. He goes there."

The guys were clearly taking the piss, but I lumbered over once more just as the bus started to edge forward.

"No, no!" he shouted, shutting the door in my face and turning tight across my path, almost running me down. I kicked the bus and spat at it and if I could have grabbed him, I would have wrung his neck. A young woman saw what happened.

"The local bus can't go to San Ysidro," she explained calmly. "It just takes you to the border and you walk across."

A short while latter I walked towards customs past an eight lane jam of overheating vehicles all heading for the United States.

"Where's your form?" demanded the US customs official, so I showed him the form I'd been given to fill in.

"No, the green one. Don't you have a green form?"

He handed me a customs declaration form and my jaw dropped in astonishment as I glanced at the questions:

Have you ever been a member of any terrorist organization?

Have you ever been a member of the Nazi Party?

Have you ever held without consent, a child of American citizenship?

Did anyone ever answer yes, and if they did, would they take them seriously? Anyway...

"Six dollars," requested the customs official.

Ah. No US currency. After explaining to him that my GB £ traveller's cheques were less popular in Mexico than cholera and that I didn't have enough pesos for a hotel, he was contemplating letting me through under escort to change the money, then come back and pay, but just at that moment the supervisor arrived.

"Can't do that...No you can't...I don't care...Go back!"

I stamped back across the road bridge and another foot bridge to downtown Tijuana. Even the name sounded foreboding. "He was heading for the USA but only made it as far as 'downtown'." I hadn't slept properly for three whole days, it was baking hot and I sweated under the weight of my heavy rucksack as I tried every bank and moneylender. The only one that showed any interest offered a derisory exchange and I refused on principle.

Maybe if I could sell my beloved guide book to one of the tourists. But they were just that; day tripping, middle class American tourists, not travellers. They were so used to snapping, "No!" at hustlers that they didn't bother to look and most of them had never even heard of Lonely Planet. I found myself in a stationery shop pleading with the assistant.

"Just give me six dollars, it's worth thirty!"

A plump, business suited guy in his sixties listened to my tale of woe. He thought for a moment then said in an oily smooth voice, "I have some ideas. I'm going to ask you to trust me."

Trust him? Why the hell should I trust him? It was detestable feeling so vulnerable, but I wandered with the stranger to a cafe, all too conscious of precious banking hours ticking by.

We sat down and he ordered us both a coffee without the least sense of urgency, but before it arrived the thought occurred to me to call American Express and find out whether they had an office in town. I went to the phone booth in the corner of the room; another sodding card phone.

"Here," he called from behind the partition, holding out his phone card. "Why won't you trust me?"

How could I tell him, 'My senses scream that there's something wrong about you. You're far too relaxed, overconfident'. The businessman wanted to chat and sip coffee, quite unconcerned that if I couldn't change my last traveller's cheque that afternoon I'd be sleeping rough in downtown. Maybe that was part of his plan. My subconscious was being extremely unhelpful, filling my head with names like rent-boy and midnight cowboy and the images made me shiver.

We got into a cab and made our way to American Express. There were actually two AMEX offices at opposite ends of town and if I hadn't panicked early on, I probably would have already made it to one of them. Only when I finally held seven crispy new 10$ notes in my hand did I relax enough to thank the businessman and shake his hand. I still doubted his motives, I couldn't help it, but it made no difference. I was on my way, back on a bus to the border.

CALIFORNIA COAST

Finally setting foot on American soil, I was pleasantly surprised to find that a Greyhound bus could take me all the way up the coast to San Francisco for just $39 - I wouldn't even have to hitch-hike - and we pulled in to Oakland bus station at 4.30 on a cool Friday morning. It was an awkward hour to be turfed out of the warm, relatively comfortable bus. Lucky arrivals moved on to connecting transport or were greeted by friends and loved ones. The waiting room seats were hard and uninviting and anyway, I was wide awake now. It was too early to phone my paraglider friend Jill whom I'd met three years earlier in Annecy, France - didn't want to piss her off. So, what to do for the next couple of hours?

"German?" asked the large black guy, sprawled upright on the bench beside me.

"No, English. South west London."

"Oh, OK. Anywhere near Hayes? I been tu Hayes for a month last year, visitin' friends."

"Nearer Croydon really. Do you know Croydon?"

I got chatting with big Darrel as he waited for his connection. We discussed crime, gun laws, Northern Ireland and American support for the terrorists. Darrel was pretty open-minded about racial issues.

"There are just as many assholes in black society as in white. We're all here. We just gotta learn to get along."

He did his Cockney impersonation for me.

"Politics is all a lowd of bollocks, mate."

And I retorted with my black dude slang,

"Wut-up fow. Yo muvva-fucka, wass hapnin'."

When I finally got through on the phone her mum told me Jill was away on a paragliding competition but would be back in a couple of days, so I sat back down with Darrel.

371

"Right here is a bad neighbourhood," he said gravely. "You could go to the university and hang out there. They got cafes an' shit and lots of students to talk to."

I didn't really want to stay in the area the way Darrel described it; cheap hotels were rented by the hour and had security bars and peep holes on the door. Darrel showed me to the bus stop. As he walked away he turned and called back,

"Be strong! ...And don't let anyone fuck wid' you!"

Thanks Darrel!

Making my way to the underground station, two guys started shouting at one another in the middle of the crowded street.

"Yeah, I got somethin' faw yo bitch ass!" yelled the black dude.

"Oh, you got somethin' for me?" shouted the white guy, standing his ground.

"Yeah. Right here muvva-fucka!"

Everybody carried on walking past them barely taking any notice, as if this was perfectly normal behaviour. I was scared one of them might have a gun and did the same.

The escalator emerged from the dark underground labyrinth of *BART* onto Powell Street and I blinked in strong sunlight. Skyscrapers stretched upwards making me feel like a toddler looking up from between its father's legs. Assorted city people queued around a giant turntable, waiting for the next cable-drawn tram to trundle down the steep hill. Vagrants whose brains were fried from years of drugs and alcohol abuse frequently burst into shouting fits amid the elegant architecture. It might have been funny if it wasn't so alarming and sad. Continuing along Market Street past an army of homeless camped out in doorways or pushing trolleys loaded with rags and personal belongings, I found the Central Hotel, now a decrepit hostel run by Asians, and moved in.

BART - Bay Area Transport.

Pier 39 on Fisherman's Wharf was a sickly tourist trap, grown up around the ferry tour industry to infamous Alcatraz. Either side of the busy ferry terminal sea lions basked lazily on fenced off jetties, occasionally waking to bark loudly at one another. Looking eastwards a retired Second World War submarine moored to a pier now functioned as a museum. Further along lay a proudly restored tea clipper from a time when these vessels raced across the Pacific carrying spices, cotton and slaves and in the distance San Francisco's most famous landmark, Golden Gate Bridge, grew out of a misty shoreline.

Heading away from the waterfront, in Kennedy's Irish Pub the jukebox played Jane's Addiction and The Waterboys, and a pint of Guiness cost half what it did back home. The restaurants and bars of Columbus Avenue thronged with the city's young and well-to-do. Silver-grey clouds raced like ghosts unnoticed over the tops of tower blocks while down below, America talked loud and stuffed its face.

Some of the guests at the Central Hotel felt very intimidated by the homeless on Market Street but for the most part they were harmless enough and I found myself instead wondering what was their story, what had caused them to fall out of society: shattered life, breakdown, drink or drugs. I watched a junkie stalking a middle-aged Mediterranean-looking guy as he withdrew money from a hole in the wall. As soon as the guy turned to walk away with his cash, the junkie moved in close buzzing around him like a bluebottle. All of a sudden the would-be victim turned and screamed,

"You want some eh? You want trouble, you fuckin' freak?"

The junkie leapt back in shock then loped away muttering to himself, so stoned he'd never really been a serious threat.

It was still too early to go to bed so I stopped in a quiet burger bar a few blocks from the hotel. Seated next to the window, a white guy in his forties wearing a fishing hat covered in small metal badges was joined by the black guy who'd been yelling outside and drumming on an array of empty boxes and tins. Inside, the drummer was much subdued and warmly shook his friend's hand. The white guy slid the book he'd been reading across the table and you didn't have to be a detective to know that an exchange was being made. Opening the book the black guy whispered gruffly,

"Aw, thank you man. That's good man. That's good."

"Is that good for you?" persisted his friend, milking every drop of appreciation.

"That's good man. That's fine."

The two carried on at an inaudible level for some time, then I heard the white guy ask,

"Can you handle that?"

"Yeah. That's fine man, don't worry."

I wondered what little errand had to be performed. They may have been talking about painting and decorating, but it was probably just another minor drugs deal that helped keep the down-and-outs of Market Street off their face.

Next morning I teamed up with a young Russian backpacker called Lena and we walked to Aquatic Park on the waterfront, for a picnic. Perhaps as a result of running the Market Street gauntlet, Lena was in curt, defensive mode and as we sat eating lunch on a grassy bank looking out at grey, imposing Alcatraz prison, an athletic looking man approached us.

"Do you have a minute to talk about the battered wives and children of San Francisco?"

"No!" barked Lena.

I was embarrassed and even the hardened fundraiser was shocked by the harshness of Lena's tone.

"Well, thanks for thinkin' about it though," he said indignantly and turned to walk away.

"I'd like to hear about them," I called after him.

He turned back and when he realised it was safe, sat down and joined us...for over two hours. Andre had pockmarked skin and a deep scar over his left cheek. He told us he had been abused by his father until the age of nineteen when he fought back and was thrown out of the house.

"Ninety percent of women homicides are murdered by their husbands," he said. "If the wife is abused the children usually are too."

From abuse of women and children to black civil rights and slavery. Andre believed the boycotting of cotton and timber by Britain and France was instrumental in the downfall of the south during the American civil war.

"Otherwise we'd all still be slaves." he said ominously.

We talked about Vietnam. Andre was there from 1974 to 1975 and his eyes sparkled as he remembered the horror of it.

"Things were gettin' pretty hot then. I was door gunner on one of those big twin rotor jobs...the Chinook. Chinook is big an' slow so it's an easy target. Every time we came back from a mission we'd just count the holes and fix the damage."

One of Andre's jobs had been to load wounded troops on and off the choppers...and the dead.

"The bodies were held in metal caskets, un-refrigerated, sometimes for months before goin' home. In the aircraft hangers there were thousands of them, stacked up to ten high."

Traumatised by the war, Andre still took medication for a shrapnel wound near the spine and worn out knee cartilage from jumping onto the Chinook's flight deck hundreds of times a day. Now he devoted much of his energy to collecting for the battered wives' and children's refuge.

On our way back to the hotel, Alligator Del Ray and his excellent Blues Band were giving a free concert behind the American Express building on Market and 7th Street. Alligator had a leadless guitar and mike and he weaved among the growing audience of office staff and passers-by, teasing the ladies with his antics and wowing us with seductive guitar riffs.

Eventually he followed one office worker right into the building and disappeared altogether.

Late that afternoon while eating in a quiet Chinese restaurant I felt my bench seat shudder, but looking around there was no one close enough to have moved it.

"Did you feel that?" asked the young black guy sitting opposite.

"Earthquake!" we cried in unison.

"I thought I was goin' out of my mind," said my neighbour.

I suppose we shouldn't have been so surprised, after all, San Francisco sits right on top of the highly active San Andreas Fault. On the TV news later I heard that an earthquake in western Turkey killed four thousand people.

CONDOR PEOPLE

I finally caught up with Jill, my paraglider pilot friend and she took me to meet her boyfriend Surhan, a professional tandem pilot from Turkey. Since we last met, Jill had clocked up another five hundred hours air time to my twenty and 'kicked ass' in height and distance competitions around the USA. Her latest toy was an oxygen supply kit so she could fly to the magic 6,000 metres.

At the American/Chinese Food-to-go restaurant on Hoddle Street next morning, a middle-aged black vagrant tapped his way through the doorway to an empty table using a white cane. In his left hand was a black plastic bag containing his worldly possessions and under his arm was a large electric keyboard. The young Chinese waitress brought him breakfast and in a bustling world that rarely had time for those who fell by the wayside, it was heartening to see her treat him with patience and compassion.

A little while later a huge black guy walked in and was ordering food at the counter when a doddery old chap shuffled in carrying a lady's coat over one arm. He tapped the huge guy on the shoulder.

"I strongly recommend you buy this coat faw yo' wife."

The huge bloke collected his food and ushered the old man to the door.

"I strongly recommend you get the hell outa' my sight! How you like 'dat, ol' chief?"

But he didn't mean it and his face broadened into a grin. They chatted as they re-entered Food-to-go and at the counter the huge bloke asked,

"How much for a medium coffee?"

"Fifty cents," said the girl.

"Better give this old fella' a coffee then. I aint givin' 'im no money though."

"Hey, I don't want yaw' money!" protested the old man.

I moved in with Jill and her housemate Patrick, an environmental consultant, at her home in the suburbs. Back in town that afternoon Melissa Etheridge gave a soul concert outside Civic Hall, drawing a huge crowd of all the young and old hippies in San Francisco. Stopping for a coffee afterwards a young, Asian waiter took my order.

"How are you today?" he asked pleasantly.

"Bored and depressed. It's my last day here. I go home to England tomorrow."

"I always wanted to visit there," he said.

"Well, it's cold and wet. And expensive!"

"I don't care, I just want to get out of America. I been here so long."

"What, you want to go back to China?"

"I not from China!" shrieked the young man, feelings terribly hurt. "I from Thailand."

"Oh! Sorry…How long have you been here?"

"Lo-ong time. I already illegal here. My last name on tax form Robin Hood."

"Yeah," I whispered, leaning across the counter, "be careful who you tell though."

"I don't care anymore. I travelled through five states already and they all suck. They so racist!"

On my way back to Jill's place I bought a Street Sheet, San Francisco's equivalent to the Big Issue, from a tall, thin black guy on College Street. At first when he told me all our Western world woes were, "'Cos of the can!" I thought he was a little crazy, but what he meant was, 'can culture'. Total wastage of materials, total consumerism and extreme capitalism. The Street Sheet seller wasn't so crazy. He wasn't crazy at all.

Jill arrived home around mid-afternoon in her Jeep.

"I'm glad you're back early," she said beaming a broad smile. "Surhan has loaned me a large canopy and some gear so now you can fly too!"

I felt nervous as hell at the site they called 'the dump', looking out from the cliff top over a choppy Pacific Ocean. There I was with Jill, la suprema sky goddess and a wing I'd never flown before, as memories of my near fatal accident at Annecy three years earlier came flooding back. Putting a bold face on it I laid out the canopy on some clear ground above take-off and gave it a thorough pre-flight inspection. Harness…no reserve - might have guessed - speed system, maillons, risers, lines, canopy and when I'd finished I checked it all over again. Jill shushed overhead, legs dangling just a few metres above me.

"Come on Andy," she yelled. "Get your ass in the harness!"

A happy flashback of John Clees in Fawlty Towers suddenly filled my head.

'It's always about bottoms with you people'.

Slipping over the shoulder straps I adjusted their length, then snapped the leg straps and waist buckle shut. At the end of the short runway a streamer fluttered steadily up the slope indicating ideal take-off conditions. I took one last glance at the canopy laid out in a horseshoe shape behind me as Jill passed over again from the opposite direction, already quite high.

Running forwards the canopy snapped back catching the wind and I leaned against it bringing it up over my head using the risers. A touch of brakes to stop her over-flying and I craned my neck left and right checking for collapses or line tangles. All OK, I ran like hell for the horizon.

Off the ground and flying I put in left and right beats gaining height all the time. Soon I was up there with Jill and we soared together like condors. The sun retreated behind a wall of cloud on the horizon leaving a vivid orange glow in its wake and the wind speed steadily increased, pushing the lift band higher and further in front of the coastal ridge, taking us higher. High as a skyscraper above take-off. With the Jeep a mere speck in the car park and the land behind it looking more like a road map, we started to circle one another, cranking ever tighter turns until centrifugal force swung our bodies out at forty-five degrees. The fear was gone now and it was better than sex, something quite extraordinary, the giddy feeling you get when you're drunk on emotion. Round and round we swung, high above chalk scarred coastline and endless blue ocean, our lives dangling so precariously from sixty slender cords.

Next morning I hugged and said goodbye to Jill, then Patrick drove me to San Bruno Mountain where his company was working to preserve an area of natural habitat. In 1973 the Endangered Species Act was introduced in North America to help protect wildlife from uncontrolled land development, and under the new law, when developers wanted to build on a greenfield site they had to pay for an environmental survey to prove the area wasn't already home to threatened species.

San Bruno Mountain, a series of gentle hills just to the north of San Francisco, supported a small population of rare mission-blue and calypies butterflies in its mantle of billowing golden grass and wildflowers and so was protected under the bill. Permission had been granted to develop twenty percent of the low-lying mountain area on condition that future home owners would pay indefinitely for all conservation work in the area.

When Patrick's survey was carried out, very little of the savannah favoured by the butterflies was left and they were dying out. The new system funded essential habitat restoration work such as removal of non-native trees and weeds and replanting host plants for feeding and egg laying, and now butterfly numbers were slowly increasing.

As we walked along Patrick showed a subcontractor thickets of brambles, gorse and non-native weeds to be removed around small conservation islands marked off with coloured flags and we spotted some of the tiny, less endangered species: echo blue, silvery blue and Ackman blue butterflies.

Back at the vehicles we met a party of ten-year-olds on a five day environmental awareness program from California's Academy of Science in Golden Gate Park and seizing the opportunity, their tutors asked Patrick to explain the work of the conservation project to the kids. Their curiosity and enthusiasm were infectious and Patrick clearly enjoyed the interaction.

Around lunch time Patrick dropped me off at Colma BART station on the edge of town and I said goodbye, shaking his hand warmly. There was just time to visit the Pacific Coast Centre to see an exhibition Jill had told me about by a photographer named Steve Lehman entitled, 'The Tibetans - A Struggle to Survive', before boarding a bus to the airport. After everything I had experienced on my journey the images of torture, oppression and suffering brought me back down to earth with a crash. There I was, penniless but free to come and go as I pleased while elsewhere, ignored by the rest of the world, genocide was being committed against a gentle, spiritual race of people.

END OF THE ROAD

It's no exaggeration that almost every time I fly home the British Isles are shrouded in claggy grey cloud, but on this morning in late August the weather was beautiful. Fleeing a golden Californian sunset the high atmosphere had been deepest mauve with a dark brown pastel line at the curved horizon. Daylight had broken in a fiery display of brilliant orange, later settling down to a more natural pale clear blue. Below us, a sea of milky white cloud like the endless snowy wastes of the arctic had stopped over France and now there was just a scattering of fluffy cumulus clouds floating like angels between our precarious silver cigar case and the ocean.

It was quick through immigration control, everyone is welcome in the UK and they barely glance at your passport. I wandered through arrivals, made my way to baggage collection and pulled my multi coloured Kenyan rucksack from the carousel for the last time. Slinging it over my shoulder, I walked through the green lane with just £2.75 in my pocket. What could I possibly have to declare?

Approaching the exit I pretended the crowd of expectant friends and relatives were waiting for me, when a tap on the shoulder made me shudder and I spun round to face two heavily built men in flak jackets with sub-machine-guns, dark rimmed police caps shadowing their eyes.

"Mr Lindsay? Andrew Lindsay? If you'd just like to stand over here out of the way Mr Lindsay."

The cops moved me to the baggage inspection counter and my fellow passengers slipped me disapproving glances as they floated past in slow motion, outside my world. "Why can't I go with them? Please let me go with them!"

"The Australian authorities have been in touch with us, Mr Lindsay. I'm arresting you in connection with the disappearance of Darren McAvoy in south west Australia earlier this year. You do not have to say anything but anything you *do* say may be used in evidence against you…"

Someone shook my shoulder and as my eyes cracked open I was hit by the muffled roar of jet engines.

"Please fasten your seatbelt sir and put your seat back in the upright position," said the stewardess with an indifferent smile. My ears popped and the noise of wind-rush over airbrakes filled my head.

* * *

Now I'm back in England fixing washing machines once again. The subject of my journey rarely comes up but when it does people say,

"Wow, that sounds great! I've always wanted to travel. Wish I could do that."

So I tell them,

"The world is out there. All you have to do is free yourself from the chains that hold you back. Go and find your adventures!"

* * *

TRAVEL SAFETY TIPS
See website: worldwidebackpacker.com

SAFETY IS YOUR PERSONAL RESPONSIBILITY

Never leave it to others and assume they will do their jobs properly. It's too late when you have been mugged or worse. All the compensation in the world won't make it right again.

Take out a good quality travel insurance - one that will fully cover all medical costs abroad or full emergency repatriation with minimal hassle. Try to find a policy that will get emergency funds to you while you are still travelling, not just when you return home.

MAKE SURE someone back home knows your itinerary: dates, places and travel arrangements as accurately as possible.

They must also have details or photocopies of your passport, drivers licence, air ticket, insurance document and traveller's cheque numbers.

Arrange beforehand how you will keep in touch and e-mail or phone regularly. Mail and items of luggage can be sent poste restante to your next destination in most countries.

MONEY

Always carry the bulk of your money in traveller's cheques and keep a record of the cheque numbers concealed separately. Don't forget to cross them off as you use them. In risky areas it is a good idea to carry a dummy wallet with a convincing amount of cash while keeping your main stash in your money belt.

Budget travel by its nature, puts you in places and situations where you are vulnerable. In some countries; parts of Africa, Indonesia and South America for example, people may be so poor that the value of the clothes you wear amounts to more than they earn in a year. Humility will get you a lot further than arrogance and flashing expensive cameras or camcorders can mark you out as a target.

ALWAYS TRUST YOUR INSTINCTS
If a situation doesn't feel right it probably isn't. Get the hell out of there and don't worry about looking foolish or being impolite. Never, ever allow yourself to be led somewhere you do not want to go.

LEARN AND REGULARLY PRACTICE SELF DEFENCE
The best self defence is to run and scream but if you are cornered or taken by surprise a good technique can be a life saver. Knowing self defence boosts your confidence so you look less like a victim and are actually less likely to get picked on in the first place.

BE EXTREMELY WARY OF INSTANT FRIENDS
In certain countries - Kenya and Thailand for example - city people being overly friendly can often be the sign of a hustle. Be polite but firm and have nothing to do with them.

NEVER ACCEPT FOOD OR DRINK FROM A STRANGER IN THE CITY
A surprising number of lone travellers visiting Nairobi have had their food or drink drugged when eating out with a 'new friend', guide or helper. If they are lucky they wake up some time later with only their wallet missing.

NEVER TAKE OFF YOUR MONEY BELT except when taking a shower and then drape it over the shower head, never the door. More frequently, tents and sleeping bags are being slashed to remove discarded money belts.
A fake wallet containing a small amount of cash can be a useful deterrent.

NEVER LEAVE YOUR BAGS OUT OF SIGHT
On buses thieves crawl under seats to get to bags. Day sacks and rucksacks are only safe if you sleep on top of them.

HEALTH

Find out which vaccinations you will need and be sure to take them well in advance. Stagger treatments where appropriate - there may be side affects - and keep a careful record in your vaccination card - available from doctor.

Decide on a malaria treatment if appropriate and stick rigidly to the regime. Some treatments have serious mental health side affects so be guided by your doctor.

It is strongly recommended that you carry a first aid kit and just as importantly KNOW HOW TO USE IT

Saint John's Ambulance run courses in first aid and you can find out when and where from their website or from your local library or doctor. Don't put it off.

Alternatively, if you live near London and are planning to travel far from civilisation you might consider the Wilderness Medical Training Course run by the Royal Geographical Society on Kensington Road.

BASIC FIRST AID KIT

Your medical details on a card i.e. blood type, allergies, conditions.

Assorted sterile syringes and needles - (for doctors use in poorer countries)

Antiseptic cream i.e. Savlon 60ml

Bandage roll 2m, assorted dressings, assorted plasters, assorted suture plasters, sterile wipes, cotton wool, pain killers i.e. Ibuprofen, sachets of re-hydration salts, scissors, safety pins, tweezers.

HEALTH TIPS

In hot countries DRINK, DRINK, DRINK. The importance of drinking as much fluid as often as you can, can't be stressed enough. (NOT ALCOLHOL as this increases dehydration of the brain) Three litres per day is an absolute minimum. When the going gets tough or you feel the least bit run down, ADD RHYDRATION SALTS...But always remember before you drink...

STERILISE YOUR WATER!

Iodine is OK to use for up to four months. It dissolves readily, is easy to carry and can also be dabbed on cuts or grazes as a disinfectant. Use three drops per litre for clear water and six for murky, suspect water. Iodine has the added advantage that other people don't like the taste and won't pester you for your precious supplies.

Beyond four months iodine carries the risk of kidney and eye damage so you should use 'sterytabs', dosage as recommended on packet.

Always remember to leave water standing for 10 minutes to allow the agent time to work and splash the neck and lid of the water bottle with treated water.

In countries with suspect water never drink unless it has been treated.

Learn to brush your teeth without water.

Avoid meat dishes unless you are certain it is fresh and has been thoroughly cooked.

Fruit is fine if you peel it yourself but avoid peeled fruit and salads unless you know for sure they have been washed in treated water.

CLOTHING and ACCESSORIES

CLOTHING

One of the most important things to remember when backpacking is that whatever you bring with you, you're going to have to carry. By keeping your clothing to a minimum and spending a bit of money on dual purpose, better quality gear you can make life a lot easier and more comfortable for yourself.

There is a lot to be said for the minimalist, wear what the natives wear approach. You will fit in a lot better and a sari in a hot country for example, is very comfortable and quite practical. If you're going to be on the move a lot however and you don't want to feel like a prat at the airport, you can't beat quality essentials.

In hot countries dark colours will make you feel hot but it's worth remembering that if you want to view shy wildlife, light or bright colours will probably scare it away. Light colours show up dirt, require frequent cleaning and so wear out more quickly.

Here's a list of essentials:

Good quality Gore-Tex walking boots with high cuff, rugged tread and Vibram sole to be worn only with thick walking socks of high wicking material.

Hat. Best all rounder is a lightweight short rimmed jungle hat. The narrow rim will keep the worst of the sun off when it's overhead and protect you from heavy rain. I prefer a lightweight baseball cap. It doesn't interfere with my hearing but it does leave me prone to burned ears and neck.

High wicking vest (base layer) available from most outdoor clothing outlets.

Light weight rugged pants with zip off legs are one of the best buys you'll make. Already you've done away with the need to carry both shorts and long trousers.

Long sleeved polar neck base layer of high wicking material with zip up front.

Good quality water repellent, light weight fleece jacket of wind stopper material, with map pockets and removable or roll up hood.

Ultra light weight over jacket and pants, ideally of Gore-Tex - but by now you've probably run out of money - so you could make do with a cheaper, breathable alternative coated with Sympatex or similar. An absolute life saver when the weather turns foul. These should come with their own tiny stuff-sacks and as they pack away very small you're more likely to always keep them with you.

Sun glasses.

Cheap sunglasses are not only a waste of money, they are also dangerous and trick your eyes into feeling they are safe while allowing your retinas to get burned.

Fleece gloves with rugged grip pads.

ACCESSORIES

As a backpacker you are very limited to what you can carry. That said, certain environments and climates will require particular variations of kit.

Basic kit:

Rucksack or Bergen

60 - 65 litres best size. If you can't get all your gear in this for normal civilian backpacking you've probably got too much kit. If you buy yourself an 80 litre bag you'll almost certainly find something to fill it.

It is possible to get by with an incredibly cheap Argos special at £22 but if you can afford a bit more you'll get better comfort and padding. Your rucksack should have two side pockets for water bottles. If you can reach them without taking the thing off, great: it's a real nuisance having to stop every few minutes and remove your rucksack for a drink of water. Otherwise you may consider an ammo belt-pouch from Silverman's for your water bottle.

The padded waist belt should sit comfortably on your hips and take most of the weight. Keep the top end close to your shoulder blades by tightening the adjuster straps. Keep the shoulder straps from sliding over your shoulders by adjusting the chest strap. Place your sleeping bag in the bottom pouch, heavy stuff in the bottom and lighter more frequently used stuff in the top.

Sleeping bag

Best value – Ajungalak 2 season for most countries in moderate temperatures, 3 season for alpine use. If you wear clothing in these it will make you sweat like mad.

Roll mat

Minimum 10mm thick of stiff durable foam. Keeps the chill off your back and smoothes out sharp bumps and lumps.

Tent

A tent opens up your options for budget travel and gets you more in touch with your surroundings. Weight and bulk can be a big downer but the more you spend, the lighter they get and the smaller they pack.

Mosquito net

Packs away to nothing and weighs nothing, so if you're passing through malarial regions, TAKE IT.

Mosquito repellent

Essential in Malarial or mosquito infested areas. I think the one I used was made by Life Systems and contained Deet. It's ferocious stuff and the mozzies really hate it but a note of caution; it melts plastic and resin watch straps.

Stove
My favourite is the little Epi Gas burner which uses self resealing cylinders. For my big trip I took a multi fuel stove and used petrol. Pretty smoky and a bit of a flame thrower to start with but you can get petrol almost anywhere. With a quick change of nozzle it will even burn diesel. Make sure your cylinders are completely empty and rinsed clean before getting on the plane and stow them in your main luggage; they'll be confiscated from hand luggage. Food became so cheap in the countries I visited that eventually I was obliged to sent my stove home.

Water Bottles
Your minimum requirement in a hot country is three litres per day so you should carry three, one litre bottles. Black plastic NATO issue bottles are the best but aluminium bottles are also pretty good. You could always make do with a couple of old plastic Coke bottles and they are surprisingly tough.

Water Filter/Pump
One of the best filter pumps on the market is the Pre Mac Travel Well. It's compact, tough and can filter all known bugs and nasties in up to 80 litres before needing replacement cartridges. In a hot country with limited fresh water or when you need to travel light, it's a life saver.

Torch
I'm afraid I don't rate the MagLite range. Heavy, easy blow bulbs, not terribly reliable. You are much better off with a sturdy, rubber switch plastic job. Always carry at least one extra set of batteries.

Gas lantern
If you do an awful lot of night time reading/ writing or if you are travelling with company and can share the carrying of luxuries, these babies are reasonably compact, give of an incredible amount of light and completely change the atmosphere after dark.

Knife
Don't rate the Super Tool. Very expensive, very heavy, incredibly soft screwdriver blades and doesn't have an adjustable spanner. There are much cheaper alternatives which now come with interchangeable screwdriver and socket bits. Very useful if you're touring with a vehicle, especially a motorbike. Swiss Army knife is still a trusty multi purpose tool with limited cutting ability.
For jungle/ woodland exploring you are much better with a single edge, six inch, sturdy blade knife with a comfortable handle, plus a parang (machete) for dense undergrowth. Obviously none of these can be taken in hand luggage on the plane.

Traveller's fold up wash bag
Containing all your hygiene essentials plus: tweezers, small mirror, small roll of toilet paper, condoms, nail clippers and lip salve for cold conditions. Plus, a medium size towel.

SHOPS
Silvermans ****
Field and Trek ****
Cotswold Camping ****
Snow and Rock ***
Youth Hostel Association ***
Blacks ***
Millets **

ACKNOWLEDGEMENTS

I would gratefully like to acknowledge the following people without whose help this book would never have been completed.

Wilfred Leng, now deceased and members of the Wilfred Leng Writers Group for their tremendous patience and incredible support: Joanna Day, Sally Esdaile, Roland Rosser, David Green, John Sturgeon, Alexandra Niewiadomski, Emma Lympany, Kahryn Hughes, Francoise Emery, Eileen Dickinson and Genevieve Fidele.

Special thanks to Karen Medweth - photographic arrangement, Andy Kempton - file arrangement,

Romano Dowbusz - for his great patience in cover arrangement and website design,

Simon Everet - additional artwork,

Adam Hill (Sunrise Paragliding) - back cover photograph,

Suzannah Fitzgerald and Ella Jane Bowden - additional edit and proof reading.

I would also like to thank:

Tony Wilkinson for giving me such an encouraging send off when I was having the biggest panic attack of my life and for giving me somewhere to stay when I finally got back to the UK, my cousin Erhard who mounted a rescue mission when he hadn't heard from me for several months and all the wonderful, amazing people I met on my journey. Some of you were kind, some of you made me laugh and some of you became great friends. Life is a collection of experiences good and bad. You made mine incredibly special.

EPILOGUE

My original aim in writing this book was to raise awareness about what we humans are doing to our fellow creatures, our environment and each other. Unfortunately there was very little description of the places I visited or what I did when I got there and the message would have been pointless because no one would ever have read it.

Luckily, I found a superb writers' group founded by a man called Wilfred Leng, and with their help turned the story into something far more descriptive and colourful. Most of the environmental message was lost in the process and haunted by that fact I found myself discussing the topic with a colleague.

"Why should I," he asked, "living here in London, give a toss about saving rhinos in Africa?"

I was stunned for a moment. The thought of not caring has never really entered my head. I care passionately about endangered species yet here was someone, a very typical someone, who didn't care about them at all and the chasm of difference between us was so great it left me wondering, "Where on earth do I start?".

"Because they're utterly amazing and they don't deserve to become extinct. Try getting close to one in the wild and you'll see what I mean. They can grow as big as a truck, weigh up to three tons and charge at almost 40mph. They're usually very peaceful but if defending a calf or territory they can be utterly ferocious. Rhinos have evolved over millions of years and the different species maintain the environment they live in through grazing back tall grass, controlling the spread of scrub, or opening up dense jungle to smaller mammals and birds. You don't have to live in Africa or Asia to love them and if we let them die out we'll have lost something truly magnificent and utterly irreplaceable!"

In the last 100 years we have wiped out more than 95% of the worlds rhino population. Three of the five different species and several subspecies are currently on the verge of extinction because we have ruthlessly persecuted them for their horn and converted most of their habitat to farmland. The horn is used to make ceremonial dagger handles in Yemen even though a number of alternative materials are readily available and medicines that ironically don't even work, in China and South-East Asia.

The slaughter of rhinos has nothing to do with natural selection and is purely commercial; in parts of Africa for example large roving gangs, remnants of war, armed with machine guns and high powered rifles, butcher adults and young alike, the tenuous logic being to force the price on the heads of the very last individuals even higher. These are the direct reasons for our devastating impact on rhino numbers and tragically the story has been repeated for so many other creatures around the world. To get a fuller picture we need to look at the underlying long term effects of our involvement.

Human population size in 2005 has far surpassed the number our planet and its resources can sustainably support and is still rising rapidly. If we fail to considerably reduce our numbers and our impact on the environment over the next few years the outcome is predictable: escalating global warming, rising sea levels and drastic climate change. There will be war as nations fight over dwindling resources and famine on a scale never seen before. We will create a world where only humans, the animals we eat and a few of the most successful scavengers survive, and all the breathtaking biodiversity that is currently hanging on by the skin of its teeth will disappear. If we don't downsize by choice nature will do it for us and the methods she uses will be catastrophic.

How can we knowingly impose that kind of future on the children and grandchildren we so lovingly nurture? If we really are 'the most intelligent species' then despite the enormous scale of the task, we must surely be able to get closer to a sustainable way of life. We urgently need to break the cycle of greed and ignorance and start living within our means. This would involve some fairly radical changes:

* Through education, wealthy countries must adopt major changes in attitude - from total capitalism and greed culture to a long term concern for the well being of each other, our amazing planet and all our fellow creatures. We must drop our obsession with economic and industrial growth because it is totally unsustainable, consolidate what we have and make much better use of our resources. We need to reduce our expectations, stop using poor countries as a source of cheap labour and raw materials and write off their loan debt to us. (This is in our interest because at the moment poor countries are decimating their rainforest and resources just to pay off the interest on those loans and *we* need the rainforest as much as they do. Also, if we take our boot off their neck then they will become less dependant on aid).

* Poor countries must abandon the culture of having large families as a pension substitute and reverse their runaway population growth. Reducing their population size will make them less dependant on aid and less susceptible to unfair trade and exorbitant loan rates from richer countries.

We all need to stop having children to improve our lives or simply because we can and adopt a culture of globally responsible family planning.

* We need to make full use of renewable energy sources (not nuclear power because it is 'dirty' and as a result extremely costly) and recycle as much of our waste as we possibly can.

* Total reversal of 'car culture' and cheap air travel to be replaced by non-polluting means of transport. (I fully accept all criticism of my own travels).

* An understanding that a healthy world requires maximum biodiversity. Wildlife, the oceans and the rainforest are not just here for us to exploit and destroy as we see fit. Every creature

and every plant has its place in nature and performs an important function. We are stewards of the planet and have a global responsibility to nurture and protect all flora and fauna for future generations so that they don't look back and say, "Those were the people who poisoned the air and sea, destroyed the balance of climate and wiped out rhinos, tigers, elephants, snow leopards, the great apes, whales, turtles, albatross, coral reefs and the rainforest" – to name but a few.

Some cynics say human nature will prevent us from making the necessary changes. It is inevitable that we will overpopulate and decimate our planet, so why bother doing anything? Part of our greatness however, is our capacity for compassion and our natural instinct to keep struggling even when the fight seems hopeless. One thing is absolutely certain; doing something positive has got to be better than doing nothing.

It is quite likely that we will reach some kind of lifestyle compromise. Most of us are not going to give up our cars, cheap air travel or the right to have as many kids and consume as much as we want until we absolutely have to. By then it may be too late, but even if the rhino's habitat is all converted into farms it is still essential to conserve the species in the hope that some time in the future something will happen to give us back our respect for our environment and our fellow creatures and we will learn to live alongside them once more.

Incredibly in 2005 we are still accelerating away in the wrong direction. The rain forests of South America, Central Africa and South East Asia are being destroyed at such a rate that they will disappear altogether within the next ten to twenty years. In Burma and the Islands controlled by Indonesia, indigenous jungle tribes are being massacred to allow the rape of the rainforest to continue unimpeded. These fragile, vibrant environments hold some of the greatest diversity of wildlife and plants on earth and are the lungs of our planet. They belong to all of us and we must take an international responsibility to protect them.

The need for action has never been more urgent. There are fewer than 475 Siberian tigers left in the world, 680 mountain gorillas and less than 500 snow leopards survive in Nepal. In Indonesia the total population of Sumatran rhinos is less than 300. There are less than 500 Sumatran tigers and fewer than 70 Javan rhinos remain. A sub species of white rhinos - the northern white rhino - of which fewer than 10 are left*, struggle to survive concerted attacks from poachers in Garamba National Park, North Eastern Democratic Republic of Congo.

At the beginning of 2005 the DRC Government agreed to allow five of the remaining rhinos to be translocated to a safe location in Kenya until the lawless situation in the north-east could be stabilised. In March however, the Government negated on this agreement leaving the way clear for the last northern white rhinos to be poached to extinction by armed rebels from Sudan. The fact that the imminent extinction of these amazing creatures barely attracts a mention by the world's press leaves the people directly involved in conservation with a feeling of utter exasperation.

Right now the most pressing task is to halt the destruction of the last rainforests and prevent critically endangered species from going extinct. They are all magnificent and have every right to live with us in our world. If we fail we will never see their like again. The handful of dedicated organisations listed below could achieve this with relatively small amounts of money but are currently woefully under funded. In the UK, all the wildlife NGOs together account for less than 1% of the total charity money raised each year. This has got to change and there must be Government as well as public support. The message is clear; these organisations (and a few others not listed) are totally above board, efficient, dedicated and know what needs to be done. Give them the money and they will save endangered species from going extinct. It really is that simple.

* As of May 2005 this species may already be extinct.

There are vast untapped resources out there; some of our film and music celebrities could afford to save entire species with their own funds and when I think of the money we spend on holidays, binge drinking, cars and other luxuries I could weep. The problem is not that we don't care, but that most of us simply don't know how desperate the situation is! Television should be bringing the message to the general public but instead it broadcasts useless consumer advertising, Big Brother and 'fluffy animal' wildlife documentaries that give the impression everything is OK. Mainstream television is the most powerful medium we have to get the conservation message across and we must convince the people in charge to let it fulfil this essential role.

In practical terms endangered animals need safe National Parks to roam free in and protection from poachers. Trade in endangered species must be made illegal, education programs introduced to encourage people to stop supporting the industry and the law firmly enforced. It is not an idle statement to say that if we can save the animals, there may also be a future for us.

If two thirds of the people of Britain alone gave just £3 a month to one of the key NGOs most of these species could be taken off the endangered list almost overnight. There is no more time to wait and see what happens or sit back and do nothing in the hope that someone else will do the necessary. We have to ask ourselves now -

"Do we want any of these creatures to exist tomorrow?"

Just as mainstream television fails to highlight the desperate situation facing endangered species and threatened environments, issues of human rights abuse are largely ignored. There are many examples of brutality and civil rights abuses around the world: Chechnya, the oppression of the Palestinian people by Israel (pretty much the root cause of 'global terrorism'), Zimbabwe, dispossession of jungle tribes in Brazil, ethnic cleansing in Ethiopia. It seems incredible that while we live in relative comfort, only a few hours flight away in Burma, Tibet and islands occupied by Indonesia, genocide is being committed.

The Korem people of Burma are being exterminated by a brutal military dictatorship while the world looks away. Indonesian armed forces are busy murdering indigenous jungle tribes on the Islands they have annexed and the Chinese, having unlawfully occupied Tibet and kidnapped its spiritual leader ten years ago when he was just six, torture and oppress the gentle Tibetan people. Instead of sending a message to China that this is unacceptable our leaders invite her ministers for discussions about commerce and we buy everything the country produces, even to the detriment of our own industry. It doesn't make any sense.

North Korea continues to brutalize its own people carrying out monstrous poison gas experiments on entire families and executing anyone who speaks out or tries to escape.

These countries must be persuaded to change their ways and the United Nations is the world's police force set up for this task. We must back it, keep it strong and not allow it to be dominated or undermined by any superpower with ulterior motives. We must demand that the media keeps us informed about civil rights abuses around the world and stops dumbing down the news so that we know what is going on and can tell our politicians when and how we want them to act. We must learn to care enough to do something about it when our fellow human beings are tortured and murdered.

Andrew Lindsay
May 2005

Some of the organisations involved in the front line of conservation and human rights issues:

Fauna and Flora International......www.fauna-flora.org
Born Free Foundation...............www.bornfree.org.uk
Save the Rhino International........www.savetherhino.org
International Rhino Foundation....www.rhinos-irf.org
World Wildlife Fund.................www.wwf.org.uk
                                   www.panda.org
Greenpeace...........................www.greenpeace.org
Friends of the Earth..................www.foe.org.uk
Rainforest Concern...................www.rainforestconcern.org
The Green Party......................www.greenparty.org.uk
The Free Tibet Campaign...........www.freetibet.org
Amnesty International...............www.amnesty.org

FINAL NOTE

Sustainability can be defined as:

*A way of life that does not cause the extinction of other species. (In Britain we passed that point about 600 years ago when we exterminated wolves, bears and wild boar, and we are still causing numerous smaller species to disappear today).

*Not creating more pollutants than the environment can neutralise or absorb i.e. carbon dioxide emissions from jet aircraft, road vehicles and power stations which accelerate climate change. High levels of fertilizer needed to grow crops for an excessive human population, entering our rivers and the sea and killing off marine life. If the population were smaller we wouldn't need to farm so intensively.

Many of us assume that because relatively cheap food is so readily available in the supermarkets everything must be fine, but this is far from true.

Supermarkets encourage us to buy far more than we actually need through clever marketing.

They encourage wastage with absurdly stringent 'use by' dates.

They exert enormous financial pressure on farmers forcing the small producers out of business and the large producers to adopt bad farming practices: Highly intensive battery style environments for livestock giving rise to high stress levels and very poor quality of life. Extensive use of pesticides and fertilizers that are absorbed by vegetables and fruit and passed on to the consumer. Destroying hedgerows and trees to squeeze every last drop of efficiency from the land.

They import food from countries that employ even more dubious farming practices; countries that often can't even feed their own population, and force all of us to use our cars to shop.

The only food that can be guaranteed chemical free, produced ethically without major impact on the environment is organic. That is the price of real food - all else is either harmful

the environment - and we should budget and plan
ngly.

Britain, short sighted governments have invited large
oers of foreign workers as a quick, cheap fix for skills
rtages. Small numbers in a sort of skills exchange have
ways been helpful and culturally beneficial but a more long
erm approach would have been to train the growing army of
unemployed with the relevant skills. In the short term,
immigration makes our economy look good at the expense of
leaving a skills crisis back in the migrant worker's home
countries. It has greatly contributed to a new rise in our
population, placing an impossible burden on the housing market
with disastrous consequences for the 'green belt', health
services and the welfare system. How can this be sustainable?

As huge new housing estates spring up all over the
countryside and every last inch of public parkland is built on in
our towns, I wonder what the future holds for the last of our
beautiful green spaces and precious wildlife. One of my dreams
has always been to see the reintroduction of wolves, bears and
wild boar - indicators of a healthy, thriving wild environment -
to the more remote parts of our island, but as more and more
land disappears under concrete and tarmac that dream is
slipping further away.